Psychic Conversion and Theological Foundations

American Academy of Religion
Studies in Religion

Thomas J.J. Altizer, Editor
James O. Duke, Associate Editor

Number 25

Psychic Conversion and Theological Foundations:
Toward a Reorientation of the Human Sciences

by Robert M. Doran

Psychic Conversion and Theological Foundations

Toward a Reorientation of the Human Sciences

Robert M. Doran

Scholars Press

Distributed by
Scholars Press
101 Salem Street
P.O. Box 2268
Chico, California 95927

Psychic Conversion and Theological Foundations:
Toward a Reorientation of the Human Sciences

by
Robert M. Doran

Library of Congress Cataloging in Publication Data

Doran, Robert M., 1939–
Psychic conversion and theological foundations.

(Studies in religion ; no. 25)
Includes bibliographical references.
1. History (Theology) 2. Christianity and culture.
3. Man (Christian theology) 4. Lonergan, Bernard J.F.
I. Title. II. Series: Studies in religion (American
Academy of Religion) ; no. 25.
BR115.H5D65 230 81-9360
ISBN 0-89130-522-X (pbk.) AACR2

Printed in the United States of America
1 2 3 4 5 6
Edwards Brothers, Inc.
Ann Arbor, Michigan 48106

To Bernard Lonergan

TABLE OF CONTENTS

PREFACE

On December 17, 1979, Bernard Lonergan celebrated his seventy-fifth birthday. While I was not able to bring this manuscript to publication in time to present it to him on that occasion, it is my privilege to express my admiration for his accomplishments in the field of methodological studies by dedicating this work to him.

My reflections flow from more than a decade of labor on Lonergan's writings. I hope that this does not render my thought inaccessible to those who have not read *Insight*[1] and *Method in Theology*.[2] Perhaps I can state in somewhat general terms the nature of my concerns and the direction of my convictions.

The problem with which I want to come to grips was set by Lewis Mumford nearly twenty-five years ago. In his book *The Transformations of Man* Mumford employs a series of ideal-types to trace the major developments of human consciousness and of the cultural forms that can be found in recorded history.[3] At the end of this overview of cultural history, he raises the question of where we go from here. He proposes two further ideal-types to help his readers imagine alternative options for human development or regression. The first he calls "post-historic man," and the second, "world-cultural man."

Post-historic humanity is one whose neurophysiology, memory, imagination, intelligence, and freedom would become ossified in patterns of behavior or--to use Lonergan's term--schemes of recurrence[4] that have been cumulatively programmed by neural, psychological, social, economic, political, conceptual, and linguistic conditioning. World-cultural humanity, on the other hand, would be the alternative that could emerge if we recognize the gravity of our present situation and move to a major transformation of selfhood. We must take our stand on the crosscultural constituents of genuine humanity and move from these foundations to appropriate and transform the major cultural acquisitions bequeathed us by the previous stages in human development. In this way the human community would be able to move to a new unity.

I have for several years been convinced of the pertinence of Lonergan's work for the emergence of a world-cultural humanity. For the central element in that work consists in a differentiation of the crosscultural constituents of genuine humanity. These elements lie in human interiority, and more precisely in the normative unfolding of that interiority that Lonergan calls "basic method."[5] But I have also tried to argue that in addition to the dimensions of cognitive, moral, and religious intentionality that Lonergan's work discloses, there is another dimension of interiority, the sensitive psyche, which must be appropriated. In my own work I have spoken of "psychic conversion" as a helpful and indeed necessary complement to Lonergan's disengagements of religious, moral, and intellectual conversion.[6] The present work synthesizes and consolidates in a systematic fashion my thoughts on psychic conversion. As related to Mumford's world-cultural humanity, psychic conversion is an instrument for the differentiation and appropriation of crosscultural modes of psychic symbolization. It thus complements the disengagement of universally human patterns of questioning found in Lonergan's intentionality analysis.

A further and ulterior purpose will become manifest as the book progresses. I wish not only to specify the foundations of a world-cultural humanity but also to initiate a movement toward the realization of a new human community. My contribution in this book is largely methodological, but not completely so. The transformation of humanity that I envision, hope for, and labor to promote will involve two dimensions. We may understand these dimensions in terms of Lonergan's distinction between the infrastructure and the suprastructure of a culture.[7]

A cultural infrastructure consists of the various transactions that constitute the fabric of everyday life. The suprastructure emerges from disciplined reflection on the infrastructure. Thus, while business transactions belong to the infrastructure, the science of economics pertains to the suprastructure; while human emotions inform the infrastructure, the science of psychology contributes to the suprastructure; while prayer is infrastructural, theology is suprastructural.

The transformations that must occur if we are to move to a world-cultural humanity affect both orders. At the infrastructural level there must occur what Lonergan calls the transformation and integration of the myriad instances of common sense.[8] At the suprastructural level there must ensue what he calls a transformation and integration of the sciences.[9] The present book is concerned only incidentally with the first of these sets of transformations. But it is deeply involved in the second. It seeks not only to offer a key to the transformation of one science, depth psychology, but to show that this transformation, joined with

Lonergan's work, will ground further interdisciplinary collaboration in the pursuit of integrated science, especially of integrated human science. This ground I call theological foundations, for reasons that will become apparent in the course of this study.

One final introductory clarification is in order. Several authors have offered the hypothesis of an axial development of human consciousness between the years 800 B.C. and 500 A.D.[10] The dates differ with different interpretations. But the authors agree in speaking of an epochal breakthrough from myth to realism that has determined the dialectic of history ever since. Two principal questions emerge for the Christian theologian who seeks to understand the Christian past within the context of an axial theory of history and to mediate the theological positions one accepts from that past as true with the current and prospective unfolding of the historical dialectic. First, is there a specifically Christian differentiation within a more generically conceived axial consciousness, and, if so, how does it relate to other axial developments? Second, what is going forward in conscious development in our own time, and how is the contemporary drama of consciousness related to the various axial advances that, in an increasingly planetized world, are becoming a relatively common heritage of humankind? I am convinced that these two questions place basic responsibilities upon contemporary Christian theology. The range of that phase of theology that mediates the past is broadened beyond the explicitly Christian past to include investigations of all the data on men and women at every time and place in history. And our conception of the alembic of foundations will enable the construction of a contemporary theology that will be both Christian and, because of its crosscultural framework and intentions, universal.

In this work I proceed from the following presuppositions regarding the first question:

1. I accept the general theorem of an axial period in the development of human consciousness.

2. In general, I leave the details regarding dates, varieties, and degrees of axial differentiation to historical scholarship and dialectical encounter, with the explicit reminder, however, that some differences in historical results will lead directly into dialectic.

3. Nonetheless, I assume that the religious component in the axial breakthrough was variously differentiated in distinct historical traditions in such a way that two possibilities emerged, each

of which is itself variously differentiated: there was *a transcendent differentiation in the noetic order* that occurred with the opening of the soul to world-transcendent reality; and there was *a soteriological differentiation in the existential order* that emerged with the discovery in human history of the initiative and response of world-transcendent reality vis-à-vis the transcendent exigence of the human mind and heart. In Western cultural history, the first differentiation is pre-eminently represented in Greek philosophy and the second in the biblical tradition.

4. That both differentiations are found and coherently related to one another in Christian tradition, I am sure; that both occur in varying degrees in other and independent traditions, I am relatively certain; that the transcendent differentiation may emerge even more clearly in some nonbiblical traditions than in the biblical, I am willing to grant; that the soteriological differentiation receives its unsurpassable fulfilment in the life, preaching, passion, death, and resurrection of Jesus and in the faith that trusts the word of the New Testament witnesses and authors, I am prepared to defend: existentially, in the sense of being prepared to give an account of the hope that is mine, and noetically, on the basis of Lonergan's heuristic structure for the identification of the complete divine solution to the problem of evil;[11] and that only the transcendent differentiation emerges with clarity in the pre-Christian Greek variant of the axial breakthrough I am also relatively certain. I must wager that the work of historical scholarship will not invalidate these admittedly crucial assumptions.

With regard to the question of the contemporary emergence of new forms of human consciousness, I assume that I have verified to my own satisfaction that something new, something that is quite distinct from any of the variants of the axial period and yet in fundamental continuity with them and dependent on them, emerges in the foundational program initiated by Lonergan. The eleventh chapter of *Insight* is epochal: it is a breakthrough to a new differentiation and specialization of consciousness, the beginning of a new series of ranges of schemes of recurrence in cognitional and ultimately in existential praxis. I hope that sufficient evidence for this conviction will present itself in the pages that follow. But I also maintain that the differentiating advances that I propose are necessary increments to Lonergan's magnificent achievement.

I wish to express my deepest gratitude to the Reverend John D. Zuercher, S.J. and to the members of the Creighton University Jesuit Community, Omaha, Nebraska, who provided me with the home and the time that I needed to complete work on this book. Finally I wish to thank Professor James O. Duke of Texas Christian University for his careful reading of the manuscript and for his many helpful editorial suggestions.

PART ONE

THE FOUNDATIONAL QUEST

CHAPTER ONE

THE SITUATION AND RESPONSIBILITIES OF A METHODICAL THEOLOGY

OUTLINE

1. Hermeneutic Consciousness and Advancing Differentiation. The place of Lonergan's methodological breakthrough within the history of theology.
2. The Threefold Mediatory Function of Methodical Christian Theology. The noetic or disclosive functions of a methodical theology.
3. Method in History: Reflections on the Third Stage of Meaning. The place of the methodological breakthrough within the history of culture. The history to date of the methodological breakthrough.
4. Methodical Theology and Authenticity. The differentiations demanded of the theologian. The transformative functions of a methodical theology. Individual and social transformation. The religion of the methodical theologian. The notion of psychic conversion.
5. The Political Responsibility of a Methodical Theology. The foundations and goal of third-stage interdisciplinary collaboration.

The intention to present a series of fairly intricate considerations regarding the construction and interdisciplinary involvement of a methodical Christian theology permeates this book. These proposals will make sense only to the extent that we are able to clarify from the outset and in a heuristic and directive manner what we mean by a methodical Christian theology. In brief, a theology will be methodical to the extent that its practitioners submit their cognitive, affective, moral, religious, and Christian consciousness to explanatory differentiation in the mode of interiority, thereby recovering with structural precision the path and the immanent intelligibility of their own search for direction in the movement of life, and that they ground their theology in the discoveries they have made and verified along that path.

1. *Hermeneutic Consciousness and Advancing Differentiation.*

Bernard Lonergan has written that "a theology mediates between a cultural matrix and the significance and role of a religion in that matrix."[1] A set of directives for a contemporary methodical Christian theology will therefore specify what is at stake when theologians, grounded in explanatory self-appropriation, mediate the Christian soteriological differentiation of consciousness with the contemporary dialectic of cultural meanings and values with which they are in contact. We must provide a way to disengage both the differentiation and the dialectic. Moreover, such a set of directives provides the maieutic for contemporary theologians to mediate both those conflicts that arose in past ages of theology and the contemporary disputes that emerge from the exegesis and historical scholarship that study the past. Introducing method into theology, then, will affect both that phase of theology that studies the past or the writings of other contemporaries and that phase that addresses itself directly to the present and the future.[2]

If method, understood as identical with the self-appropriating subject, is a new differentiation in the history of theology, then a methodical theology, a theology grounded in explanatory self-appropriation, is a new theological possibility. Methodical theology means a new age in theology, an age that has only recently begun. While the self-understanding of methodical theology will continue to gain precision as theologians advance in their understanding of what they are doing when they are doing theology, it will nonetheless be helpful for us at the outset of this book to stand back and reflect on some of the implications of the methodological breakthrough. Our first reflection--one that we will return to and amplify in a spiralling fashion in the course of subsequent chapters--will treat the place of this breakthrough within the history of theology.

The history of theology demonstrates that theologies are quite different depending on the respective theologians' philosophic and general intellectual development, on the degree of religious differentiation that they are able to mediate to a cultural matrix, on the familiarity that they have gained with the various realms of meaning,[3] and on the cognitive, moral, affective, and religious differentiations and regressions that determine the cultural matrix with which they set out to mediate both transcendent noetic and Christian soteriological significance. For these reasons, all theological endeavor is finite, hermeneutical, and when authentic, dialectically incremental. Theology is an ongoing process because religious and cultural differentiations are themselves always in a process either of advance or of regression or of struggle between advance and regression. The theologian's consciousness seems always to be a battlefield, and one's individual doctrinal positions and overall systematic understanding represent the eventual outcome of the battle within one's own person. In a methodical theology, however, the battle itself is objectified in what Lonergan calls the functional specialties of dialectic, where its roots are uncovered, and of foundations, where it achieves its resolution.[4]

To speak more precisely, and to place Christian theology within the framework of the history of human consciousness and self-understanding, we may speak of *an original experience of existential consciousness searching for direction in the movement of life*. This experience is universal to the human condition. It admits of various degrees of differentiation. It is differentiated into various realms of meaning as consciousness develops and it is compacted into a more or less undifferentiated unity to the extent that consciousness does not develop. But it can also be contracted into a distorted unity to the extent that consciousness regresses to more archaic forms after having taken some decisive steps forward.[5] The introduction of method--of differentiation in the realm of interiority--into theology enables the theologian to understand how his or her own consciousness, as well as the consciousness of every theologian in every period of theology's history, participates in the drama of differentiation and compactness. Since the terms of the drama are dictated by the specific contents that it assumes in the theologian's cultural matrix, theology is always *situated*. But method allows us to disengage a permanent structure or form that constitutes the outline of the drama in each specific instance.

A methodical theology is itself situated with respect to the terms of its own drama. The history of the symbolic forms through which cultures express their understanding of the meaning, order, direction, and responsibilities of human existence clearly manifests varying degrees of compactness and differentiation of the original search for direction.[6] The substance of the Western cultural heritage was for centuries determined by the anthropological and transcendent noetic disengagements of classical Greek philosophy, the Yahwistic differentiation of a historical order of existence under a world-transcendent God, and the soteriological differentiation that claims definitive status in the New Testament. But in our post-Enlightenment context it is clear that this Western axial heritage can neither be preserved nor made effective in individuals, cultural communities, and polities unless it surrenders its previous implicit foundational privilege and allows itself to be both criticized and reoriented on the grounds of a further degree of differentiation. This radical increment in foundational differentiation occurs as the subject advances in self-knowledge to the explanatory account of the normative exigencies of subjectivity. This advance is both enabled and necessitated by the positive gains of modernity in the areas of science (natural and human), methods of historical scholarship, and philosophy, by the dialectical problems created by these developments, and by the global communications, interdependencies, and injustices that characterize our age. Modern intellectual, technological, and socio-political developments have been coincidentally anticipating the leap in being that Lonergan has called transcendental (or generalized empirical) method, where they are reoriented, consolidated, and systematically related both to one another and to previous developments by being explicitly grounded in a set of foundations that can account for both modern and pre-modern achievements. This leap in being onto a third stage of meaning--beyond both common sense and theory--is the cognitive and existential drama of contemporary conscious subjectivity. Moreover, with this advance to explanatory self-appropriation, theology becomes methodical in a thematic manner. It gains self-conscious controls of meaning grounded not in theory but in the realm of the conscious interiority of the performing theologian. The terms of the drama dictate that the function of such foundations, if they are indeed to meet modern exigencies, must be not simply noetic, that is, disclosive of intelligibility, but also transformative of praxis.

Hans-Georg Gadamer has emphasized well, indeed profoundly, the finite and incremental character of all hermeneutic understanding.[7] But the sense in which I use the terms "method" and "methodical" obviously differs quite substantially from Gadamer's ironic use of these terms.[8] Lonergan has differentiated into a set of eight interrelated functional specialities what even for Gadamer is a more compact hermeneutical experience.[9] Moreover, Lonergan has introduced into his account of the hermeneutic experience an acknowledgment both of the opening of the interpreting and evaluating mind and heart to the realm of the divine and of the Christian discovery of God's bending to the subject and to history in grace. The opening of the mind and heart constitutes a transcendent noetic differentiation of consciousness.[10] The discovery of God's redemptive love in historical events moves Christian theology to the center of the integral hermeneutic experience and unequivocally identifies that experience as not simply interpretive but also evaluative. Because of the eightfold differentiation of an incremental hermeneutic of historical experience, Lonergan's complete hermeneutic theory goes beyond the functional specialty "interpretation" to include the various moments that occur in the collaborative framework of all eight functional specialties. The central tasks of dialectic and foundations display the normative exigencies of cognitive, moral, and religious consciousness and add to the entire hermeneutic enterprise a much needed precision of the dialectical nature of what Gadamer calls the fusion of horizons.[11] As contrasted with Gadamer, Lonergan acknowledges a methodical exigence within the hermeneutic enterprise itself.

The Christian theological moment within the integral hermeneutic experience is itself in need of clear methodological precision because of the modern developments that necessitate a new set of foundations. The classical anthropological, metaphysical, and transcendent differentiations that emerge in the Platonic and Aristotelian advances beyond myth to theory and philosophy have in the history of Christian theology symbiotically combined with the Israelite historical and the Christian soteriological differentiations of the original experience in such a way as to promote and preserve a normative notion of culture. Lonergan calls this notion classicist. He indicates how it formed the matrix of meanings and values with which past Christian and especially Catholic theology attempted to mediate the significance of Christian faith. And he notes that in fact the normative notion of culture is counter-positional to the full impact of the soteriological message of Christian revelation.[12] The sharp contrast between modern and Aristotelian ideals of science, along with the advancing differentiations of modern historical methods and human science, have invalidated the classicist notion of culture. To Lonergan's noetic disqualification of classicism, moreover, must be added a political critique that would establish the responsibility of normative notions of culture--whether they be classicist or some variant of modern common sense--for colonialism, expropriation, exploitation, and oppression. Theology is thus left with the enormous and quite new task of mediating the significance of Christian faith with ongoing and changing sets of cultural meanings and values--or, more generally, with a self-understanding of culture that is, first, more at home in principle with Christianity's advance in differentiation; yet, secondly, far more complicated than the classicist self-understanding; and thirdly, precisely because of Christianity's long symbiosis with the normative notion of culture, suspicious of or inimical to the soteriological significance of Christian faith as long as Christianity remains tied to the classicist cultural framework. The theological task is made even more difficult in that the extrication from classicism cannot be an unqualified repudiation, but must be a dialectical movement. The axial differentiations of classical philosophy are not to be jettisoned by a soteriologically differentiated, modern, methodical hermeneutic consciousness. Nonetheless, they can no longer be considered basic. They must be grounded in, derived from, and critically monitored, relocated, and reoriented by a hermeneutic consciousness that takes its stand on the explanatory self-appropriation that constitues transcendental method.[13]

The concern to introduce method into the theological component of the integral hermeneutic of historical experience, then, arises when theology is no longer taken to be a permanent achievement of the human mind but is known to be an ongoing process.[14] This process must be guided in a normative, critical, dialectical, and systematic manner that "assures continuity without imposing rigidity."[15] Moreover, since theology is a moment within a more embracing hermeneutic of historical experience, and since its concern for absolute self-transcendence as a constituent moment within the original experience of the search for direction in the movement of life introduces into the integral hermeneutic experience the functional specialties of dialectic and foundations, the introduction of method into the theological moment will also contribute to the laying of the foundations for an interdisciplinary construction of a methodical understanding of humanity.[16]

Theology has always been prone to a Protean temptation to revert to extrinsicism, nominalism, or revelational positivism. This temptation was overcome even in the classicist conjoining of reason and faith. With the complication of the theological task brought about by the breakdown of classicism, however, the temptation asserts itself again in our time. Today it is often countered by an opposed and peculiarly modern reversion to compactness, as the theologian, simultaneously acculturated and decultured, succumbs to a theological immanentism--a secular Gnosticism whose possible forms are at least as many in number as those of theological nominalism. Putting method into theology establishes the truth that cuts between extrinsicism and immanentism: "The objects of theology do not lie outside the transcendental field. For that field is unrestricted, and so outside it there is nothing at all."[17] Transcendence is not an opening one happens upon independently of the process of mediating the world by meaning, constituting the world by discerning the direction one discovers in the movement of life, and constituting oneself in the process. Nor is a theology that would mediate transcendence and culture structurally a different kind of pursuit of understanding from other integral hermeneutic performances of the human mind and heart. If a theology does not satisfy the structure imposed by the normative ordering of human inquiry in the advance of intentionality through the objectives of intelligibility, truth, and being to the intention and active pursuit of the human good, it is not a matter of knowledge but of ideology, and to be teaching or writing theology is to be promoting alienation, whether from an extrinsicist or an immanentist set of commitments.[18] What sharply distinguishes a responsibly methodical theology from either fundamentalist or secularist alienation is the seriousness with which it undertakes to bring all of the culturally available differentiations of the original experience into a dialectically integrated unity that makes yet further differentiating advances possible. Due to the modern exigence for method in general, a contemporary theology that would not be an ideology must be built on the explicit foundations of transcendental method, that is, on the explanatory self-appropriation of the normative order of the search for direction in the movement of life.

This essay is not limited, however, to extolling the advance in differentiation that occurs through the disengagements of cognitive and existential consciousness in the writings of Lonergan, nor even to recommending this advance to any theologian in search of a prolegomenon to future theology. For the integral heuristic structure of the normative interiority of the subject has not been fully disengaged in Lonergan's writings. A central intention, then, of the present work is to advance transcendental method through the discussion of psychic conversion.

2. *The Threefold Mediatory Function of a Methodical Christian Theology.*

In this section, we treat primarily the noetic, i.e., the disclosive functions of a methodical theology, even though mention of dialectic raises the issue of theology's transformative responsibilities. Detailed discussion of the latter occurs in sections Four and Five of the present chapter. Theology's intention of truth is presupposed and sublated by its contribution to world-constitutive praxis.

The term, theology, is not a Christian, but a Platonic invention. In the second book of the *Republic*, Plato distinguishes types of theology, patterns of speech about the divinity; he indicates the order of being that the soul informed by the classical experience of reason discovers as it opens to world-transcendent reality; and he insists that this opening corrects, purges of illusions, and converts to truth previous orientations that appeared in the poets and especially in Homer. The way of ignorance, myth, and falsehood is replaced by the transcendent differentiation that appears with the clearing of the order of the soul by philosophy.[19] The need for theology arises with the advance of immanently generated differentiations of human consciousness to the priority of theory over symbolic consciousness. Only as a similar theoretical exigence appeared in Christianity did there arise a notion of Christian theology as differentiated from faith.

I once defined theology as "the pursuit of accurate understanding regarding the moments of ultimacy in human experience, the referent of such moments, and their meaning for the individual and cultural life of humankind."[20] This definition covers the broadest conception of theology as a rational and disclosive discipline. In principle, it includes what is disclosed under the dominance of the transcendent noetic differentiation as well as what appears under the impulse of the soteriological existential disengagements of the original experience of the search for direction in the movement of life. But I prefer to speak now of the world-transcendent context of all experience rather than simply of those precise moments of ultimacy or limit in which this context comes to fuller clarity and emerges as a differentiated realm of meaning; or of the final anagogic setting of the world that determines the comprehensive intelligibility of all experience and expression;[21] or, with Eric Voegelin, of the Metaxy, the In-Between of cognitive and existential experience, the tension of the divine-human encounter as the basic structural determinant of the original experience.[22] This basic structure received its earliest clear and sustained anthropological-theological differentiation as the measure of the soul in Greek philosophy,[23] and its earliest historical-theological differentiation as the context of history in the experience of Israel.[24] For Christian theology, a further and definitive soteriological differentiation occurs in and because of the person and destiny of Jesus.[25]

Through the ages, the task of Christian theology had been to mediate this soteriological differentiation with the cultural matrix established by other differentiations of consciousness, including the Greek anthropological and the Israelite historical differentiations. But the cultural matrix within which Christian theology is done has been changed considerably by the development of modern natural and human science, modern historical studies, and modern philosophy, and by the situation of global communication, interdependence, and injustice that marks our age. New differentiations of human consciousness appear with each of the modern intellectual developments: the modern theoretic differentiation of science, the scholarly differentiation of historical method, and the interior differentiation of modern philosophy. Therefore, a contemporary methodical Christian theology has a more extensive task of disclosive mediation to perform than did a medieval metaphysical Christian theology. But there is also a continuity. Christian theology had, and has, always to mediate the transcendent noetic differentiation with all of the other immanently generated differentiations of consciousness, and the soteriological differentiation of the Gospel with all immanently generated differentiations, including the transcendent noetic differentiation.[26] Although the differentiations have increased, these two mediations remain, and they can now be carried out under the influence of the controls of meaning provided by transcendental method. In addition, we today find ourselves increasingly exploring the possibility of the mediation of the Christian soteriological differentiation with other historically experienced discoveries of the divine solution to the problem of evil in other religious traditions. Through its performance of these mediatory tasks, Christian theology contributes not only to its own development as a reflective discipline but also to the development of Christian doctrine.[27]

The transcendent differentiation is constitutive of post-axial religion in general. The soteriological differentiation of the Gospel is constitutive of Christianity. Other immanently generated differentiations besides the transcendent noetic differentiation--common sense, theory, art, scholarship, and interiority--are constitutive of cognitive and existential inquiry in their orientations to the knowing, appreciating, valuing, and making of proportionate being.[28] Because of its mediatory function, then, Christian theology relates in principle to all reflection on the human condition and to all of the capacities of consciousness that have emerged in the course of history.

Nevertheless, we discover that the mediations of theology, whether methodical or pre-methodical, have at different theological moments decidedly different qualities. For the transcendent noetic differentiation can itself be related in a complementary, a genetic, or a dialectic fashion to the various other immanently generated differentiations that constitute a culture's cognitive and existential relation to proportionate being.[29] And even though the Christian soteriological differentiation cannot be related genetically to the integrity even of the transcendent noetic differentiation,[30] it may nonetheless stand either in a complementary or a dialectical relationship with all immanently generated differentiations.[31] Finally, the emerging dialogue among representatives of the great world religions may well indicate an overall complementarity between the Christian soteriological differentiation and other manners in which the divine solution to the problem of evil has found a home in human consciousness.

In summary, then, Lonergan specifies the task of theology as a mediation between a cultural matrix and the significance and role of a religion within that matrix. This task involves three sets of mediatory operations. First, there is the mediation of the transcendent noetic differentiation with other immanently generated differentiations of consciousness. This mediation may itself be complementary, genetic, or dialectical. Second, there is the mediation of the Christian soteriological differentiation with all immanently generated differentiations. This mediation may be either complementary or dialectical. Third, there is the task of reaching explicit complementarity between the Christian soteriological differentiation and other conscious realizations of the divinely originated solution to the problem of evil.[32] Because all of these differentiations are themselves in a process of mediated development, Christian theology is an ongoing process. And because there has emerged in our time the modern philosophic differentiation that is consolidated in the work of Lonergan, the ongoing process that is theology can be governed normatively by the leap in being that is transcendental, or generalized empirical, method.

3. *Method in History: Reflections on the Third Stage of Meaning.*

The inner structure or immanent intelligibility of a cultural matrix, when culture is defined empirically as the operative meanings and values that inform a way of life,[33] is a function, first, of the degree to which the various immanently generated differentiations and the soteriological differentiation have emerged in that culture, and, secondly, of the fidelity or infidelity of human subjects to the transcendental imperatives through which advancing differentiation, and so cultural development, occur. These imperatives--Be attentive, Be intelligent, Be reasonable, Be responsible, Be in love--constitute the normative order of the human search for direction in the movement of life.[34]

A culture, then, is a function of the development of human consciousness. Cultural advance is rooted in differentiation, cultural regression in a reversion to unmediated or less mediated compactness. Consciousness is simply experience, the subject as subject; but the subject may or may not have learned, depending on the mediation of education in its various forms, to operate in various differentiated realms of meaning. The culture that flows from undifferentiated consciousness is either archaic and mythical or regressive, depending on whether or not the differentiation of various realms of meaning is part of the heritage that it could have appropriated.

Eric Voegelin has called attention to a disturbing feature of modernity, a feature that I would include in the list of factors that necessitate the advance to transcendental method. He refers to the Gnosticism of modernity, by which he means its neglect of the world-transcendent measure of the soul and of the consequent psychic measure of society. This Gnosticism, he says, actually develops out of recessive strands immanent in the Christian heritage itself.[35] Evidence of this Gnosticism can be found in almost all major representatives of specifically modern forms of thought.

At the center of this Gnosticism of modernity, it seems to me, is an illusion about consciousness and its development, an illusion that has been spotted and relentlessly attacked by Lonergan. Expressed in Cartesian terms, the illusion is that consciousness is objective self-consciousness, "the primary because most immediately evident *object* which disposes instrumentally of ideas and representations by means of a technical orientation." According to the illusion, consciousness is "reducible to an objective awareness of itself."[36] Lonergan's cognitional analysis, however, makes it clear that one may be the conscious subject of the operations of knowing without knowing what one is doing when one is knowing. And psychotherapy makes it clear that one may be the conscious subject of certain feelings, without knowing what one feels. In either case, what is already conscious becomes known, i.e., becomes an object, not by an inward look, but by quite complex operations of mediation through which consciousness is objectified. The objectification is the result of intelligent inquiry and reasonable affirmation, and it therefore results in a mediated differentiation of consciousness in the mode of interiority. The notion that consciousness is objective self-awareness is rooted in the blunder that knowing is like taking a good look. "Its origin lies in the mistaken analogy that all cognitional events are to be conceived on the analogy of ocular vision; consciousness is some sort of cognitional event; therefore, consciousness is to be conceived on the analogy of ocular vision; and since it does not inspect outwardly, it must be an inward inspection."[37]

Thus in speaking of culture as a function of consciousness, we are not positing apodictically a transcendental ego that is creative and constitutive of meanings and values in a manner independent of the historical relativity of situatedness, tradition, and incompleteness. Consciousness is simply the presence of the subject to himself or herself in all of the operations of which he or she is the subject. Consciousness is no more supremely creative and constitutive than are these operations. An adequate analysis of human intentionality, of the operations of the human subject, will reveal that in both its origins and its processes, consciousness is as receptive as it is constitutive, as traditional as it is originative. In Gadamer's phrase, it is effective-historical consciousness.[38] The self-transcendence of consciousness, wherein lies its authenticity, its participation in the true order of being, is constituted by the tense unity of its receptive and constitutive features. There is even a relative dependence of the constitutive capacity on the active receptivity of inquiry through which the real world is mediated by meaning to the conscious subject. Both the cognitive and the existential experience of the subject are partly constituted in their integrity by the active receptivity that conditions the normative order of inquiry.

What allows us to say that a leap in being occurs in transcendental method is that this normative order of inquiry is itself mediated to consciousness through an explanatory differentiation that is unique to our age. The various operations that constitute consciousness as cognitive and as existential are intentional operations. Transcendental method offers a reflexive technique by means of which consciousness is able to bring the operations as intentional to bear upon the operations as conscious. Through such a technique, what was conscious becomes known and willed, i.e., appropriated in both the cognitive and moral orders. Because what was conscious is the structuring operator of all human knowledge and decision, rendering it known and willed provides the self-appropriating subject with a set of foundations for knowledge and decision that enables a new series of ranges of schemes of recurrence in human cognitive and existential praxis. And it is precisely in the context of the theory of emergent probability that we may speak of the explanatory interior differentiation of consciousness as something beyond the various axial differentiations and equally worthy with them to the title of a leap in being.[39] Consciousness is the arena of history, which itself is a dimension of proportionate being, subject to the laws of emergent probability. When world process becomes human history, blind alleys do not cease to be travelled; breakdowns are still suffered, but now personally, socially, and culturally; and yet through it all we may discern, even if at times only dimly, the course that *through differentiation* leads to new capacities, to expanded consciousness, and to more precise self-articulation and that *through integration* leads to temporary plateaus of relative wholeness on the part of the differentiated self-possession of consciousness. Following this course through successive differentiations and integrations, the upwardly directed but indeterminate dynamism of intelligent emergent probability heads toward an ever more nuanced and artistically delicate balance of limitation and transcendence[40] with an increasingly more self-possessed conscious subjectivity. There are novelties along the way, leaps in being, new forms of differentiated awareness, more sophisticated integrations of the capacities of consciousness. In the limit, these constitute axial periods. Who knows how many there were before those that allowed a recorded history to preserve the memory of their occurrence? The leap in being that occurs in transcendental method means in part that intelligent, reasonable, responsible emergent probability can come to understand itself, can work out the laws and patterns of its emergent process, and can thus direct itself from a more secure basis of self-knowledge, freedom, and responsibility.[41] As ignorance and neglect of the transcendental imperatives give way to an appropriation of the laws of intelligent emergence, the probability is increased of cutting a path of genuine advance. A new set of conjugate forms in the individual and new patterns of relations in the human community, a higher integration in the being of the subject and a new series of ranges of schemes of recurrence in human knowing and human living, become attainable. In transcendental method, the course of this expansion of consciousness passes through the intelligent, reasonable, and responsible differentiation and integration of the various spontaneities and cultural acquisitions of human consciousness.

Consciousness, then, is not the objective self-consciousness of some fictive inward perception. In fact, in itself it is not knowledge at all, but simply the presence of the human subject to himself or herself in all of the operations and feelings, compact or differentiated, of which he or she is the subject. This presence is not that of any object. It need not be intended in any operation for it to be experienced. The operations have objects, but consciousness is not an operation. The presence in question makes consciousness distinct perhaps from the condition of dreamless sleep or of a coma, but not from the condition of ignorance. Whenever we are neither dreamless nor comatose, we are surely conscious, however ignorant we may be. The presence of consciousness through operations and feelings to objects is an intentional presence, but the presence of consciousness to itself is simply experience. The experience, however, varies considerably depending on the kinds of operations that the conscious subject is performing and on the quality of the feelings that orient the subject dynamically to the objects of these operations. Therefore, to speak of culture as a function of consciousness is to state that the meanings and values that inform and constitute a given way of life will be dependent on the relative differentiation or compactness of the realms and functions of meaning in the consciousness of the men and women of that culture.

Transcendental method takes its stand on the recognition that human living provides the manifold of conscious data that remain purely coincidental events from the standpoint of the physical, chemical, biological, and psychological sciences. There are events of dreaming, sensitive perception and imagination, inquiry, insight, conceptualization, formulation, reflection, judgment, deliberation, evaluation, decision, action, love, prayer, and worship. There are the feelings that permeate these operations. There is a difference between being intelligent and stupid, reasonable and silly, responsible and selfish. There is the insightful discovery on the part of the developing adult that it is up to oneself what kind of person one will be. As the basic science of humanity transcendental method posits that a person makes a work of art out of his or her life when the way one takes is the way of insight, reflection, and humble commitment; that the deepest desire of the human heart is for this dramatic artistry, this existential authenticity;[42] and that neglect of its conditions is failed artistry, breakdown and collapse, the failure of one's very life.[43] Transcendental method recognizes that the data on men and women as selves will be understood not by studying physics, chemistry, biology, or even sensitive psychology, but by questioning the data of human consciousness itself, by bringing conscious operations as intentional to bear on conscious operations as conscious, by "(1) experiencing one's experiencing, understanding, judging, and deciding, (2) understanding the unity and relations of one's experienced experiencing, understanding, judging, deciding, (3) affirming the reality of one's experienced and understood experiencing, understanding, judging, deciding, and (4) deciding to operate in accord with the norms immanent in the spontaneous relatedness of one's experienced, understood, affirmed experiencing, understanding, judging, and deciding."[44] From this basic and prolonged exercise in explanatory self-understanding,[45] there slowly emerges an expanding differentiation of the various realms and stages of meaning,[46] an elaboration of the structure of the human good,[47] a theory of culture and a dialectical account of history,[48] and a metaphysics that assembles the integral heuristic structure of proportionate being, that unifies scientific inquiry, and that provides a dialectical basis for the hermeneutic appropriation, purification, and promotion of social, cultural, and religious traditions.[49] Finally, from this exercise emerges a set of foundations, indeed theological foundations, that ground a collaboratively realized comprehensive reflection on the human condition.[50] These foundations enable us to speak of transcendental method as a leap in being.

The foundations result from the objectification, in the way of interior self-differentiation, of an "*original normative pattern of recurrent and related operations* that yield cumulative and progressive results."[51] The objectification gives us "basic method."[52] What is objectified is "the subject in his conscious, unobjectified attentiveness, intelligence, reasonableness, responsibility" and relation to transcendent being.[53] Any objectification of this "rock"[54] will, of course, be culturally conditioned and incomplete, and so it will admit further clarifications and extensions.[55] But these will neither affect the structure of the rock itself nor refute the essential elements that basic method discloses.[56]

In order to present in detail the foundations that emerge from the objectification of the original unity of consciousness in its search for direction in the movement of life, we would have to summarize all of *Insight* and most of *Method in Theology*. An interpretation of the development that occurred in Lonergan's thought between these two works will be offered in the next chapter. But what can be done now is to discuss five examples of how extension and clarification of the basic method have already been effected without invalidating the fundamental breakthrough to the new control of meaning.

First, there is Lonergan's own differentiation of a fourth level of consciousness. In his later works, he has disengaged existential consciousness in its concern for judging and effecting value and distinguished this concern from the levels of consciousness whose objective is ascertaining what is, understanding correctly, i.e., knowing. In *Insight*, existential or deliberative consciousness is collapsed into intelligent and reasonable consciousness. As a result, decision becomes a specialization or extension of intellectual activity,[57] and the good is identified with the intelligent and the reasonable.[58] In *Method in Theology*, however, the notion of value is distinguished from the proximate objectives of the desire to know. The sense of constraint that we feel in reading the last chapters of *Insight*, especially when we read with the knowledge that later developments expand the order of intentionality in such an enriching manner, appears almost from the beginning of Lonergan's movement from epistemology to metaphysics. For explicit metaphysics is defined as "the conception, affirmation, *and implementation* of the integral heuristic structure of proportionate being,"[59] and yet the operations that constitute "implementation" have not yet been differentiated. Implementing what one has affirmed to be true demands evaluation, deliberation, and decision. Moreover, as we read on in *Insight*, we meet other instances of the manner in which the account of intentionality is more compact, less differentiated, than the later objectifications that recognize the distinctness, and even the primacy, of the existential in human consciousness. In the chapter on ethics, we find an almost Kantian distinction between affective and effective attitudes,[60] and, as Lonergan himself has acknowledged,[61] an insufficient portrayal of the context in the experience of the heart for the movement to a philosophy of God. These shortcomings are corrected in Lonergan's later works.

Although we cannot overestimate the significance of the emergence of an explicit existential concern in Lonergan's later writings, we must stress that it does not diminish the crucial significance of the basic positions of *Insight* on knowing, the real, and objectivity.[62] And we must remember that it is not Lonergan's last word on the differentiation of the order of intentionality. Since *Method in Theology*, there has been emerging the affirmation of yet a fifth level of consciousness, distinct from and sublating even the heart's concern for what is good. This is the dynamic state of being in love with God, the achievement of what even in *Method in Theology* is called "a basis that may be broadened and deepened and heightened and enriched but not superseded."[63] Its differentiation constitutes the second instance of extension of the basic method.

The third instance perhaps results from these expansions of the differentiation of interiority. It consists in the acknowledgment of the reciprocity of movements within the structure: a creative movement from below upwards and a therapeutic movement from above downwards.[64] The acknowledgement begins with *Method*'s recognition that the Latin tag *Nihil anatum nisi praecognitum* is of minimal relevance,[65] and it extends in post-*Method* developments to the affirmation of the reciprocal conditioning of creating and healing in human history. Lonergan writes:

> . . . Human development is of two quite different kinds. There is development from below upwards, from experience to growing understanding, from growing understanding to balanced judgment, from balanced judgment to fruitful courses of action, and from fruitful courses of action to the new situations that call forth further understanding, profounder judgment, richer courses of action.
>
> But there also is development from above downwards. There is the transformation of falling in love: the domestic love of the family; the human love of one's tribe, one's city, one's country, mankind; the divine love that

> orientates man in his cosmos and expresses itself in his worship. Where hatred only sees evil, love reveals values. At once it commands commitment and joyfully carries it out, no matter what the sacrifice involved. Where hatred reinforces bias, love dissolves it, whether it be the bias of unconscious motivation, the bias of individual or group egoism, or the bias of omnicompetent, shortsighted common sense. Where hatred plods around in ever narrower vicious circles, love breaks the bonds of psychological and social determinisms with the conviction of faith and the power of hope.[66]

Moreover, "just as the creative process, when unaccompanied by healing, is distorted and corrupted by bias, so too the healing process, when unaccompanied by creating, is a soul without a body."[67] Again, we find a more differentiated expression of a structure and of processes that were already recognized in a somewhat more compact unity by the end of *Insight*.

Fourth, there is talk of conversion--of the religious, moral, and intellectual varieties of radical about-face that occur, respectively, when the transcendent exigence of human consciousness[68] is met by the saving response of otherworldly love, when the criterion of one's decisions shifts from satisfactions, with all their ambiguities, to genuine values despite the sacrifices entailed in realizing them,[69] and when one replaces the cognitive myth that knowing is like taking a good look with the self-affirmation of a consciousness that at once is empirical, intelligent, and rational.[70] The conversions are related to one another, both in their usual order of occurrence and in their relations of sublation within a single consciousness.[71] As we shall see in the next chapter, the recognition of a triply converted subjectivity as foundational enables Lonergan to move, however inchoatively, from the position of speaking of the *foundations of theology* to that of talking about the *theological foundations* of a comprehensive, collaborative reflection on the human condition.

Fifth, in my own work, I have introduced the notion of psychic conversion. I have done so simply by extending the basic pattern of the levels of intentionality not upwards, but downwards, in order to include dreaming consciousness and to explain the possibility of the transformation that allows even human sensitivity to participate in the divine solution to the problem of evil.[72]

I have carried forward from *Insight* a precision that one might overlook in *Method in Theology*, namely, the distinction between a soteriological existential differentiation that is cleared by the Christian discovery of the divinely originated solution to the problem of evil, and the transcendent noetic differentiation that is cleared by classical philosophy's opening of the soul to world-transcendent reality. Such a distinction would seem necessary if we are to speak, as I believe we must, of a specifically Christian conversion as a process in the cumulative establishing of foundational reality.[73]

And so the objectification of the rock, the transcendental infrastructure of the subject as subject, the original experience of the search for direction in the movement of life, goes forward. What is cumulatively being established is a position on the human subject as subject, an explanatory differentiation of consciousness that uncovers the terms and relations that obtain in the order of human interiority. But the basic leap in being that establishes the explanatory interior differentiation occurs in Chapter Eleven of *Insight*. Subsequent extensions and clarifications by Lonergan himself and by others will not invalidate the very condition of their possibility. "All such clarifications and extensions are to be derived from the conscious and intentional operations themselves."[74]

4. Methodical Theology and Authenticity.

As we have said, the methodical mediation of the Christian faith with the variety of contemporary cultural matrices involves, first, an articulation of the relationships that obtain between the transcendent noetic differentiation of consciousness and the relative differentiation or compactness of the other immanently generated realms of meaning that inform a way of life; second, the mediation of the soteriological differentiation of the Christian Gospel in its relation to all of the immanently generated differentiations of consciousness; and, third, the search for mediated complementarity between the Christian soteriological differentiation and other historical realizations of the divine solution to the problem of evil. If, as Eric Voegelin has argued, history finds its substance "in the experiences in which man gains the understanding of his humanity and together with it the understanding of its limits,"[75] then history is mutilated when the various experiences of the noetic opening of the soul to the divine order of being as well as the various discoveries of a saving response to the transcendent exigence of consciousness are forgotten or neglected. Voegelin retrieves the manner in which these differentiations have affected the substance of history in the West:

> Philosophy and Christianity have endowed man with the stature that enables him, with historical effectiveness, to play the role of rational contemplator and pragmatic

> master of a nature which has lost its demonic terrors. With equal historical effectiveness, however, limits were placed on human grandeur; for Christianity has concentrated demonism into the permanent danger of a fall from the spirit--that is man's only by the grace of God--into the autonomy of his own self, from the *amor Dei* into the *amor sui*. The insight that man in his mere humanity, without the *fides caritate formata*, is demonic nothingness has been brought by Christianity to the ultimate border of clarity which by tradition is called revelation.[76]

Nonetheless, the transcendent noetic and soteriological differentiations by no means suffice to constitute the articulation of the conscious interiority of the contemporary theologian. With the help of these differentiations, the theologian must critically appropriate the ambiguities of common sense and work through and transcend the pre-philosophic and in a sense pre-Christian biases caused by neurosis, egoism, social transference, and shortsighted practicality.[77] Otherwise these biases will readily mingle with one's theoretical inclinations in such a way as to mask themselves as systematic theological competencies. But the theologian must also acquire personal familiarity with the various immanently generated differentiations of consciousness that enter into the constitution of the substance of history: with mythic consciousness in its various forms, with art and scholarship, with the specialization and refinement of the theoretic differentiation in modern science, with what would seem to be an emerging moral-ecological differentiation that will have enormous consequences for the economic and social, political and institutional order of human life,[78] and with interiority itself in all of its operations and states. Christian theology demands of its practitioner the most subtle and delicate differentiation of consciousness in the mode of interiority, if it is not to degenerate into an ideological justification of some blend of the many alienations that are available to the contemporary mind and heart. The explicit need for such nuanced differentiation imposes on theology the task of providing the foundations of a comprehensive collaborative reflection on the human condition in the context of the full substance of history.

To speak of alienation and ideology, however, is to insist that our linking of the differentiations of consciousness with the realms of meaning does not limit theology to the role of a purely disclosive discipline. The key to the method that Lonergan puts into theology is the notion of authenticity.[79] A methodical theology has a transformative objective. This objective, implicitly introduced in the previous sections, must now be explored more fully.

Cultures obviously originate from consciousness in a hermeneutical fashion. Consciousness is not autonomously or originatively constitutive of a way of living. Nonetheless, culturally situated consciousness is effective-historical consciousness: the preservation and advance of meaning occurs through complementary, genetic, and dialectical fusions of horizons. Cultures are produced by a doubly operative functioning of consciousness through whose relatively differentiated or compact agency the world is both mediated and constituted by meaning. Particularly significant for the constitutive function of meaning is the evaluative or existential level of consciousness. At this level, certain ways of understanding, living, acting, and projecting possibilities are deemed worthwhile and others are rejected as useless and even evil. To speak in more general terms, we can say that the notion of authenticity enables us to disengage the relative dialectical autonomy of constitutive meaning. A lengthy quotation from Lonergan will serve to explicate our meaning:

> As it is only within communities that men are conceived and born and reared, so too it is only with respect to the available common meanings that the individual grows in experience, understanding, judgment, and so comes to find out for himself that he has to decide for himself what to make of himself. This process for the schoolmaster is education, for the sociologist is socialization, for the cultural anthropologist is acculturation. But for the individual in the process it is his coming to be a man, his existing as a man in the fuller sense of the name.
>
> Such existing may be authentic or unauthentic, and this may occur in two different ways. There is the minor authenticity or unauthenticity of the subject with respect to the tradition that nourishes him. There is the major authenticity that justifies or condemns the tradition itself. In the second case history and, ultimately, divine providence pass judgment on traditions. . . . The unauthenticity of individuals becomes the unauthenticity of a tradition. Then, in the measure a subject takes the tradition, as it exists, for his standard, in that measure he can do no more than authentically realize unauthenticity.[80]

The notion of authenticity becomes crucial in the functional specialty of dialectic, where the issues of the intellectual, moral, and religious conversion of the theologian are explicitly raised. These issues are clarified in the functional specialty, foundations, where the self-appropriation of human interiority and, consequently, the objectification of converted subjectivity in its opposition to unconverted subjectivity come to the center of the theological enterprise. The task of theological foundations is, of course, a distinctly third-stage enterprise. The dramatic quality of the exigence which these foundations meet appears in Lewis Mumford's typology of the alternatives that lie before us: post-historic and world-cultural humanity.[81] But it is Lonergan who explains what is required in order to move to the second alternative: the expansion, heightening, differentiation, integration, conversion, and self-appropriation of human consciousness as the key to a new set of controls of meaning.

Because of the centrality of the notion of authenticity, the center stage of the drama of the emergence of world-cultural humanity is not to be located exclusively in the social order. Only individual human subjects are conscious intelligently, reasonably, and responsibly. Consciousness is the unity of the subject's presence to himself or herself in all of his or her human operations and feelings. The unity is more or less differentiated. In either a compact or a differentiated condition of genuineness or authenticity,[82] it begins its upward movement with the sublation of the consciousness of the dream by waking memory into the consciousness of the empirical subject. It extends through the unfolding of intentionality on the empirical, intelligent, and rational levels to its fulfilment in existential and religious consciousness. From an even more basic therapeutic point of view, it is the unity effected when the mediation of God's saving love with existential responsibility sharpens one's dedication to values, overcomes the biases that infect one's pursuit of intelligibility, truth, and the good, and reaches down even into unconscious neurophysiology to stimulate and release the symbols that empower the creative upward movement of empirical, intelligent, rational, existential, and religious intentionality. The constitutive arena of the drama of an emerging cultural epoch lies in the consciousness of the individual human subject. It is there that the struggle of our time is taking place, there that the emerging epoch is taking form, there that the successive breakthroughs that would promote world-cultural humanity are being accepted or refused. What is going forward in our time, most fundamentally, is the struggle for a qualitative leap in conscious being. The successful outcome of this struggle would lead to transformations in styles of living and relating and in the organization of human affairs that would promote existential and social liberation from the suffocating pressures of a cultural epoch that has seen its day but that is holding to its hegemony over conscious subjects with a tenacity that can be broken only by the subtlest and most delicate, because most resolved, resistance.

If this depiction of the deepest meaning of the universal cultural drama of contemporary humankind is accurate, then it is precisely with such a cultural matrix that a contemporary Christian theology must mediate the significance and role of Christian faith. If individuated and self-appropriating authenticity alone can assume responsibility for a differentiating advance of humanity in our time, then the religion that theology mediates with this cultural exigence must be shown to have a crucial significance, an enabling power, with respect to the tasks of advancing full conversion and, consequently, of promoting the self-appropriation by individuals of their conscious subjectivity.

It is clear, then, that the religion of the subject who is emerging into differentiation in the way of interiority fulfills the definition of "rational religion" offered by Alfred North Whitehead: what the individual does with his or her own solitariness.[83] Whether in a compact or a differentiated form, religion has been, as Whitehead recognized, "an unquestioned factor throughout the long stretch of human history." It has always been concerned with what, through Christian mediation, we have come to call justification, with the transformation of character that sets one right with the order of being.[84] In its compact form, religion is primarily a social fact. As such, it achieved expression both in the rituals and myths of the cosmological societies and in the early Israelite embodiments of the historical differentiation effected by the Exodus from Egypt and by the Sinaitic revelation. But because of the advances in differentiation embodied in the prophets of Israel, the tragedians and philosophers of Greece, and the Incarnation of the divine Logos in Jesus, a religion that today "sinks back into sociability" is a religion in its decay.[85] "The age of martyrs dawns with the coming of rationalism."[86] "All collective emotions leave untouched the awful ultimate fact, which is the human being, consciously alone with itself, for its own sake. . . . If you are never solitary, you are never religious."[87]

Even the axial religions stressed the element of individuation in religion. But what is the religion of the theologian to be when theology has responsibility for grounding in self-appropriation the methodical mediation of the significance and role of Christian faith with the contemporary dialectic of meanings and values? For the individual whose participation in the substance of history is a hermeneutic appropriation of the epochal differentiations of the past into a consciousness that promotes a further enriching differentiation in the way of interiority, what the individual does with his or her own solitariness must include the discerning constitution of world-cultural humanity in the retrieval of authenticity that passes through the explanatory self-appropriation of interiority. The individuating emergence of theological foundations is a process founded in religious commitment. It is also a process indispensable to fulfilling the responsibility of carrying emergent probability to a new series of ranges of schemes of recurrence in human life. Solitariness is not apolitical.

The specifically religious component in this exercise of theological responsibility must satisfy Kierkegaard's requirement of authentic faith: "by relating to its own self and by willing to be itself, the self is grounded transparently in the Power which posited it."[88] With advancing differentiation, religion has been disengaged as intrinsic to the process of constitutive meaning. It is not something one does over and above, or unrelated to, the existential project of world-constitution and concomitant self-constitution. The stage of constitutive meaning grounded in the multiform appropriation of the order of intentionality will demand and exhibit the most differentiated religiosity that the substance of history to date permits.

How is it, though, that "by relating to its own self and by willing to be itself, the self is grounded transparently in the Power which posited it?" Ernest Becker has lucidly studied Kierkegaard's notion of faith in relation to the contrasting power of inauthentic cultural traditions, psychological transferences, and the flaccid attempts of psychological religionists to heal the individual consciousness of the other-power to which it succumbs in order to render itself oblivious to the inevitability of death.[89] But for Becker the groundedness of the self in transcendent being is not transparent. It is a "creative illusion"--the best projection indeed, but still a projection.[90] What is it then about authentic world- and self-constitution that make them religiously self-authenticating? This question calls for a basic clarification that a contemporary theology must be prepared to offer.

The best answer to such a question will be found in narrative form, even in the third stage of meaning. But the new control of meaning through the self-appropriation of interiority extends even to the telling and making of the story of one's own life. The key to this explanatory objectification of one's story is to be found in the further differentiating advance upon Lonergan's intellectual conversion that I have called psychic conversion. Foundational reality in the third stage of meaning, then, is dependent not only on Lonergan's maieutic of intentionality, but also on a complementary mediation of the sensitive psyche, a mediation that is engaged in in explicit dependence on intentionality analysis. The heuristic structure of such a mediation will be presented in Part Two. It is a maieutic of the sequence of sensations, memories, images, emotions, conations, associations, bodily movements, and spontaneous intersubjective responses that renders these events--which we will summarize under the term, the psyche--luminous to themselves in a manner both similar and complementary to that in which Lonergan has enabled us to clarify our intelligence, our rationality, and our desire for the good, for what is truly worth while.

This clarification of the stream of sensitive consciousness is relevant to the self-appropriation of both the first and the fourth levels of intentional consciousness in Lonergan's explanatory scheme of consciousness. It is relevant to the first level, because this sensitive stream constitutes precisely what Lonergan means by "experience" or "the empirical level of consciousness" that is sublated by and thus permeates successive operations of intelligent inquiry, rational reflection, and responsible deliberation. It is relevant to the fourth level, because what in Lonergan's later writings is called existential consciousness we shall correlate psychically with what in *Insight* he calls the dramatic pattern of experience, that pattern for which the stream of sensitive consciousness is of such crucial significance.[91] The dramatic pattern of experience is sensitive consciousness sublated by the fourth level of intentionality: it is that organization of the sequence of sensations, memories, images, emotions, conations, associations, bodily movements, and spontaneous intersubjective responses whose cohesive principle is the intentionality of dramatic artistry, the desire to make of one's life with others a work of art. The sensitive stream thus considered has been granted existential significance in *Method in Theology*, where there is acknowledged the indispensable role of feelings and symbols in our existential response to values.

The mediation of the stream of sensitive consciousness that follows upon Lonergan's intentionality analysis first *effects*, and then is enabled to proceed further by virtue of, a change in the subject that I call psychic conversion. The change is *from* a one-sided hypertrophy of ego-consciousness *to* a tense unity in consciousness of the opposed principles of transcendence and limitation[92] in one's development as a person. The source of transcendence lies in one's capacity for intellectual, rational, and deliberative activity. The source of limitation resides in one's sensitive consciousness or psyche. The tense unity means that there is an aesthetic dimension to all intellectual, rational, and deliberative activity. Neglect of this dimension is conducive both to inauthenticity in one's specifically human operations and to the failure of dramatic artistry in one's constitution both of the human world and of oneself.

Psychic conversion consists in the development of the capacity for internal communication in the subject among spirit (intellectual, rational, deliberative, and religious consciousness), psyche (sensitive consciousness), and organism (the unconscious), by means of the attentive, intelligent, rational, and existentially responsible and decisive negotiation of one's imaginal, affective, and intersubjective spontaneity. At the moment, however, I want to call attention to the adjectives: attentive, intelligent, rational, and existentially responsible and decisive. Psychic analysis in the third stage of meaning follows upon intentionality analysis in the cumulative establishment of the full position on the subject, i.e., on *oneself*. Without the qualifications suggested by these adjectives, concern for one's imaginal and affective spontaneity ends one up on an endless treadmill of self-analysis, dooms one to a narcissistic and romantic agony that is without purpose, without direction, without fruit. As transcendence without limitation leads one to a one-sided hypertrophy of ego-consciousness, so limitation without transcendence displaces the tension of consciousness in the opposite direction, entrapping one in a psychological *cul-de-sac* whose only issue is a perpetually renewed psychic stillbirth.

5. The Political Responsibility of a Methodical Theology.

With this requisite addition to the position that will be formulated in Christian theological foundations, we turn to the question of the historical responsibility of the community of self-appropriating subjects. What is it for a community of such subjects to assume collaborative responsibility for the human world? What is it *for them* to be responsible, to fulfill the exigencies of the notion of value as that notion is concretized in their consciousness? I propose this answer to these questions: the existential responsibility of intentionally and psychically self-appropriating subjects in the third stage of meaning consists in collaborative interdisciplinary cognitive and existential praxis oriented to the promotion of the concrete process that is the human good. The human good is a process, at once individual and social, that is engaged in in freedom and that consists in the making of humanity, in humanity's advance in authenticity, in the fulfilment of human affectivity, and in the direction of human labor to genuine terminal values, that is, to particular goods and to a good of order that are really worth while.[93] The meaning of each of these components will be clarified in the next two chapters. For the moment, I choose to indicate how this responsibility is to be fulfilled.

Third-stage interdisciplinary collaboration can be specified by drawing upon Lonergan's treatment of metaphysics in Chapter Fourteen of *Insight:* the collaborative responsibility of subjects who meet on the common ground of intellectual, moral, religious, and psychic self-appropriation is to implement the integral heuristic structure of proportionate being by reorienting contemporary common sense and by reorienting and integrating contemporary scientific knowledge.[94] Let me explain this prescription under five points.

First--and here we repeat a point made earlier in this chapter--without the personal labor involved in arriving at one's own general theological categories that have to do with the immanent intelligibility of generalized emergent probability, theology, in all eight of its functional specialties, runs the risk of a new nominalism--an extrinsicism, a revelational positivism, a supernaturalism in the sense in which David Tracy has employed this term to refer not to the medieval speculative theorem of the supernatural but to an unmediated, uncorrelated semi-vision and hence alienating distortion of the Christian faith.[95] Nominalism in contemporary theology represents a desperate and ultimately futile attempt to escape from the exigencies of historical responsibility into some form of systematic and/or practical theology that is, in Lonergan's terms, not doctrinal but dogmatic,[96] and that proceeds as though the discovery of transcendent and redemptive reality and of the truth of ourselves in relation to that reality is something we happen upon independently of the intentional quest through which we constitute the human world and ourselves in the process. Nominalism manifests itself in theological positions that reveal no appreciation for the theological significance of human intentionality and psychology, of the dialectic of history, of economic relations, of the sociology of institutions, and of the dynamics of political power--in sum, of the operations, decisions, and relationships by which we constitute this world in which we live. The theological field is a dimension of the transcendental field, which is the field intended by the human mind and the human heart. Thus general as well as special theological categories, categories concerned with the immanent intelligibility of generalized emergent probability as well as with the absolutely transcendent establishment of the Kingdom of God, are essential to responsible theologizing.

Second, there is demanded of a theology that would methodically mediate the significance and role of Christian faith with the contemporary dialectic of meanings and values, what we might call, adapting a phrase from Eric Voegelin, an exodus of theology from theology.[97] By this expression, I mean that theologians must realize that their work in the functional specialties of research, interpretation, and history as well as of doctrines, systematics, and communications is but one moment in a more embracing evaluative and transformative hermeneutic of historical experience. It is not a comprehensive reflection on the human condition. A comprehensive hermeneutic will necessarily be interdisciplinary and collaborative.

Third, the basis for this collaborative interdisciplinary hermeneutic *is* provided in the *theological* functional specialties of dialectic and foundations. These functional specialties, precisely as *theological* specialties, become differentiated tasks within the framework of an interdisciplinary hermeneutic of historical experience, because (1) it is theology that inescapably raises the concern for authentic inquiry in all disciplines, and (2) concern for authentic inquiry in any discipline is necessarily connected with issues that are intrinsically theological. Such concern moves the inquirer to answer the question concerning the religious, moral, intellectual, and psychological constitution and integrity of his or her own being. It is in dialectic and foundations, then, that the radical contribution of theology to the comprehensive reflection on the human condition occurs.

We are not saying, of course, that there is no place for doctrinal and systematic theology in an integral hermeneutic of historical experience. But theology's ownmost contribution to interdisciplinary collaboration does not emerge here. When economists or sociologists or psychologists or philosophers ask--as they seldom do, partly because of the way we usually answer them--"What are the theologians saying that is pertinent for this or that issue before us?", the radical theological response will not be a systematic theory of creation or grace, not a point of doctrine, not a moral position, but a foundationally theological and theologically foundational prescription: differentiate your own consciousness, and then advance the positions and reverse the counterpositions that constitute your alternatives.[98] Theologians who know what they are doing when they are doing theology will say, most radically: come to know your own mind and your own heart; come to live your own life on the basis of an affirmation of the exigencies of your own intelligence, rationality, and existential openness and transcendence; and out of that discovery in its fullness find your own answers as economists, sociologists, psychologists, philosophers. It is in this sense that the foundations for interdisciplinary collaboration are theological foundations and that theological foundations are foundations not simply of a few functional specialties within theology but of collaborative interdisciplinary cognitive and existential praxis.

The role of doctrinal and systematic theology within collaborative interdisciplinary praxis, then, is derivative. These represent the theologian's mediation of both transcendent-noetic and soteriological-existential significance with the dialectic of cultural meanings and values. But theology has a *foundational* role to play in interdisciplinary praxis. The theological specialty, foundations, will lay the foundations also of the collaborative reflection on the human condition that issues from the third stage of meaning, which theological foundations itself inaugurates. This theological responsibility demands differentiation in the various realms of meaning on the part of the theologian. Theology requires more than a finely developed religious or soteriological differentiation of consciousness, however necessary that may be. It is also necessary that the theologian be differentiated in modern science, in historical scholarship, in art, and above all in interiority.

Fourth, we find in Lonergan's own development a warrant for the statements we are making. Lonergan's commitments to the classical, the Christian existential, and the Christian theoretic differentiations are obvious in all of his writings. But equally obvious is his effort at displacing these axial developments from a foundational to a derivative position. A new and more differentiated ground emerges in an explanatory self-appropriation of human interiority, of the subject-as-subject. Moreover, Lonergan's own development from *Insight* to *Method in Theology* can be interpreted as a differentiation out of cognitive compactness of the existential intention of value as both the basis and the ulterior objective of cognitional praxis. Coincident with this development in his thought is a movement from concern with the intellectual foundations of theology to an emphasis on the theological foundations of knowledge and, consequently, of interdisciplinary collaboration.

In *Insight*, foundations are a matter of cognitional theory, with its three basic positions on the knowing subject, on being, and on objectivity. These positions remain foundational in the later development, for the modern necessity of the foundational quest is in large part an intellectual necessity that emerges from the breakdown of classical and the development of modern ideals of science, history, and philosophy. But the foundations set forth in *Insight* are not complete. Even in *Insight* there is an implicit recognition of the *existential* genesis of the counter-positions and of the *therapeutic* finality of dialectic. But explicit acknowledgment of the existential dimension of foundations has to wait until *Method in Theology*, or at least until the post-1965 developments, where there is differentiated the distinct structure of the existential intention of value and of its objective correlative in the concrete process of the human good. Concomitant with the development is a significant differentiation of the range of our affectivity, whose reach matches and informs the unrestricted desires of our intentionality. This differentiation, as we shall see, is precisely what enabled me to develop my position on psychic conversion.

Fifth, this development in Lonergan's thought has crucial implications for praxis. These implications can be specified in terms of the effects of this development upon the understanding of explicit metaphysics that appears in *Insight*. There we are told that explicit metaphysics is the conception, affirmation, and implementation of the integral heuristic structure of proportionate being. By the time this definition of metaphysics is introduced, we already know what proportionate being is, what a heuristic structure is, what an integral heuristic structure would be, and what operations are included under the rubric of conceiving and affirming. But only with the later development do we begin to know in differentiated fashion what it is to *implement* a knowledge that one has affirmed to be true. In *Insight*, the operations that constitute implementation are compacted into those that constitute conception and affirmation. The distinct existential intention that must ground the cognitive praxis of implementing, by which one reorients contemporary common sense, and reorients and integrates contemporary scientific knowledge, is not clarified.

As a result, the transformative impact that this movement to explicit metaphysics has, not only on oneself but on the human world that one constitutes through one's insights, judgments, and decisions, does not become clear. With the later development, explicit metaphysics becomes a semantics for the transformation and unification of the results of both cognitive and existential praxis. With this realization, the foundational questions reappear in a new form. Lonergan speaks of the cognitional theoretic question, what am I doing when I am knowing? This is followed by the epistemological question, why is doing that knowing? His later development disengages the existential theoretic question, what am I doing when I am setting my values and following through on them? and the ethical question, why is doing that moral? Talk of religious conversion makes explicit the religious question, what am I doing when I transcend to the known unknown? and the Christian theological question, how is all of this affected by the identification of the life, preaching, death, and resurrection of Jesus of Nazareth as the revelation of the divine solution to the problem of evil? Then the metaphysical question, which in Lonergan's early writing followed immediately on the epistemological question, emerges in a more differentiated form: what do I know as I move toward true judgments of fact *and* toward authentic judgments of value? Finally, a distinctive form of foundational question arises: what do I do when I know all that? when I have answered the cognitional theoretic and the epistemological, the existential theoretic and the ethical, the religious, the Christian theological, and the metaphysical questions? The answer is: I implement the integral heuristic structure of proportionate being by reorienting contemporary common sense and by reorienting and integrating contemporary scientific knowledge through the development of positions and the reversal of counter-positions. The basic positions are now more differentiated than they were in *Insight*. The position on the subject is no longer limited to the self-affirmation of the knower; the position on being is differentiated from the position on the good, for we can approve of what is not and disapprove of what is; and the position on objectivity includes the account of existential self-transcendence, of affective detachment, of universal willingness, of moral, religious, and Christian authenticity.

We have now moved beyond *Insight*'s concern with the cognitional theoretic foundations of metaphysics, ethics, and theology to focus on the theological foundations of the cognitive and existential task of interdisciplinary collaboration in the knowing and making of being. Such implementation of the integral heuristic structure of proportionate being is the existential responsibility of the subject in the third stage of meaning. Its objective is to specify, initiate, promote, and sustain new ranges of schemes of recurrence in human cognitional and existential praxis. The schemes have taken generic form through the leap in being that occurs in the self-affirmation of the knower. But an advancing differentiation has promoted this leap in being from the discrimination of the order of knowing to the appropriation of the full order of human praxis, thus placing existential consciousness in a place of primacy in the determination of personal value. Thus foundations must objectify not only the intellectual differentiation but also, as grounding the intellectual, an existential, a transcendent-noetic, and a soteriological differentiation of consciousness.

We have been attempting to indicate the political responsibility of a methodical theology. Theological foundations will result from the efforts of human subjects to enter into and consolidate their stance in the third stage of meaning--that is, from the efforts of human subjects who have brought and are bringing their conscious operations as intentional to bear upon their conscious operations and states as conscious and who thus come to affirm with explanatory precision the normative exigencies of their own subjectivity. Such subjects bear collaborative responsibility for cognitive and existential praxis that will promote the human good, especially at a juncture in history when the human good depends upon the transcultural discovery of the normative order of inquiry through which human consciousness searches for and discovers the direction that is to be found in the movement of life. There will arise a community of men and women who find in the developing position on the human subject the common ground on which their minds and hearts can meet. This community will be establishing Christian theological foundations. A concluding word about the historical and political significance of psychic conversion will complete this introductory discussion of theology's vocation beyond itself, its political function.

Because the articulate structure of foundations now highlights existential interiority as the fountain of objectivity, the integral heuristic structure that can be conceived and affirmed because of intellectual conversion can also be implemented because of existential self-appropriation. Because of this possibility, the human good can be promoted through third-stage praxis; for men and women who intend to think and decide on the level of history now have a common ground on which to meet. The ground is the explanatory objectification of the normative order of intentionality. Because of the dependence of creativity on healing, of personal value on religious value, the transcendent and soteriological differentiations--the discovery and account of the divine solution to the problem of evil--receive absolute foundational primacy, and it is for this reason that we must recognize foundations themselves as *theological*.

The work that appears below in Part Two, the attempt to indicate the heuristic structure for the understanding of human affectivity and symbolic consciousness, is an instance of what I mean by implementing the integral heuristic structure of proportionate being. I would argue, moreover, that it is still a foundational instance, since here we are still dealing with the realm of interiority. Moreover, this work will affect both contemporary common sense and contemporary science: common sense, because psychic conversion is the key to dramatic artistry and existential authenticity in the third stage of meaning; science, because I will deal explicitly with the key to the reorientation and integration of the discoveries of key figures in the history of modern psychology.

The responsibility to think, to judge, and to act on the level of history itself--the responsibility that falls inevitably to the subject in the third stage of meaning and that demands commitment to a collaborative enterprise of interdisciplinary cognitive and existential praxis--cannot be met without an affective detachment that matches the disinterestedness of the desire to know and of the intention of value. This affective detachment can be promoted through psychic conversion, which, by enabling one to disengage the symbolic ciphers of one's dramatic participation in the dialectic of history, provides a set of defensive circles to safeguard the self-transcendence of one's participation. The task before us is not easy. It is particularly difficult for our sensitive spontaneity. If it is to be an enterprise to which we can commit not only the whole of our minds but also all our heart, we are going to have to learn to acknowledge, to live with, to negotiate those reasons of the heart that speak in our elemental symbols.

The difficulty of the task that we face at these crossroads in the development of human consciousness may be described by quoting from Lonergan's lectures on the philosophy of education. The context of the quotation is a discussion of alienation in modern society. Lonergan says:

> Things have slipped beyond the human scale and the average man tends to find it incomprehensible. He speaks about 'they are doing this, they are doing that.' But who are the 'they?' Nobody knows. That leads to frustration. It is very hard to form small groups of men who will work for particular purposes at the present time because they know it is no use trying. 'You cannot beat the machine.' You can't get anywhere. There is no significance to it. Control power is too centralized. There is no room for personal decision, personal achievement, personal taste, personal significance. *It is a case of economic determination resulting from a lack of the existence of individuals who know their own minds and live their own lives.* In other words, economic determination as affirmed by Marx, as something necessary, is a mistake; but economic determinism as resulting from people not having minds of their own, not insisting that human intelligence and reason and free choice are to be the ultimate determinats of what human life is to be--if that breaks down, then human life becomes mechanical.[99]

Third-stage subjects, too, will find it difficult to join together into small groups to work for the particular purposes that are contained in a vision of interdisciplinary collaboration oriented to the conversion of common sense and the integration of the sciences on the foundations of the basic positions. We are all afflicted by bureaucracies, including University administrations, that have slipped beyond the human scale and have become instruments of alienation, that do not know what they are doing, that are staffed by persons who do not know their own minds and hearts and do not live their own lives. We cannot expect resounding success. We will have to take the way of simplicity, of steadfastness, of ever-renewed transcendence. But when the alternative is post-historic humanity, the price is worth paying. We must be ready for poverty, contempt, and humiliation; but in this way we will gain that freedom from a dying order that is essential if we are to promote the development and sustainment of the new conjugate forms in human consciousness that emerge from the leap in being that first occurred when the operations of human consciousness as intentional were first brought to bear in explanatory fashion upon the operations and states of human consciousness as conscious. Psychic conversion, I trust, will promote that freedom.

6. *Concluding Summary.*

In this chapter we have attempted to detail the situation and responsibilities of a methodical Christian theology, i.e., a theology governed by the theologian's self-appropriation of the normative exigencies of his or her cognitive, moral, affective, religious, and Christian interiority. In the first section, we assigned to such self-appropriation a hermeneutic significance that meets the demands posed by our age for an utmost and a novel differentiation of consciousness in the way of interiority. In section two, we indicated that this differentiation will enable theology to perform three tasks of disclosive mediation: the mediation of transcendent noetic significance (or natural knowledge of God) with other immanently generated differentiations of consciousness; the mediation of the Christian discovery of the divinely originated solution in Jesus to the human problem of evil with all immanently generated differentiations including the transcendent noetic; and the mediation of the Christian discovery with discoveries made by other religious traditions of God's gracious initiative in the world-constitution and self-constitution that comprise history. In the third section, we identified the explanatory self-appropriation of transcendental method as a leap in being, that is, as a qualitative mutation in the development of human consciousness. We located its consolidating moment in the explanatory self-appropriation of the knower that is articulated in Chapter Eleven of Bernard Lonergan's *Insight*. And we specified the major developments that have occurred since this leap forward was first taken. In the fourth section, we discussed the transformative role of a theology grounded in self-appropriation, emphasized the centrality of individual transformation vis-à-vis social change, and set forth some characteristics of the religion of the methodical theologian, indicating the need of psychic conversion if the methodical exigence is to be brought full circle. Finally, in section five, we further specified the transformative role of a methodical theology by locating as its political responsibility the laying of the foundations of an interdisciplinary collaboration. By reorienting contemporary common sense and by reorienting and integrating contemporary scientific knowledge, this collaboration would promote the pursuit of the human good, i.e., of a process at once individual and social that is engaged in in freedom and that consists in the constitution of humanity, in humanity's advance in authenticity, in the fulfilment of human affectivity, and in the direction of human labor to particular goods and to a social order that are really worth while.

CHAPTER TWO

BERNARD LONERGAN: FROM FOUNDATIONS OF THEOLOGY TO THEOLOGICAL FOUNDATIONS OF INTERDISCIPLINARY PRAXIS

OUTLINE

1. Vetera et Nova. The need for new foundations. The development of Lonergan's notion of foundational subjectivity.
2. The Existential Determinants of Cognitional Praxis. The existential differentiation. Existential consciousness as objective and basis of cognitive consciousness.
3. *Insight:* Cognitive Foundations. The three basic positions emanating from cognitional theory.
4. The Possibility and Necessity of Cognitive Foundations. Transcendental method as a distinctly modern possibility and exigence.
5. Foundations as Existential and Theological. The implicit existential problematic of *Insight*. Its explicit acknowledgment in *Method*. Existential consciousness in the third stage of meaning.
6. The Structure of Existential Consciousness. The transcendental notion of value.
   - 6.1. The Order of Value. Existential self-transcendence and the scale of values. The order of differentiation and the order of conditioning.
   - 6.2. Affective Intentionality. Feelings in *Insight*. A psychology of orientations. Intentional feelings and their differentiation. Affective self-transcendence and the scale of values. Affective development. The aesthetic base of morality.
   - 6.3. The Knowledge of Value. Questions for deliberation. Judgments of value: foundational and derived. Horizontal and vertical liberty, and their contexts. Major authenticity. Judgments of value and judgments of fact.
7. Existential Consciousness and the Explicit Metaphysics of the Third Stage of Meaning. Modernity and the question of metaphysics. Being and the good. Implementing the integral heuristic structure of proportionate being.
8. The Theological Foundations of Interdisciplinary Collaboration. The function of interdisciplinary collaboration. Science, common sense, and history.

The work of Bernard Lonergan sets the context for the methodological and theological proposals that are put forth in this work. In this chapter, I expand on the suggestions offered at the end of the previous chapter regarding Lonergan's development. I interpret Lonergan's position on foundational subjectivity in the genetic fashion that outlines a development in another's thought. Only then can I move responsibly to articulate more fully a further differentiating advance that complements Lonergan's achievement. We cannot hope to offer a more inclusive horizon than that cleared by Lonergan. What could be more inclusive than the unrestricted notion of being? But we can contribute incrementally to the development of a fully differentiated and integrated position on the subject. In doing so, I will attempt to follow as far as possible the pedagogical technique of the moving viewpoint employed by Lonergan in *Insight*, for I am motivated by a similar intention to write a book that will aid a personal development.[1] But I do not need to begin with the minimal context that disengages the elements of insight, for I can presuppose not only that minimal context but also the full development of *Insight* into basic positions on knowing, the real, and objectivity, into a dialectical account of a history that has been transformed by the entrance into human consciousness of the divine solution to the problem of evil, and into the dialectic of evaluative hermeneutic consciousness unfolded in *Method in Theology*. But a moving viewpoint is not a moving target. I must therefore root all that follows in an interpretation of Lonergan's own advancing differentiation.

1. *Vetera et Nova*.

Even minimal familiarity with Lonergan's writings discloses some of his fundamental commitments. He surely intends, for example, to preserve, monitor, and reawaken in modern culture the differentiations of consciousness that are displayed in the writings of Plato and Aristotle, in the Christian Gospel and the development of dogma in the Church, and in the classic Christian theologies of Augustine and Aquinas. And he insists persuasively that a consolidation of the positive gains of modernity, as well as a commitment to meeting its peculiar exigencies in the cognitive, existential, and social orders, will shift these classical and Christian advances from a foundational position to a derivative status in any theological reflection that would mediate Christian faith with modern culture. The Christian theologian must move beyond the differentiations that constitute the substance of his or her heritage, and must do so precisely for the sake of preserving the heritage while meeting problems in our understanding of reality and our constitution of the human world with which this heritage is not equipped to deal unless it is purified by a more radically foundational alembic.

Modern science, modern human studies, modern philosophy, and modern politics and economics call for a new and more differentiated ground on which people of intelligence can meet[2] than is available in the premodern philosophical and theological achievements of the Christian tradition. Lonergan found this ground, it is true, by reaching up to the mind of Aquinas;[3] but it is a ground that Aquinas himself did not and could not cultivate with the differentiation that modern developments make possible.

> Aquinas explicitly appealed to inner experience and, I submit, Aristotle's account of intelligence, of insight into phantasm, and of the fact that intellect knows itself, not by a *species* of itself, but by a *species* of its object, has too uncanny an accuracy to be possible without the greatest introspective skill. But if Aristotle and Aquinas used introspection and did so brilliantly, it remains that they did not thematize their use, did not elevate it into a reflectively elaborated technique, did not work out a proper method for psychology, and thereby lay the foundations for the contemporary distinctions between nature and spirit and between the natural and human sciences.[4]

The thematization, technique, method, and foundations here referred to emerge in Lonergan's writings with a systematic explanatory clarity that allows him to speak of a third stage of meaning, i.e., of a new and quite modern series of ranges of schemes of recurrence in the control of mediating and constitutive meaning.

Those familiar with Eric Voegelin's stinging critique of the Gnosticism of the Third Realm[5] need not fear that Lonergan falls into the modern trap of trying to grasp the *eidos* of history and ends up with an immanentization of the transcendent finality of the human spirit. Lonergan recognizes that the three stages of meaning are not simple descriptions of reality but ideal constructs that may help one to describe and explain reality;[6] moreover, all of the variants of modern Gnosticism represent a falling back on "a less differentiated culture of spiritual experience" than that informed by the classical and Christian traditions.[7] Nevertheless, Lonergan's solution to the problems set by modernity's derailment of the differentiations of existence in the search for direction in the movement of life is not simply to be equated with Voegelin's concern to resurrect the classical experience of reason. The basic difference between the two intentions is the capacity, opened precisely by the new differentiation that Lonergan clears, to advance the positions and reverse the counter-positions in modern developments.[8] This further differentiation, dependent upon, resembling, but not identical with theory, and possible only as a result of the development of the human mind in modern science and philosophy,[9] clears a realm of meaning, a sphere of being, that Lonergan calls interiority.[10] The basic clarification takes the form of a position on the human subject as subject.

Lonergan first differentiated the cognitional operations that constitute the subject as knower. In his later works he expands the order of interiority to include distinct levels of moral and religious, and so existential, orientation. The key to the development that I will spell out in detail in Part Two is to be found in Lonergan's own differentiating advance in the assembly of a position on the subject. I have already mentioned that Lonergan's definition of explicit metaphysics shows the need for a further differentiation of interiority. His treatment of metaphysics follows upon his articulation of the positions on knowing, the real, and objectivity in *Insight*.[11] An exegesis of the pages on the definition of metaphysics in *Insight* will reveal that Lonergan's later expansion of the basic position on the subject is already present there, but in an inchoate and more compact form. It is collapsed into the position on knowing, but it is straining to burst the bonds of this intellectualist stricture. *Insight* covertly admits into its formulation of foundational subjectivity intentional operations that are not accounted for, thematized, objectified in the articulation of cognitive subjectivity's foundational adequacy, but that are properly credited only in Lonergan's later position on foundational subjectivity. When we move from *Insight* to *Method in Theology*, we find a development from cognitional analysis to an intentionality analysis that includes but sublates cognitional analysis into a more inclusive and expansive account of the normative order of interiority. The later position, I believe, is not simply a homogeneous expansion that involves no change in notions already employed; it is a higher viewpoint that involves "a complex shift in the whole structure of insights, definitions, postulates, deductions, and applications."[12] The shift no more falsifies the earlier cognitional theory than algebra invalidates basic arithmetic.

By reason of this development, foundational subjectivity is no longer said to be constituted exclusively by intelligence and rationality, but is acknowledged to include intentional operations that are not objectified in cognitional theory. In his later works, Lonergan acknowledges levels of conscious intentionality distinct from the empirical, intelligent, and rational levels that constitute the subject as a knower. There is a fourth level of intentionality whose concern is good and evil and whose operations radically constitute the subject as authentic or inauthentic. And there is a fifth level of consciousness, where the subject withdraws into prayer, into the *ultima solitudo* of the mystic in love with God. When foundations embrace only cognitional subjectivity, one talks about the cognitive foundations of theology. When foundations embrace the existential and the mystical levels, one discusses the theological foundations of interdisciplinary collaboration. It is this significant development that we must interpret in this chapter.

2. The Existential Determinants of Cognitional Praxis.

The expansiveness of an articulate position on authenticity determines the relative differentiation or compactness of one's account of foundations. What is essential, it seems, is an adequate heuristic structure of foundational subjectivity. For obviously the precise detailing of the "lower blade" with regard to specific operations and states of the subject will continue to gain accuracy and precision with further philosophical and genetic-psychological research. But if the upper blade of heuristics is not sufficiently differentiated, the interpretation of empirical data will be distorted by reason of an overly compact account of the possible structuring of the operations.[13] If the heuristic structure is more compact than the data of consciousness whose intelligibility is to be framed on the basis of that structure, the theory that one develops will be constrained, for the heuristic structure and the unfolding account of the empirical data will necessarily be isomorphic. The upper blade of heuristics must be precisely marked in such a way that its structural arrangement is fitted to the object under investigation.

Heuristic structures, however, do not arise out of nowhere. Nor are they "discovered by some Platonic recall of a prior state of contemplative bliss. They result from the resourcefulness of human intelligence in operation. They are to be known only by an analysis of operations that have become familiar and are submitted to examination."[14] They advance only by the discovery of new methodical precision. Their development, moreover, becomes more complex when the heuristic structure in question is fitted to the study of consciousness itself, to the account of heuristic structures themselves, when what is at stake is bringing the operations as intentional to bear upon the operations as conscious, thus effecting an objectification of what one is doing when one is a subject. Then the concern is a heuristic structure for foundations.

The advancing differentiation that appears in Lonergan's work consists precisely in a more adequate marking off of the upper blade of method. The recognition of existential and religious levels of consciousness, distinct from yet related to empirical, intelligent, and rational levels, frees the theory of consciousness from the constraints imposed by the relative compactness of the earlier heuristic structure. We can only assume that the resourcefulness of Lonergan's own intellect led him to analyze operations that were already quite familiar to him but that were not adequately accounted for in his earlier theory. This analysis results in the advancing differentiation of method that made possible the book *Method in Theology:* for the cardinal chapters of that book deal with the two functional specialties, dialectic and foundations, that correspond to the dimension of consciousness that was cleared by the development in the heuristic structure. "The basic idea of the method we are trying to develop takes its stand on discovering what human authenticity is and showing how to appeal to it."[15]

The existential differentiation, then, will be our principal concern in this discussion of Lonergan's development. This differentiation gives an account of the moments of conscious experience in which, beyond and sublating one's knowledge of human and non-human reality, one discovers oneself inevitably confronted with the task of discriminating what is truly worth while from what is only apparently good, and even inescapably bound at certain moments to the pursuit of a fundamental option upon which the significance and value of one's own life and actions depend. Evaluation, deliberation, decision, and conscious fidelity to decision are already familiar operations or states of which one is the subject. They deal not so much with the knowing of being as with the making of being. In and through such operations, one constitutes oneself as good or evil. In moments of existential self-discovery one finds that one has to decide for oneself what one is to make of oneself. And it is precisely because of such moments that "individuals become alienated from community, that communities split into factions, that cultures flower and decline, that historical causality exerts its sway."[16] The clearing of the existential differentiation, then, is explanatory of the course of human affairs in history. Moreover, without this clearing, something remains too obscure in the account of an intelligent emergent probability challenged to think and act on the level of history. Once this clearing has been made, the heuristic structure of historical understanding and decision can be established.[17]

The objective of existential consciousness is the human good. Lonergan details the elements that are at play in heading toward this objective: one intends it in questions for deliberation, aspires to it in feelings, knows it in authentic judgments of value, and brings it about by decisions executed with fidelity.[18] Existential consciousness integrates the affective and cognitional dimensions of consciousness. "Just as intelligence sublates sense, just as reasonableness sublates intelligence, so deliberation sublates and thereby unifies knowing and feeling."[19] Decision synthesizes elements of our conscious being that, without existential self-discovery, remain opposites,[20] and in this integration itself is to be found the criterion of authentic decision. It is at the level of existential consciousness that there is achieved the creative tension of conscious limitation and transcendence that constitutes the genuine or authentic person.[21]

The human good that is the objective of existential consciousness is, as concretely intended, a process that is at once individual and social, that is engaged in in freedom, and that consists "not merely in the service of man [but in] the making of man, his advance in authenticity, the fulfillment of his affectivity, and the direction of his work to the particular goods and a good of order that are worth while."[22] The structure of cognitive consciousness receives its proper integration when the distinctiveness of existential consciousness is recognized, for the advancing authenticity, the fulfilled affectivity, and the responsible direction of one's work that mark the flourishing human personality are functions of a decision to implement the capacities of conscious intentionality for detachment, disinterestedness, and objectivity at each level. Therefore, the integrative moment in the retrieval of oneself in transcendental method occurs not when one affirms the reality of one's experienced and understood experiencing, understanding, judging, and deciding, but when one decides to operate in accord with the norms immanent in the spontaneous relatedness of one's experienced, understood, affirmed experiencing, understanding, judging, and deciding.[23]

Neither the basis nor the objective of cognitional praxis in existential praxis emerge with clear differentiation when Lonergan confines himself, as he does in *Insight*, to cognitional theoretic. questions and their epistemological and semantic derivatives.[24] They are not absent from *Insight*'s analysis, but they are present in a more compacted form. One would not get the impression, for example, from *Insight*'s discussion of patterns of experience[25] that the dramatic pattern is to be assigned a priority over the other patterns, including the intellectual. But this is precisely what emerges from the later expansion, for then one realizes that what *Insight* called the dramatic pattern of experience is the sensitive psychological correlative of the existential dimension of intentional consciousness.[26] And yet who can deny that the author of *Insight*'s chapters on common sense, ethics, and special transcendent knowledge was an existential subject, not short of but beyond the intellectual pattern and sublating it,[27] sharing with us his concern for the *drama* of insight, and sublating his objectification of the intellectual pattern itself into his account of the structure of the unfolding drama of human history? But only in Lonergan's later writings does this dramatic finality emerge in differentiated fashion, for there it becomes clear that the existential concern for the drama sublates the concern for the intellectual and rational pursuit of understanding and truth.

With this development, the transcendental notion of value is given priority over the unrestricted desire to know that is the notion of being,[28] in that the implementation of the desire to know is a function of the recognition of intelligibility and truth as good. The primordial struggle between the desire to know and the flight from understanding that is so central to the dynamics of *Insight* can be adequately appropriated only when one realizes that it is a struggle of existential-dramatic consciousness, a struggle of the heart, more radically than it is of the mind; it is a dialectic of willingness and refusal. Then one can begin to appreciate with due respect the mutual interrelations of the two vectors in one's consciousness that in a post-*Method* development are called creating and healing.[29] Prior to this recognition that the existential-dramatic concern is distinct from and constitutive of the orientations of one's cognitive subjectivity, the struggle--no matter how deeply one feels it from reading *Insight*--cannot be adequately appropriated. The heuristic structure needed to appropriate it is too compact. The *feeling* one gets of the struggle from reading *Insight* needs to be mediated in an account of existential consciousness that recognizes that *feelings* are intentional responses to values.[30] The opening of the existential differentiation is liberating for a consciousness that has followed Lonergan along the path of self-appropriation. One is provided with a heuristic structure much better fitted to elements of one's being with which one became *empirically* familiar in a heightened manner even under the compactness of the previous heuristic structure. It is partly for this reason that I think it not inaccurate to say that in Lonergan's later writings a higher viewpoint appears in the expanded account of the order of intentionality.

Among the values that may be aspired to, acknowledged, decided on, and pursued by existential consciousness are the objectives of the preceding three levels of intentionality. It is under the guidance of existential consciousness that sensitivity, intelligence, and rationality interlock with one another to generate incrementally the knowledge of the real. One is authentically and consistently a knower because one has *decided* to be a self-consistent and self-transcending intelligent and rational inquirer. When its existential character is acknowledged, this decision for cognitive self-transcendence is understood as making a constitutive contribution to the human good. Moreover, the flight from understanding that generates decline now receives the existential name of alienation.[31] Cognitional consciousness is existentially determined in that it is dependent for its exercise upon operations other than those that immanently constitute it as knowledge.

3. *Insight: Cognitive Foundations.*

Although *Insight* can be read on its own as a comprehensive systematic philosophy, or, better, as a workbook intended to introduce the reader to a new control of meaning, it can also be studied as a moment within Lonergan's intellectual development. From this perspective, *Insight* is a preliminary work required for the execution of Lonergan's consuming ambition to work out a method for a contemporary Christian theology. As Lonergan wrote in 1970, "I . . . wrote a long book on methods generally to underpin an as yet unfinished book on method in theology."[32] We are here studying *Insight* in this developmental context, and we are focusing on what would become in the later work the issue of foundations.

Insight pivots around the three chapters which introduce its second part, "Insight as Knowledge." These three chapters treat three notions which are subsequently said to provide the basis for all metaphysical, ethical, and theological pronouncements.[33] These notions concern, respectively, the subject, being or the real, and objectivity. Commitments in their regard are immanent within any cognitional theory, and a cognitional theory is the at least implicit basis of any philosophy and of any philosophical stand on metaphysical, ethical, and theological issues. Our present task is simply to examine these three positions and ask why they are assigned a foundational role. Then, convinced that they are indeed foundational within the modern context (section 4), we must ask why they are not sufficiently foundational (sections 5 and 6), and we must inquire further as to how their insufficiency becomes apparent even in *Insight* (section 7).

Cognitional theory seeks to answer the question, What am I doing when I am knowing? The answer begins with a descriptive account of the experience of certain cognitional operations, but it moves quickly to an explanatory elucidation of the knowing subject by relating these described operations to one another in such a way that the operations fix the relations and the relations fix the operations. Consciousness provides immediate access to an entire range of data on the subject. Thus, description elucidates the event of insight as satisfying, sudden and unexpected, dependent on inquiry, pivoting between the concrete and the abstract, passing into the habitual texture of the mind, combining with other insights, open to systematic formulation.[34] But description yields to explanation when one locates data, percepts, and images as the material concerning which one inquires and into which one has insight, when one further recognizes that concepts, definitions, and formulations are dependent on inquiry and insight, when one proceeds to grasp that formulations in turn give way to a set of further questions of a different kind concerned with the adequacy of one's understanding, and when these further questions are acknowledged as entailing the reflective operations of checking, marshalling and weighing the evidence, grasping that the conditions for affirming one's understanding either are or are not fulfilled, affirming or denying that "this is the case," or judging that one is not yet ready for such an affirmation or denial. Cognitional theory becomes a matter of definition by relation, and such definition provides an explanatory account of human knowledge.[35]

The proximity of the evidence renders such an explanatory account more secure than explanations of the data of sense.

> Explanation on the basis of sense can reduce the element of hypothesis to a minimum but it cannot eliminate it entirely. But explanation on the basis of consciousness can escape entirely the merely supposed, the merely

> postulated, the merely inferred. . . . What is excluded [in cognitional theory] is the radical revision that involves a shift in the fundamental terms and relations of the explanatory account of the human knowledge underlying existing common sense, mathematics and empirical science.[36]

Cognitional theory, then, details an interlocking set of operations which, while many and diverse, can all be located on one of three levels of consciousness: empirical consciousness (experience of the data of sense and of the data of consciousness); intelligent consciousness (inquiry, insight, conceiving, defining, formulating); and rational consciousness (critical reflection, marshalling and weighing evidence, grasping the unconditioned, affirming or denying). All of the operations at each level are intentional. They intend objects and make them psychologically present to the subject. This presence is qualitatively different from one level to the next. The operations are also all conscious: they make the subject who performs them present to himself or herself, but as subject rather than as object. The three levels differ qualitatively from one another in that there is a different and fuller self who emerges as one moves first by inquiry from observation to understanding, and then by reflection from understanding to judging. Binding the three levels together into a coherent unity is the dynamism of inquiry, the pure, detached, disinterested, and unrestricted desire to know which governs cognitional process. The affirmation that such an account is explanatory of one's own knowing, that one is oneself an empirical, intelligent, and reasonable conscious unity--the intelligent and reasonable affirmation, "I am a knower"--constitutes the basic or foundational position on the subject.[37]

There are two other basic positions immanent in cognitional theory, and they are consequent upon the position on the subject. The first is the position on being, and the second the position on objectivity.[38]

When I understand correctly, I know what is so. The term of cognitional process is the affirmation of a conditioned whose conditions have been grasped as fulfilled, i.e., of a virtually unconditioned. Short of that affirmation, I continue raising questions. With that affirmation, my questions on a particular issue come to term. When I reasonably affirm that a particular formulation of my understanding hits things off correctly, I know what is so.

Being, then, is the objective of the pure desire to know.[39] Being is whatever can be intelligently grasped and reasonably affirmed.[40] In its totality, being is what would be known by the totality of true judgments,[41] by the complete set of answers to the complete set of questions;[42] being includes all that is presently known and all that remains to be known.[43] Every true judgment is a complete though minute increment in the knowledge of being.

It is the exigence of the desire to know that promotes the subject to the true judgments in which being is known. The desire to know is prior to all answers, all insights, concepts, formulations, reflective grasp of the unconditioned, and judgments. It is the pure question that

> . . . pulls man out of the solid routine of perception and conation, instinct and habit, doing and enjoying. It holds him with the fascination of problems. It engages him in the quest of solutions. It makes him aloof to what is not established. It compels assent to the unconditioned. It is the cool shrewdness of common sense, the disinterestedness of science, the detachment of philosophy. It is the absorption of investigation, the joy of discovery, the assurance of judgment, the modesty of limited knowledge. It is the relentless serenity, the unhurried determination, the imperturbable drive of question following appositely upon question in the genesis of truth.[44]

As the pure question that comes to rest only in assent to the unconditioned, the desire to know is a notion of being, a heuristic anticipation of what is to be known by intelligent grasp and rational affirmation. It can be denied or perverted, it can become narrowly interested or attached, it can be ulteriorly motivated in its performance or guided by a hidden agenda. But then it will not be given free rein in its own domain, where accurate understanding is pursued for its own sake, where the pure desire is "the source not only of answers but also of their criteria, and not only of questions but also of the grounds on which they are screened. For it is intelligent inquiry and reasonable reflection that just as much yield the right questions as the right answers."[45]

To define being in terms of the desire to know, then, is not to assign the *idea* of being[46] but to differentiate a *notion* of being that precedes all ideas and to specify how to go about determining what is so in any given instance. The position on being is thus a corollary to the position on the subject. Nonetheless, the definition of being that arises from identifying the notion of being with the subject's desire to know is not simply indeterminate. The structured process guided by the pure desire is a determinate one, and the definition assigns to being several quite determinate characteristics: being is all-inclusive, in that apart from being there is nothing; being is completely concrete, in that over and above the being of anything, there is nothing more of that thing; being, while concrete, is completely universal, in that apart from the realm of being, there is simply nothing.[47] Of course, the definition of being is determinate only at a second remove, through the position on the subject. "Being admits no more than a definition of the second order."[48] Such a definition specifies that being is what is to be known in correct judgments. It does not determine what those judgments are. "The notion of being does not determine which position is correct; it merely determines that the intelligently grasped and reasonably affirmed is being."[49] The notion of being, the intention that underpins and penetrates all cognitional contents and constitutes them as cognitional, the core of all meaning, is the subject as consciously attentive, intelligent, and rational, as pursuing understanding and wanting to get things right, as dissatisfied with bright ideas and insisting on evidence, as careful, persistent, cautious, but not indecisive in his or her intellectual commitments, as on the watch for further questions, and as ready to face them when they arise. As consciousl empirical, intelligent, and rational, I not only desire an objective named being, but I have and indeed am a notion of what I desire, a set of criteria for discerning when I have and have not reached that objective in any particular instance. Because my orientation is neither unconscious nor merely empirically conscious but intelligent and rational, "there is not only an orientation towards being, not only a pure desire to know being, but also a notion of being."[50]

The third foundational position immanent within cognitional theory is the position on objectivity. As the position on being is dependent on the position on the subject, so the position on objectivity is dependent on both previous positions. It combines with the position on being to answer the epistemological question about the validity of knowledge: "Why is doing that knowing?"

The principal notion of objectivity is located within the context of a plurality of judgments that exhibit a determinate pattern. The pattern contains at least three judgments: a judgment in which I know myself, a judgment that this or that being exists, and a judgment that I am not this or that being. "There is objectivity if there are distinct beings, some of which both know themselves and know others as others."[51] One knows oneself not in experiencing oneself nor by thinking about oneself, but in making true judgments about oneself. One knows other beings in exactly the same fashion. One knows oneself and anything other than oneself by following precisely the same pattern of operations, by "heading for being within which there are positive differences and, among such differences, the differences between object and subject."[52] If all three of the judgments are correct, then I know both myself and beings other than myself. My knowledge is objective if it is correct, and transcendent of myself if the being that I know in the second judgment is correctly affirmed in the third judgment to be other than myself. The problem of how one gets "beyond oneself" to a known is thus a misleading question--one that has had disastrous consequences in the history of philosophy.

There are three aspects to objectivity. First, every correct judgment is endowed with an *absolute objectivity*. If it can reasonably be affirmed that I am the only being, then this judgment is absolutely objective. If it is reasonably affirmed that I am, that you are, and that I am not you, then each of these judgments is absolutely objective. Absolute objectivity, then, is but a partial aspect of the principal notion of objectivity, whose validity is derived from the set of *de facto* absolutes: I am, this is, I am not this.

Second, from a *normative* point of view, objectivity is a property of a subject. Normative objectivity consists in giving free rein to the pure desire to know; in withstanding "the subjectivity of wishful thinking, of rash or excessively cautious judgments, of allowing joy or sadness, hope or fear, love or detestation, to interfere with the proper march of cognitional process";[53] in opposing "the obscurantism that hides truth or blocks access to it in whole or in part," "the inhibitions of cognitional process that arise from other human desires and drives," "the well-meaning but disastrous reinforcement that other desires lend cognitional process only to twist its orientation into the narrow confines of their limited range."[54] Positively, to be normatively objective is

> to distinguish between questions for intelligence that admit proximate solutions and other questions of the same type that, at present, cannot be solved. Similarly, it is to distinguish between sound questions and, on the other hand, questions that are meaningless or incoherent or illegitimate. For the pure desire not only desires; it desires intelligently and reasonably; it desires to understand because it is intelligent and it desires to grasp the unconditioned because it desires to be reasonable.[55]

Normative objectivity, then, is fidelity to the imperatives that attach to one's empirical, intelligent, and rational being.

There is, finally, an *experiential* aspect to objectivity. It consists in the given as given. It lies outside and prior to the intelligent and reasonable levels of cognitive process. It is simply the flow of empirical consciousness, unscreened by inquiry, equally valid in all of its parts, differently significant in different parts. But its differences have yet to be assigned by intellectual activities.[56]

4. The Possibility and Necessity of Cognitive Foundations.

The explanatory account of cognitive subjectivity is a peculiarly modern possibility. Only as a result of modern intellectual history--modern science, modern human studies, modern philosophy--could the three basic positions immanent in cognitional theory be disengaged in this manner, with the positions on being and objectivity rooted in the position on the subject. Modern intellectual history has made possible a sharp formulation of antitheses in which the basic positions are set against their respective counter-positions. The antithesis to the basic position on the subject lies in "the native bewilderment of the existential subject, revolted by mere animality, unsure of his way through the maze of philosophies, trying to live without a known purpose, suffering despite an unmotivated will, threatened with inevitable death and, before death, with disease and even insanity."[57] The counter-position on being defines the real as correlative to the biological extroversion of the bewildered existential subject: the real is a subdivision, along with the apparent, in a vitally anticipated "already out there now."[58] And the counter-position on objectivity follows suit: objectivity is taking a good look at what is already out there now, seeing everything that is there and nothing that is not there. It is "the unquestioning orientation of extroverted biological consciousness and its uncritical survival not only in dramatic and practical living but also in much of philosophic thought."[59]

The sharp formulation of these antitheses in explanatory fashion did not occur prior to the development of the human mind in modernity. Obviously the antitheses themselves are existentially and dramatically involved in an implicit and compact manner in the counsel and wisdom of the ancient philosophers and Scriptures, in the sophisticated commonsense self-knowledge of an Augustine's *Confessions*, and in the spiritualities that flow from the transcendent noetic and soteriological differentiations in any stage of intellectual maturity. But prior to the modern period, an explanatory pursuit of the truth of reality and of a maieutic to discriminate reality from appearance took its stand on theory and issued directly in a metaphysics. The metaphysics may happen to hit things off fairly well. Lonergan maintains, for instance, that the metaphysical systems of Aristotle and Aquinas did precisely this, within the contexts permitted by the development of the human mind that was their historical heritage.[60] But the relative adequacy of their metaphysics is due to their genius rather than to a control of meaning that thematizes genius itself, that accounts for originality, that articulates in explanatory fashion the very process of intellectual activity that could issue in an accurate metaphysics. And yet that process really was the foundation of the metaphysics. A metaphysics, like any theory, is derivative and not foundational. Its source is the cognitional praxis of the human mind in operation. The transcendental recovery of the process of those operations that issue in theoretical understanding lays bare *the foundations of systematic meaning*. The foundational quest, then, is post-theoretic, but not in the sense of regressing to unmediated immediacy. Rather, theory is carried forward in the foundational quest in order to aid in the mediated and explanatory return to immediacy that is the finality of intentionality analysis.[61]

The peculiarly modern character of the possibility of the foundational quest appears in *Insight* itself in a number of contexts. The sharp formulation of the antitheses on the basic positions occurs only after the lengthy and often painfully difficult phenomenology of knowing that occupies Lonergan in the first ten chapters and that answers the cognitional theoretic question, What am I doing when I am knowing? And that phenomenology itself, we are told, was

> prepared and supported in a manner unattainable in earlier centuries. The development of mathematics, the maturity of some branches of empirical science, the investigations of depth psychology, the interest in historical theory, the epistemological problems raised by Descartes, by Hume, and by Kant, the concentration of modern philosophy upon cognitional analysis, all serve to facilitate and to illumine an investigation of the mind of man. But if it is possible for later ages to reap the harvest of earlier sowing, still before that sowing and during it there was no harvest to be reaped.[62]

Further light on the movement from theory to interiority appears in the "Introduction," where Lonergan tells us why he begins his study by concentrating on insight in mathematics and natural science. His reasons are three. First, these are "the fields of intellectual endeavour in which the greatest care is devoted to exactitude and, in fact, the greatest exactitude is attained,"[63] and therefore one's apprehension of the activities of one's own intelligence is apt to be more precise if one focuses on such rigorous pursuits of the human mind. Second, nowhere else than in modern science and mathematics does the duality of human knowledge emerge so clearly. The transition from mechanism to relativity and from determinism to statistical laws is concomitantly a transition from the assumption that the objects of scientific inquiry must be imaginable entities moving through imaginable processes in an imaginable space-time to the realization that these objects can be reached "only by severing the umbilical cord that tied them to the maternal imagination of man."[64] Finally, it is best to begin a book on methods with an account of those areas of intellectual pursuit where the human mind itself is most methodical--not in order to set up an analogy of science in one's account of methodical inquiry but in order to form a preliminary notion of method from which one can then advance to the more fundamental question of the procedures of the human mind itself.[65] It is for these reasons that the modern mathematical and scientific developments of the human mind are granted a privileged place among the conditions of the possibility of the foundational quest.

The foundational quest is not only possible; it is necessary. Its necessity can be understood by comparing the context of modernity with the stage of intellectual development that was quite content to take its stand on theory and to base its explanatory elaboration of the order of reality in a metaphysics. What is it about modern culture that calls for the foundational control of meaning? Why is it that we not only do not need but cannot assimilate or tolerate a control of meaning by theory? Once again, it is modern science that lies behind the foundational quest, but now not in the sense of providing the condition of its possibility but in the sense of necessitating our engagement in the movement beyond theory to the post-theoretic account of the mind whose capacities include theoretical understanding. Lonergan has discovered that an age that could be satisfied with a theoretic control of meaning was an age that entertained a quite different notion of science from that which emerges from the appropriation of the methods of modern natural science.

The classical ideal of science is articulated in Aristotle's *Posterior Analytics*. For Aristotle, science is true, certain knowledge of causal necessity. The fact that there are many things in the universe that are not necessary but contingent means that this universe is divided between necessity and contingency, and the human mind is split between science and opinion, theory and practice, wisdom and prudence. Lonergan summarizes the Aristotelian position as follows:

> Insofar as the universe was necessary, it could be known scientifically; but in so far as it was contingent, it could be known only by opinion. Again, in so far as the universe was necessary, human operation could not change it; it could only contemplate it by theory; but in so far as the universe was contingent, there was a realm in which human operation could be effective; and that was the sphere of practise. Finally, insofar as the universe was necessary, it was possible for man to find ultimate and changeless foundations, and so philosophy was the pursuit of wisdom; but in so far as the universe was contingent, it was a realm of endless differences and variations that could not be subsumed under hard and fast rules; and to navigate on that chartless sea there was needed all the astuteness of prudence.[66]

The Aristotelian theoretic ideal belongs to a culture that conceives itself as normative, perhaps because of its genuinely stupendous breakthrough to systematic controls. The classicist notion of culture assumed that "at least *de jure* there was but one culture that was both universal and permanent; to its norms and ideals might aspire the uncultured, whether they were the young or the people or the natives or the barbarians."[67] Native existential bewilderment could be healed, or at least pacified, by accepting as normative this culture's "canons of art, its literary forms, its rules of correct speech, its norms of interpretation, its ways of thought, its manner in philosophy, its notion of science, its concept of law, its moral standards, its methods of education."[68]

In all of these dimensions, however, classicist culture has simply broken down. Modern science is not only the sharpest illustration of the breakdown, but also probably the most effective catalyst for the dismantling of classicist culture. And yet modern science itself is still theory, and theory can no longer function as a maieutic of meaning and value. A brief summary of the characteristic features of modern science will show precisely why this is so. Lonergan summarizes them:

> Modern science is not true; it is only on the way towards truth. It is not certain; for its positive affirmations it claims no more than probability. It is not knowledge but hypothesis, theory, system, the best available scientific

> opinion of the day. Its object is not necessity but verified possibility. . . . , not what cannot possibly be otherwise, but what in fact is so. Finally, while modern science speaks of causes, still it is not concerned with Aristotle's four causes of end, agent, matter, and form; its ultimate objective is to reach a complete explanation of all phenomena, and by such explanation is meant the determination of the terms and intelligible relationships that account for all data.[69]

So it is that, instead of contrasting with Aristotle science and opinion, we speak of scientific opinion. For the differentiation of theory and practice we substitute a continuum from basic research to industrial activity. Rather than thinking of philosophy as the search for changeless ultimates, we find our philosophers concerned with existential authenticity, the hermeneutic of cultural objectifications, and the relative adequacy of models, paradigms, and explanatory frameworks. The extension of existential philosophy into concrete living obliterates the old distinction between wisdom and prudence, so that "the old-style prudent man, whom some cultural lag sends drifting through the twentieth century, commonly is known as a stuffed shirt."[70]

The techniques that have effected the breakdown of classicist culture, then, are not limited to the domain of natural science. More existentially pertinent, at least from a proximate point of view, is the shift from a human science that focused on the essential, necessary, and universal to a study that concerns itself with "all the men of every time and place, all their thoughts and words and deeds, the accidental as well as the essential, the contingent as well as the necessary, the particular as well as the universal."[71] What classicist culture thought to be normative is now seen to be an arbitrary standardization of the human person that obscures our nature, constricts our spontaneity, saps our vitality, and limits our freedom. We have even set aside or at least relativized the classical definition of man as a rational animal and have come to prefer an understanding of ourselves as symbolic animals or incarnate spirits. Through depth psychology, we have recovered the profound existential significance of mythopoetic understanding and expression, and in phenomenology we have retrieved the primal dimensions of our corporeal and intersubjective reality. But this wealth of existential discovery leaves us normless. The breakdown of a theoretic control of meaning in the context of a proliferation of theoretic meanings leaves us "bewildered, disorientated, confused, preyed upon by anxiety, dreading lest we fall victims to the up-to-date myth of ideology and the hypnotic, highly effective magic of thought-control."[72] For all the wealth of detail that their investigations have provided us about ourselves, "the psychologists and phenomenologists and existentialists have [only] revealed to us our myriad potentialities"--what *Insight* calls the polymorphism of human consciousness and identifies as the root of the foundational dilemma[73]--"without pointing out to us the tree of life, without unraveling the secret of good and evil. And when we turn from our mysterious interiority to the world about us for instruction, we are confronted with a similar multiplicity, an endless refinement, a great technical exactness, and an ultimate inconclusiveness."[74] No amount of theoretic refinement can remove, nor simply as theory even alleviate, the moment of profound existential self-discovery, "when we find out for ourselves that we have to decide for ourselves what we by our own choices and decisions are to make of ourselves."[75] No definitions or doctrines can be taken as foundational, for they are qualified by the techniques of modern culture to the point of relativism and skepticism. We know their histories and their adventures of development and decline. Authorities, too, are historical beings, and as such they are no more immune from commentary, interpretation, exegesis, suspicion, and criticism than the rest of us. The emerging modern mediation of meaning is one

> . . . that interprets our dreams and our symbols, that thematizes our wan smiles and limp gestures, that analyzes our minds and charts our souls, that takes the whole of human history for its kingdom to compare and relate languages and literatures, art-forms and religions, family arrangements and customary morals, political, legal, educational, economic systems, sciences, philosophies, theologies and histories.[76]

But while countless scholars and scientists devote themselves to the task of understanding meaning, the individual is left alone when it comes to judging meaning and to deciding. "There is far too much to be learnt before he could begin to judge. Yet judge he must and decide he must if he is to exist, if he is to be a man."[77]

The necessity of the foundational quest within the modern context emerges sharply from this discrimination of classical ideals from modern developments. The need is clearly for a maieutic that pushes relentlessly back behind the theories and the techniques, the symbols and the possibilities, to the disengagement, in the way of explanatory self-mediation, of the order of the intentionality that gave rise not only to the modern developments but to the classical breakthrough and even to the mythic elaborations that classicism succeeded. The need is for *a science of consciousness itself* that sublates the sophisticated theoretic capacity of modernity into a post-theoretic control of meaning. The need is for a theory that is both existentially reorienting and immune to fundamental revision. Such a theory can emerge only from the application of the theoretic differentiation to the data that are both closest to us and most elusive--so elusive that they are denied scientific relevance by several of the theoretical variants competing without warrant for status as foundational maieutic. These are the data of consciousness. The leap in being that is transcendental method occurs when our conscious operations, developed to the point of delicate refinement by the modern sciences, are applied as intentional to our conscious operations as conscious. Such an extraordinary procedure brings about an intellectual liberation from the mistaken counter-positions on the subject, reality, and objectivity. This liberation is so radical that it is properly called in Lonergan's later writings a variant of conversion. As conversion it begins a new series of ranges of schemes of recurrence in one's knowing and one's living, founded in the acquisition of "the mastery in one's own house that is to be had only when one knows precisely what one is doing when one is knowing. . . . It opens the way to ever further clarifications and developments."[78]

The antithesis of basic positions and counter-positions is rooted in the polymorphism of human consciousness. The positions presuppose the differentiation of an intellectual pattern of experience. And, as we have just seen, even to formulate the antithesis there was needed much that has occurred in modern intellectual history. Before the basic issues had been sharply formulated, philosophers could base their pronouncements in metaphysics, ethics, and theology only on more or less implicit options regarding cognitional theory. Now that these basic issues have been made explicit, a thorough reformulation of the methods and foundations of metaphysics, ethics, and theology can be undertaken. This is the task initiated in the final seven chapters of *Insight*.

The method of philosophy made possible by the clarification of cognitive foundations enables the many, contradictory, and disparate philosophies, ethical theories, and theologies to take their place as contributions to the elucidation of polymorphic consciousness. A sweeping articulation of dialectical method brings the contradictory contributions into a complex unity in the mind of the philosopher, ethicist, or theologian whose own intellectual development has produced a clarity on the basic antitheses. This unity is heuristically specified and anticipated by the principle that affirmations coherent with the basic positions are to be developed, while those that are incoherent with the basic positions are to be reversed. The reversal ultimately runs its course back to an exposition of the dialectic of concept and performance on the part of the mind of the erring philosopher, ethicist, or theologian.[79] The impetus for both the development and the reversal is to be found in the operating intelligence and reasonableness of the inquiring, critical, self-affirming subject, for whom counter-positions *invite* reversal and positions development. Such a subject can structure the dialectic in which "the historical series of philosophies would be regarded as a sequence of contributions to a single but complex goal."[80] A subject whose mind has mastered its own manifold can determine what utterance is, what is uttered, and the relation between what is said and what is meant. From these determinations, one can find significant discoveries in the formulation of both positions and counter-positions. Moreover, one can enrich the unified, cumulative structure resulting from the positions by adding to it the discoveries that were initially expressed as counter-positions, once one has separated these discoveries from the oversights or biases that led them to be formulated in counter-positional utterance.

Metaphysics, ethics, and theology, then, are all dependent on and expansions of the explicit or implicit cognitional theory of any given metaphysician, ethicist, or theologian. Immanent within that cognitional theory are the thinker's basic philosophic commitments with regard to the subject, being, and objectivity. The disengagement of these philosophic commitments, however implicit they may be, will reveal the ultimate foundations of a thinker's metaphysics, ethics, or theology. The foundation ultimately lies in the position on the subject, which is the position on knowing.[81] The other two foundational positions are rooted in and consequent upon the self-affirmation of the knower, which is the most fundamental assertion of all.

5. *Foundations as Existential and Theological.*

Even in *Insight* we glimpse *the existential or dramatic genesis of mistakes in cognitional theory*, and so we are prompted to push back behind the position on knowing to a more radical existential foundation. The basic positions on being and objectivity are rooted in a position on the subject that is dialectically antithetical to *the pathos of existential bewilderment.* This position calls the disoriented mortal animal back to oneself, there to discover dimensions of intelligent and rational capacities that would, if given free rein, mediate to one a world that, in the limit, one would find completely intelligible.[82] The basic counter-positions on being and objectivity find their ground in the neglect or oversight of the mind through which the real world is mediated by meaning to a human subject. Empirical consciousness is only the substratum for an intellectual pattern of experience governed by the intention of meaning and truth. In short, the search for meaning and truth is existentially motivated. Its finality already is implicitly acknowledged to be ulterior to the immanent finalities of the intellectual and rational levels of consciousness; the latter function in the service of the existential quest for direction in the movement of life. Already the labor of formulating as sharply as possible the basic antitheses on philosophic issues has an ulterior dramatic finality to it, namely, the therapeutic finality of mediating the retrieval of self, the recovery of the order of interiority, that will relieve the bewildered existential subject of his or her desperation. A therapy of self-possession is established over against the unrestrained biological extroversion impelled by fear and anxiety, motivated by animal desire, preoccupied with survival, and oblivious of the dramatic artistry that is its ontological flourishing. Such extroversion is at the root of personal alienation.

Method in Theology explicitly acknowledges this more radical existential foundation. In it the basic position on the subject is expanded to include not only the position on knowing, but also the position on existential consciousness, on moral and religious conversion. From a condition of native bewilderment in *Insight*, a state prior to the grasp of the normativity of intelligence and rationality, the existential subject has been elevated in *Method in Theology* to a position of primacy. The operations of existential consciousness initiate and sustain, but also follow upon and sublate, those of cognitional consciousness. The existential intention of value needs and so sublates the knowledge of reality that has been attained by the exercise of intelligence and rationality. Because of this sublation, existential consciousness is a fuller and richer condition than knowing consciousness. Concomitant with this development is the explicit acknowledgment that theology is no longer founded in cognitional analysis alone, but in an intentionality analysis that objectifies moral and religious consciousness as well. And such an objectification is referred to, not as the basis or foundation of theology, but as theological foundations.[83]

The new notion of existential consciousness means that the specialty of foundations includes an objectification of moral and religious conversion as well as an intellectual self-mediation. Cognitional analysis becomes but one component, however necessary, in theology's foundational functional specialty. A shift has occurred: Lonergan moves from speaking of the cognitional foundations of theology to discussing the theological foundations of--among other things--interdisciplinary collaboration. The development in Lonergan's thought, I believe, is quite momentous. It is, in fact, the most significant moment in the foundational quest, for it grounds as well the specific differentiation of *existential consciousness in the third stage of meaning*. All existential consciousness emerges "when judgment on the facts is followed by deliberation on what we are to do about them."[84] But third-stage existential consciousness comes about by "deciding to operate in accord with the norms immanent in the spontaneous relatedness of one's experienced, *understood, affirmed* experiencing, understanding, judging, and deciding."[85] As third-stage cognitional consciousness emerges from answering the questions, What am I doing when I am knowing? Why is doing that knowing? What do I know when I do that?, so third-stage existential consciousness assumes the responsibility that one acknowledges as one's own when one answers the question, *What ought I to do when I know that*, i.e., when I have answered with Lonergan the cognitional theoretic questions and analogous questions about the moral and religious dimensions of my being. The answer to this question grounds third-stage praxis, whether cognitional or existential-dramatic. Such praxis, on the way toward the constitution of a world-cultural humanity, consists in the explicit implementation of the integral heuristic structure of proportionate being.

6. *The Structure of Existential Consciousness.*

Before we can speak any further of the specific differentiation of existential consciousness in the third stage of meaning, we must follow Lonergan in his disengagement of the transcendental structure of all existential consciousness. As intelligent consciousness is the transcendental notion of the intelligible, as rational consciousness is the transcendental notion of the true and the real, so existential consciousness is the transcendental notion of value.

6.1. The order of value.

The intention or notion[86] of value is complex, for existential consciousness is intentionally correlative to the concrete historical process that is the human good. Moreover, this process itself has both a transcendent-noetic and a soteriological significance. Despite its complexity, however, the criterion of authentic existential performance is analogous to that which obtains for cognitional activity: the difference between what is truly worth while and what is only apparently good is measured by the *self-transcendence* of the intending subject. As intelligent consciousness is a self-transcendence beyond empirical consciousness, as rational consciousness brings one to the affirmation of what is so and thus to a cognitive transcendence of what one feels or thinks or supposes, so existential consciousness concerns itself with the further reach of self-transcending subjectivity in decision and responsible action. Consciousness is promoted to each successive level by the transcendental notions.

> Beyond questions for intelligence--what? why? how? what for?--there are questions for reflection--is that so? But beyond both there are questions for deliberation. Beyond the pleasures we enjoy and the pains we dread, there are the values to which we may respond with the whole of our being. On the topmost level of human consciousness the subject deliberates, evaluates, decides, controls, acts. At once he is practical and existential: practical inasmuch as he is concerned with concrete courses of action; existential inasmuch as control includes self-control, and the possibility of self-control involves responsibility for the effects of his actions on others and, more basically, on himself. The topmost level of human consciousness is conscience.[87]

Obviously not all existential consciousness is self-transcending intentionality. Inquiry can be "limited to determining what is most to one's advantage, what best serves one's interests, what on the whole yields a maximum of pleasure and a minimum of pain."[88] In such cases, we do not have self-transcendence but the individual bias of the egoist.[89] Or one's infectious deliberations can be biased by transference, by the cheap heroics of group-embeddedness[90] that Lonergan calls group bias.[91] But to the extent that one is existentially self-transcendent, one's response is to values, to the effective promotion of that concrete historical process that is the human good. The complex structure of the human good dictates a differentiated scale of values, and existential consciousness entails the artistic structuring of one's responses in accord with this scale. The scale itself is based in a differentiation of the existential criterion: there is a scale of values because there are degrees of existential self-transcendence. It would seem--and at this point, I am offering an interpretation not explicitly found in Lonergan's writings--that the levels of value disengaged by Lonergan are related as follows: *the differentiation of their ascending order* is a matter of emergent probability; but the actual functioning of the levels depends upon the fact that lower order values are conditioned by the successful functioning in a social order of the intention of the higher values. From below upwards, then, there are the vital values of health and strength, grace and vigor, without whose functioning there cannot be differentiated a response to the social values, the good of order, that condition the vital values of a human community. The differentiation of the problem of order frees existential consciousness to inquire into cultural values; the meanings and orientations that inform human living are discovered and expressed, validated and criticized, corrected, developed, and improved. There arises the possibility of the disengagement of the question of authenticity, of the self-transcending subject who originates value in himself and in his milieu. And from the pursuit of personal value as an end in itself there is differentiated the quest of "a basis that may be broadened and deepened and heightened and enriched but not superseded,"[92] the intention of religious value as a differentiated realm. The order of conditioning is inverse to the order of differentiation. The realization of religious values is the condition of authenticity. Authenticity is the condition of genuine cultural values. Cultural values are the condition of a just social order. And a just social order is the condition of the realization of the vital values of the whole community. Explicitly to intend the human good, then, is to differentiate a response to a process, at once individual and social, in which higher values condition the realization of lower values, while the realization of lower values conditions the possibility of the differentiation of the ascending scale of values. Responsible existential subjectivity is a complex though never abstract task, in which one's capacities for mature commitment are continually subject, it seems, to the possibility of greater refinement. In the mutual conditioning of higher and lower levels of value, we are perhaps afforded the explanatory core of a theology of history.[93]

6.2. Affective Intentionality.

In section two of this chapter we presented something of what it means to respond to personal value, to choose authenticity and promote it in oneself. For among the values that may be aspired to, acknowledged, decided on, and pursued under the direction of existential consciousness are the objectives of the three prior levels of the unfolding of conscious process. Under the dynamism of the desire to know, sensitive, intellectual, and rational consciousness interlock with each other, thereby generating the affirmation of the virtually unconditioned in the true judgments in which the real world becomes known. The interlocking of the levels of cognitive consciousness is so compact that their differentiation occurs only by analysis;[94] moreover, "it is only by a specialized differentiation of consciousness that we withdraw from more ordinary ways of living to devote ourselves to a moral pursuit of goodness, a philosophic pursuit of truth, a scientific pursuit of understanding, an artistic pursuit of beauty."[95] Finally, the differentiation that occurs through intentionality analysis brings one to the explanatory self-possession that mediates the precise judgment of value that it is worth while to be attentive to the data of sense and of consciousness, intelligent in pursuing the relations among data, and reasonable in affirming one's formulated insights in accord with available evidence. The desire to know is a personal value that can be implemented by the responsible existential subject and differentiated as a distinct value by the subject in the third stage of meaning. Third-stage consciousness understands the exercise of the desire to know to be the fruit of an existential decision in favor of personal value. The choice of authenticity bids the inquirer assemble the constituent parts of the knowledge of the real. This knowledge is reached incrementally as the operations of rationality come to term in true judgment. *Method in Theology* thus expands the position on the subject to include but sublate the position on knowing into a differentiation of the order of intentionality that accords primacy to existential consciousness.

What I now wish to call attention to is the manner in which the expanded position on existential consciousness constitutes a new account of our affectivity. Whether the human self will emerge in the fullness of personal being as responsible constitutive agent of the human world, thus promoting the concrete process whose immanent intelligibility lies in a mutual conditioning of lower-level and higher-level values--whether the subject will assume personal responsibility for community and history, for progress and decline, for justice and oppression, for culture and deculturation--, is in no small part a function of affective development. For it is in feelings that values are aspired to, and it is by feelings that the scale of values is distorted. The delicate refinement of one's existential engagement in the making of humanity is a task of dramatic artistry.

The criterion of developed affectivity lies, again, in self-transcendence. One's constitutive contribution to the course of human affairs is ambiguous to the extent that it is not attended by a detachment and disinterestedness in the realm of dramatic action that match and sublate the native orientation of the intention of truth. In *Insight* this praxio-critical detachment is called "universal willingness."[96] But only in *Method in Theology* does the positive contribution of differentiated affectivity to world-constitutive agency begin to emerge in its own right. In *Insight*, Lonergan "asserts emphatically" that his account of the identification of the good with being "bypasses human feelings and sentiments to take its stand exclusively upon intelligible order and rational value."[97] In *Method in Theology*, however, the notion of the good is distinguished from the notion of being,[98] and, instead of bypassing human feelings, the account of the good, and implicitly of its ontology, begins with them. The essential difference between the two accounts, it would seem, lies in a differentiation of the range of human affectivity. Although it would be simplistic to maintain that *Insight* ignores the rich potentialities of both human feeling and its neural base, feelings and sentiments are there explicitly correlated intentionally with somewhat restrictively conceived objects of desire.[99] An illuminating passage, already quoted in part, will clarify the issue:

> Unless one's antecedent willingness has the height and breadth and depth of the unrestricted desire to know, the emergence of rational self-consciousness involves the addition of a restriction upon one's effective freedom.
>
> In brief, effective freedom itself has to be won. The key point is to reach a willingness to persuade oneself and to submit to the persuasion of others. For then one can be persuaded to a universal willingness; so one becomes antecedently willing to learn all there is to be learnt about willing and learning and about the enlargement of one's freedom from external constraints and psychoneural interferences. But to reach the universal willingness that matches the unrestricted desire to know is indeed a high achievement, for it consists not in the mere recognition of an ideal norm but in the adoption of an attitude towards the universe of being, not in the adoption of an affective attitude that would desire but

> not perform but in the adoption of an effective attitude in which performance matches aspiration.[100]

Notice that the positive role of affectivity in the latter attitude is not acknowledged. The range of feeling is explicitly constricted, it seems, to a form of adolescent amoric idealism. The agapic subjectivity of universal willingness is not explicitly recognized as *affectively* oriented toward the universe of being in an *effective* manner. There is, as we have said, something Kantian about the distinction between an affective attitude and an effective orientation, something that suggests moreover that feelings can be overriden, something that neglects the constitutive role of affective development in the emergence of universal willingness. True, the neglect appears mainly by way of overtone, for the very notion of persuading oneself and submitting to the persuasion of others implies the delicate task of negotiating one's feelings. But even the overtone is transcended in *Method in Theology*, which heuristically opens the possibility of what Eric Veogelin has called a psychology of orientation, in contrast to a psychology of passional motivation. This is a contrast between the ontologically appropriate psychology and the incomplete psychologies of modernity which deal "only with a certain pneumopathological type of man."[101] A psychology of orientation would differentiate the affectivity and imagination that are ordered by their participation in the normative order of human inquiry. But psychologies of motivation, which Voegelin roots in Thomas Hobbes' drastic derailment of the Western cultural tradition's discovery of the soul, provide little more than an account of "the man who was intellectually and spiritually disoriented and hence motivated primarily by his passions."[102] Such a psychology, and the persons of whom it is true, are constitutive--to the extent they remain on the purely passional level--not of world-cultural but of post-historic humanity. These psychologies acknowledge no higher order of values than the social value of the good of order, and some of them neglect even this level of value. Since autonomous cultural, personal, and religious values are a threat either to spontaneous passional desire or to the good of order, they must be relegated to a realm of oblivion. The technique of forgetfulness consists in nothing less than a redefinition of the nature of the person, which restricts human desire to the limits of passional motivation, to which even the sometimes acknowledged requirement of civic order is reduced.

In Lonergan's disengagement of the affective component of existential consciousness in *Method in Theology*, however, we find in addition to motivation by passion and by the fear of death the *orientation by intentional feelings*. Let us explore and amplify what he says.

The reach of intentional feelings corresponds to the order of intentionality itself in its native desire for the intelligible, the true and real, the good, and the divine. These feelings arise out of perceiving, imagining, or representing particular objects or courses of action. Their appropriation begins by distinguishing these intentional feelings from those affective states or trends respectively rooted in causes or directed to goals that are recognized only by belated reflection. The Kantian-sounding distinction between an affective attitude and an effective orientation that we found in *Insight* is overcome when intentional feelings are acknowledged to be a constituent feature of our conscious orientation to understand, to judge, and to decide. Such feelings are the *effective* orientation of our being.[103] Intentional feeling

> . . . gives intentional consciousness its mass, momentum, drive, power. Without these feelings our knowing and deciding would be paper thin. Because of our feelings, our desires and our fears, our hope or despair, our joys and sorrows, our enthusiasm and indignation, our esteem and contempt, our trust and distrust, our love and hatred, our tenderness and wrath, our admiration, veneration, reverence, our dread, horror, terror, we are oriented massively and dynamically in a world mediated by meaning. We have feelings about other persons, we feel for them, we feel with them. We have feelings about our respective situations, about the past, about the future, about evils to be lamented or remedied, about the good that can, might, must be accomplished.[104]

The very massiveness of our affective orientation, however, risks a compactness that would contract intentional consciousness into undifferentiation. The distinction of intentional and non-intentional feelings is only the beginning of affective differentiation. There is needed also a series of differentiations within the field of intentional feelings. For their objects, their normative order, and their development are complex.

The *objects* of intentional feelings are twofold. Affectivity may respond to what is satisfying and agreeable, on the one hand, or to what is worth while, on the other. But the objects of intentional feelings are complex because the satisfying and the truly worth while are not inevitably exclusive of one another. What is satisfying may also be truly worth while. In fact, a fully developed moral consciousness would not only find eminent satisfaction in all that is genuinely of value but be able to regard its very satisfaction as a sign of genuine value. Yet it is also often the case that "what is a true good may be disagreeable."[105] And, to compound the issue, the phenomenology of conversion would show rather abundantly that dissatisfaction, too, may well be a symptom of an orientation to what is less than good and so may mark the first stages of a transformation for the better of one's existential consciousness and of its participation in the concrete process that is the human good. For this reason, although we must differentiate between the satisfying and the worth while, we will find the criterion for what is good neither in satisfaction nor in dissatisfaction. That criterion, again, is located by Lonergan in the degree of self-transcendence to which our intentional feelings carry us. In any instance of response to "the ontic value of persons or the qualitative value of beauty, understanding, truth, virtuous acts, noble deeds,"[106] affective self-transcendence may be an agreeable or disagreeable experience, depending on one's education and on the effective measure of sensitive detachment to which one's existential development has brought one. But its *character* as a response is not located here but simply and exclusively in the extent to which our response carries us beyond ourselves. Only by long work on one's feelings does one come to a relatively stable point of detachment where even one's inner sensitivity in its radical spontaneity responds to objects with that matter-of-factness that is not uncommitted indifference but universal willingness.[107] In fact, as Lonergan argues persuasively and in continuity with ancient religious insight, such universal willingness has as its condition one's repeated assent to the invitation to participate ever more deeply in the divinely originated solution to man's problem of evil. But even without such spontaneous detachment of desire, one's effort at self-transcendence is a symptom and function of an authentic orientation. Lonergan puts it quite simply: "Most good men have to accept unpleasant work, privations, pain, and their virtue is a matter of doing so without excessive self-centered lamentation."[108] It is the orientation and not the degree of its spontaneity that supplies both the criterion of the value of objects or of proposed courses of action and the *normative order* of affective response.

Nonetheless, affective *development* is a matter of achieving affective responses that are *both* spontaneous *and* self-transcendent. Since self-transcendence, particularly as it affects our feelings, is quite complex, we will do well to anticipate several difficulties. Self-transcendence is not at all of the same order as the psychological perversion of masochism. Nor is it equated with the lesser disorientations of compulsive perfectionism and legalism, or with denials and rejections of the undifferentiated side of the human psyche, and so of human limitation. Nor is it, finally, to be equated with that denial of the order of intentionality as arbiter of the social and cultural domain which reverts to the pathetic decentering of the individual in the Leviathan of political other-power. The culturally automatic person who seeks protection from the threat of meaninglessness and death in the web of social institutions is *not* the self-transcending person. Self-transcendence, rather, has been differentiated by Lonergan in line with the normative ordering of inquiry that promotes it. Thus an intentional response to value can meet the requirements of intelligent, rational, and responsible inquiry. The order of intentional consciousness is a grid for the existential discernment of affective response. This grid marks a self-transcendent affective response to objects and courses of action as a response of a person who is normatively objective, inquisitive, non-obscurantist. Only a culturally effective ideology of alienation could identify self-transcendence as a psychological perversion. In fact, perversions are perversions precisely because they neglect or overrule the normative inquisitiveness of a self-transcendent response. They are, by definition, flights from understanding, refusals or inabilities to face further relevant questions. Universal willingness, however, is the achievement of a habitual affectivity in co-operation with the normative objectivity of the order of inquiry. Nor is it normatively objective for a person to bury one's talents in the social web of other-power, to hide one's light under a basket, to refuse to walk the solitary path of becoming the individual. Precisely through the connection of affective response with the normative order of inquiry, the subject as subject remains normative when one moves from a discussion of cognitive performance to an elucidation of concomitant affective orientations.

This normative objectivity conditions the construction of the preferential scale of values discussed above. This scale constitutes an objective order for the determination of one's participation in the concrete process of realizing the human good. The objectivity of the order is constituted by the self-transcendence to which the subject attains in responding to the different values. Once again, then, physical and psychological health and strength, grace and vigor, constitute a level of vital values. These can be acquired, maintained, and restored only by self-discipline, but such self-control is worthwhile because these values are to be preferred to their opposites. The vital values of a community of people, however, are contingent upon a good of order, a social system that demands contributions on the part of the subject that go beyond procuring one's own vital values. Thus, social values call for a more self-transcending response than do vital values. But since a good social order is constituted by genuine meanings, the cultural values which offer meaning and purpose to living and acting rank higher than social values, and their pursuit calls the subject beyond a practical, common-sense concern with the social order to the discovery, expression, validation, criticism, and correction of the meanings and values that constitute a given social order. The cultural pursuit of meaning and purpose, moreover, is objective only to the extent that the subjects engaged in it are themselves intelligent, reasonable, and responsible, and so the cultivation of authenticity in oneself and in others ranks yet higher, as a response to personal value. Finally, sustained authenticity in human living is impossible without growth in a loving relationship with the source of all meaning and value, without the vertical self-transcendence of the openness of one's intentionality to the divine, and without the discovery of a response in grace to the pure question that one is. A realm of transcendence can be differentiated and cultivated in human living because

> there is to human inquiry an unrestricted demand for intelligibility. There is to human judgment a demand for the unconditioned. There is to human deliberation a criterion that criticizes every finite good. So it is . . . that a man can reach basic fulfilment, peace, joy, only by moving beyond the realms of common sense, theory, and interiority and into the realm in which God is known and loved.[109]

Lonergan's discussion of the preferential scale or objective order of value occurs, significantly, in the context of his treatment of intentional feelings. It represents that differentiation and expansion of the range of feelings that are in large part constitutive of the expanded heuristic structure for the study of the subject that distinguishes *Method in Theology* from *Insight*.

Although feelings are intentional, they are not operations, and so their development is something other than that of operations. In discussing the development of operations, Lonergan distinguishes between mediate and immediate skills. Operations in the world of immediacy regard objects that are present at hand. But imagining, understanding, formulating, and judging are operations through which a world is meant, and meaning mediates that world to the operating subject, who operates immediately with images, symbols, concepts, and words, but mediately with respect to the world that is meant, represented, signified, symbolized. Linguistic skills introduce the child to a far vaster world than the immediate world of one's prelinguistic habitat. The development of mediating operations can proceed to the point where the person's home is the universe and where one's overriding concern as an existential subject is the fulfilment of some purpose that is uniquely one's own within a universal order. But even short of such admirable philosophic, moral, and religious development, the world mediated by meaning sets the context for differentiating cultural advance in accord with reflexive techniques that operate on the mediating operations themselves. So, in a higher culture, not only does language mediate being, as it does even in less advanced human cultures, but also "alphabets replace vocal with visual signs, dictionaries fix the meanings of words, grammars control their inflections and combinations, logics promote the clarity, coherence, and rigor of discourse, hermeneutics studies the varying relationships between meaning and meant, and philosophies explore the more basic differences between worlds mediated by meaning [play, common sense, theory, art, transcendence, the common sense world of others, and subjective interiority]."[110] As we have shown, the reflexive techniques of classical Western culture regarded themselves as universally fixed for all time and thus as normative for cultural development. Modern reflexive techniques, however, are developed with the awareness that they are involved in a constant process of refinement. The problem of assuring their objectivity is precisely what calls for the leap in being that is transcendental method.

Although the development of feelings is distinct from the emergence of all of these operations, it is not unrelated to it. Intentional operations and intentional feelings are inseparable from one another. All of the means employed in the development of feelings will satisfy the general rule of *operating on our feelings*, reinforcing them by advertence and approval or curtailing them by disapproval and distraction. By operating on one's feelings in an intentionally responsible manner, one gradually brings one's own spontaneous scale of values into closer harmony with the objective order of values that flows from the normative order of inquiry itself. Education contributes to one's effectiveness in operating on one's feelings to the extent that it makes one critically aware of the various objects to which feeling responds and thereby enlarges and deepens one's apprehension of values. That the curtailment of feelings through disapproval is something other than what psychoanalysis calls repression should be obvious. It is a matter not of ignoring feelings, but of taking full cognizance of them and of negotiating them in an intrasubjective dialogue that heads toward a psychic integrity of affective response. Moreover, the objective order of values to which the developing feelings of the flourishing adult respond makes it possible that "there are in full consciousness feelings so deep and strong, especially when deliberately reinforced, that they channel attention, shape one's horizon, direct one's life."[111] No small part of the task of operating on one's feelings consists in the awakening in consciousness of the orientation of love that can become the binding force of psychic integration.

Intentional feelings, then, have a precise place and role in the normative order of intentional inquiry. As the apprehension of value, they mediate existential consciousness. The ethical implication of this insight is that there is an aesthetic base in the order of intentionality itself for the character of one's moral being. A psychology of orientations will thus assume as its principal task the differentiation and refinement of this aesthetic intentionality.

6.3. The Knowledge of Value.

With this discussion of feelings, we are only at the beginning of our discussion of the structure of existential consciousness. Related to the apprehension of possible value in intentional feelings are questions for deliberation. Moral inquiry activates the intention of value into a genuinely personal orientation. I ask whether the object or course of action apprehended affectively is truly good or only apparently good. The notion of value as transcendental intention of a true judgment of value goes into operation. The subject is promoted to existential consciousness, to the discernment of what is good, to the discovery of personal responsibility for the world and for the character of one's own being. Like questions for intelligence and reflection, questions for deliberation provide consciousness with the criterion of their answer. In existential inquiry, this criterion is found in the integrity of conscience when confronted with the normative order of inquiry. The morally developed person is aware of "the limitation in every finite achievement, the stain in every flawed perfection, the irony of soaring ambition and faltering performance." But the person is also confident of the self-transcendent process that extends over a lifetime and even through death to "an encounter with a goodness completely beyond [one's] powers of criticism."[112] Sustained participation in this process is the fruit of a long moral development whose aim is the emergence of an existential consciousness that would involve one in the concrete process of the human good; one becomes an originating value, a principle of benevolence and beneficence, capable of genuine collaboration in the advancement of human flourishing.[113]

The intention of what is truly worth while reaches a decisive turning point in judgments of value. Such judgments would seem to fall into two classes. Some are basic or fundamental; others are categorial or derived. Fundamental judgments of value occur when one is moving toward the selection of a determinate horizon or existential stance. At stake here is one's vertical liberty, "the set of judgments and decisions by which we move from one horizon to another."[114] In fundamental judgments of value, one is "determining what it would be worth while for one to make of oneself, and what it would be worth while for one to do for one's fellow men. One works out an ideal of human reality and achievement, and to that ideal one dedicates oneself."[115]

The movement from one horizon to another may be a development out of the inherent potentialities of one's former horizon, and in that case the difference between the new horizon and the old is genetic.[116] But the movement may also be an about-face, a change that repudiates the characteristic features of the old horizon and begins a new series of ranges of schemes of recurrence in one's response to value--a conversion. In this case, the old and the new horizon are related dialectically. "What in one is found intelligible, in another is unintelligible. What for one is true, for another is false. What for one is good, for another is evil."[117] The foundations of one's particular judgments of value about what is good or better[118] lie in these genetic or dialectical exercises of vertical liberty in which one selects one's horizon. Categorial or derived judgments of value are, then, concerned with the exercise of a horizontal liberty within the horizon that one has chosen.

Both vertical and horizontal liberty are exercised in contexts established by the hermeneutic capacities of the individual engaged in appropriating his or her social, cultural, and religious heritage. Thus only the historical development of humankind and the individual's relationship to it give to one's judgments of value their proper context, their clarity, their refinement. "To such contexts we appeal when we outline the reason for our goals, when we clarify, amplify, qualify our statements or when we explain our deeds."[119] Nonetheless, to speak of a vertical exercise of liberty is to imply an originating capacity on the part of the subject's authenticity. The vast context of beliefs within which one's own immanently generated knowledge of fact and value is embedded constitute tradition. But among the fundamental decisions that a maturing adult is called upon to make is the question of the stance that is to be taken towards one's heritage itself, and indeed this question may be said to be the most basic of all human judgments of value and of all decisions. It is the option where major authenticity is at stake.[120]

What was originally an authentic social, intellectual, or religious tradition meeting the criteria established by the normative order of inquiry can be corrupted by the unauthenticity of subjects with regard to the tradition itself. The corruption stems "from a selective inattention, or from a failure to understand, or from an undetected rationalization,"[121] and from the continued usage of the language of the tradition, which suffers a consequent devaluation, distortion, or watering down. As the process of corruption continues, "the unauthenticity of individuals becomes the unauthenticity of a tradition. Then, in the measure a subject takes the tradition, as it exists, for his standard, in that measure he can do no more than authentically realize unauthenticity."[122] The historicity of human understanding and evaluation, then, does not shift the criterion of objectivity away from the immanent order of the subject's intentionality by virtue of which one retains the singular prerogative of being responsible for originating and promoting the realization of what is really worth while. We can discover that our beliefs were erroneous; we can exercise what Paul Ricoeur calls a hermeneutic of suspicion regarding our social, cultural, intellectual, and religious traditions;[123] we can uncover the carelessness, credulity, and bias through which we accepted an inauthentic tradition; we can replace the corruption of our own minds and hearts with the pursuit and promotion of the true and the good. And we can do all this because the immanent order of our own intentionality is the source and criterion of human authenticity and of cognitive and moral objectivity. The potentiality for adopting a critical and selfless stance toward even one's own social, cultural, intellectual, and religious tradition means that the immanent order of intentionality is the radical foundation of authentic existential consciousness. This affirmation does not minimize the importance of belief in general nor does it deny the complementarity of a hermeneutic of retrieval to a hermeneutic of suspicion.

The determining factor of the quality of the context of one's judgments of value, then, is whether one grows or backslides in the domain of personal value. The person in the way of growth is developing his or her knowledge of human living and operating and is finding an advance in affective self-transcendence that opens one's moral feelings to more inclusive horizons of value. One discovers the significance of personal value itself, and at the summit of one's discovery one reaches the transcendent and soteriological base that cannot be surpassed but only enriched and deepened. That base is "the deep-set joy and solid peace, the power and the vigor, of being in love with God."[124] Growth in religious love consolidates one's affectivity, and the religious saint reaches the relatively stable condition of self-transcendent affective apprehensions of value appropriately ordered according to the immanent proportions of human intentionality itself, the coincidence of value and satisfaction, where "values are whatever one loves, and evils are whatever one hates."[125] The person in the way of breakdown, on the other hand, is so affected by neurotic need, external circumstance, lack of practical insight, and antecedent refusal to grow that one's preference scales become distorted, one's feelings sour, and one's self-understanding so corrupted by bias, rationalization, and ideology that one "may come to hate the truly good, and love the really evil. Nor is that calamity limited to individuals. It can happen to groups, to nations, to blocks of nations, to mankind. It can take different, opposed, belligerent forms to divide mankind and menace civilization with destruction."[126] At the root of the distorted context of judgments of value, frequently enough, is the familiar affective aberration that Max Scheler, following and reinterpreting Nietzsche, calls *ressentiment*.[127]

Judgments of value--the affirmation or denial that some objective is truly good or better than another--have the same structure as judgments of fact. In both, the criterion of knowledge lies in the self-transcendence of the knowing subject in search of the virtually unconditioned. In both, the term is independent of the subject. In both, the course of one's movement to judgment is a process promoted by inquiry from apprehension through insight to the point where there are no further relevant questions for a self-transcending subject. Finally, in both, the movement toward becoming a good judge is a self-correcting process of learning.

At the limit of moral development, however, moral knowledge is a matter of affective insight and even of affective judgment. The locus of evidence that enables existential inquiry to come to an authentic judgment of value is found in the intentional response to values in feelings on the part of a subject whose scale of preferences accords with the objective scale that derives its very objectivity from self-transcending intentionality's immanent order of inquiry. But the meaning or content of judgments of value differs from that of judgments of fact, despite the coincidence of their respective structures. The differentiation of existential consciousness in *Method in Theology* means, as we have said, that "one can approve of what does not exist, and one can disapprove of what does."[128]

We must now move beyond exposition to interpretation. It is necessary to investigate the implications of this distinction for our notion of the integral heuristic structure of proportionate being.

7. *Existential Consciousness and the Explicit Metaphysics of the Third Stage of Meaning.*

Method in Theology has expanded the account of the immanent and normative order of human inquiry beyond that given in *Insight*. Since the latter account grounded an outline of explicit metaphysics, and since we have already identified the existential responsibility of the subject in the third stage of meaning to be the implementation of the integral heuristic structure of proportionate being, we must now pursue the metaphysical implications of the further differentiation that appears in Lonergan's later work.

Surely the first questions that arise have to do with the value of such an investigation. Why is it important to work out foundations for metaphysics? Is the labor involved worth while? Are we not embarking on a detour that postpones getting to the point? Can anything come of this circuitous route of inquiry? Is anything more to be gained than the elaboration of an intellectual exercise that may be of interest only to a few philosophers with minds already refined beyond the point of integral human well-being? After all, as the argument goes, metaphysics has been of interest to moderns largely because of a supposed pretence on the part of the human mind's estimate of its own powers, or at least because of a historically conditioned and now permanently laid-to-rest manifestation of the human tendency to misplace and absolutize its partial, fleeting, and relative achievements. Metaphysics may perhaps have been indispensable at a certain point in the historical unfolding of human consciousness or of Being itself as it comes to light in consciousness, but sooner or later it is seen to be futile and in need of being surpassed by a new response to what is still the irretrievably historically relative enterprise of human thought.

Such questions are crucial, for they pinpoint both the need we encounter to take a stand on precisely what is going forward in modernity and the possibility at our disposal to direct the course of the advance of human consciousness, knowledge, and action. The question of metaphysics forces an issue that is inescapable if modernity is to advance to maturity in its intellectual and existential praxis.

If we take the questions seriously, we will come to an expansion of the account of the integral heuristic structure of proportionate being, beyond that provided in *Insight*. By confronting the question of the isomorphism between existential consciousness and the real, we will be able to define with precision the existential responsibility of the subject in the third stage of meaning. This expansion affords us the proper context for appropriating the task of reorienting and unifying the results of the modern experiment in science, in human studies, in politics, and in philosophy. In the third stage of meaning, metaphysics becomes not only cognitive but also existential praxis, for we acknowledge the distinct significance of *implementing* the integral heuristic structure of proportionate being as contrasted with conceiving and affirming this structure.

But we first needed a satisfactory account of the operations of implementing themselves, and of the objective correlative in the ontological order that is isomorphic with these operations. It is precisely this account that Lonergan offers in his expanded notions of existential consciousness as the notion of value, and of the correlative, objective structure of the human good. The new account of value permits us to speak of the operations of implementing. We will investigate the structure of the good at the beginning of the next chapter.

There is a residual neglect of the *existential as foundational* in the last seven chapters of *Insight*. But this relative oversight is manifest not in the insistence on speaking of metaphysics, or in the argument for the existence of God, as some might want to claim, or even so much in the context for raising the question of God, which Lonergan himself has subsequently admitted to be inadequate. Rather, a non-existential metaphysics arises, I believe, because Lonergan restricts himself to the cognitive dimensions of foundations and so affirms an unqualified identification of *being and the good*.[129] From the standpoint of the immanent intelligibility of the universe of proportionate being, which consists in emergent probability, this identification can stand. But when emergent probability becomes intelligent and free, the human world, the real world, in so far as it results from the neglect of the transcendental precepts, is not a good human world. Recognition of the distinct quality of existential foundations leads to a distinction between the real human world as it is and the good human world as it is to be realized. Commitment to the human world as it is to be realized is not the same as satisfaction with the human world as it really is. This fairly obvious distinction, however, depends for its critical grounding on locating the distinct function of the existential dimensions of foundations as contrasted with cognitional foundations.

The qualification of the ontology of the good that arises from the recognition of the primacy of the notion of value will have implications for formulating the existential task of the subject in the third stage of meaning, and even for permitting us to preserve the articulation of this task in terms of conceiving, affirming, and implementing the integral heuristic structure of proportionate being. A metaphysics that identifies the real and the good without further existential qualification limits its transforming and unifying effects to the order of knowledge. It does not extend itself thematically to integrating and changing what we do as existential subjects. And so it is not unimportant that in *Insight* the grounding position on the subject is the position on knowledge.

Our concern for metaphysics and its foundation is valuable, then, because it leads us to a semantics for the transformation and unification of the results of human cognitional *and* existential praxis. If an integral human wisdom is worth while and possible, then our concern for metaphysics is neither anachronistic nor useless. But the differentiated position on the human good presented in *Method in Theology* shows that a metaphysics grounded in cognitional analysis alone is premature. As we indicated in our first chapter, the order of the basic questions is to be expanded. There remains the cognitional theoretic question: what am I doing when I am knowing? This is to be followed by the epistemological question: why is doing that knowing? And there then arise other questions: the existential theoretic question, what am I doing when

I am setting my values and following through on them?; the ethical question, why is doing that moral?; the religious question, what am I doing when I transcend to the known unknown?; the theological question, with whom or with what am I related when I do that?; and the question peculiar to Christian self-understanding, how is all of this affected by the identification of the life, preaching, death, and resurrection of Jesus of Nazareth as the revelation and enactment of the divine solution to the problem of evil? Only then does the metaphysical question become properly differentiated: what do I know when I arrive at true judgments of fact *and* at authentic judgments of value? And the metaphysical question is followed by a new existential question, a question raised by a subject who by reason of the former questions has been elevated into the third stage of meaning: what do I do when I know all this, when I have answered correctly the preceding set of questions? The answer to this final foundational question is already compacted into Lonergan's definition of explicit metaphysics: the existential responsibility of the subject in the third stage of meaning is to implement the integral heuristic structure of proportionate being. And the immanent intelligibility of the task of implementation is also already provided in *Insight:* one implements the integral heuristic structure of proportionate being by reorienting contemporary common sense and by reorienting and integrating contemporary scientific knowledge. Both tasks are accomplished through the application of the heuristic principle that positions are to be developed and counter-positions reversed. But in *Method in Theology* basic positions and counter-positions are more differentiated than they were in *Insight*. The basic position on the subject sublates the analysis and affirmation of empirical, intelligent, and rational consciousness into the context afforded by the recognition of the primacy of existential consciousness. The cognitional theoretic question alone cannot provide the basic position on the subject. It must be complemented by the existential theoretic question. The basic position on being remains what it was in *Insight:* being is the objective of the pure desire to know, what can be intelligently grasped and reasonably affirmed. But the basic position on the good can no longer be reduced without remainder to the position on being. The good is the objective of the notion of value. It is what is known in the judgments of value made by a self-transcending existential subject. The notion of being is subordinated to the notion of value. And the basic position on objectivity sublates the position on cognitional objectivity into a more embracing horizon determined by the notions of existential objectivity, of universal willingness, of moral and religious authenticity.

It follows that, for Lonergan, foundations themselves become a matter of the objectification of intellectual, moral, and religious conversion and that the objective correlatives of these positional statements on the subject assume a threefold structure: the objective correlative of intellectual conversion is proportionate being, the world as it is; the objective correlative of moral conversion is the concrete process of the human good; the objective correlative of religious conversion is the source and destiny of all proportionate being and of all that is good. From such a foundational perspective we can derive the general and special categories of a methodical theology. Even more significantly, with this expansion of the foundational domain, we move beyond *Insight's* concern with the cognitional foundations of metaphysics, ethics, and theology to *Method in Theology*'s focus on the theological foundations of the cognitive and existential task of interdisciplinary collaboration in the knowing and making of being. The objective of this collaboration is the integration of being and the good. But such an integration cannot be assumed to be the starting-point. We start from the real human world as it is, and we intend the real human world as it ought to be.

In *Insight*, the basic counter-positions on being and objectivity are grounded in the basic counter-position on the subject, "the native bewilderment of the existential subject, revolted by mere animality, unsure of his way through the maze of philosophies, trying to live without a known purpose, suffering despite an unmotivated will, threatened with inevitable death and, before death, with disease and even insanity."[130] From our analysis of *Insight*, however, we recognize that this existential subject who sets the foundational problem is not thematically disengaged in his existential determination. At the root of the cognitional-theoretic counter-positions on being and objectivity is a subject who lacks the *existential* resources needed to affirm the order of his or her own intentionality as arbiter of meaning and value. These existential resources only begin to be afforded one through the correct position on one's own intelligence and rationality. Only an affirmation that cuts to the depth of one's being with the same precision as the self-affirmation of the knower and also involves the existential realization of one's desire and constitutive responsibility for the human good meets the exigence of alienated existential consciousness. But this affirmation concerns primarily not the notions of the intelligible, the true, and the real, but the notion of value. It is an affirmation of the ulterior existential finality of one's development. It is an appropriation of the basic dialectic of desire in its own most radical domain of existential consciousness, rather than in the derivative domain of the conflict between the intention of being and the flight from understanding. Even the self-affirmation of the knower, as we have seen, hinges upon the issue of decision. I am a knower to the extent that I have decided to be attentive, intelligent, and reasonable.

What *Insight* lacks, then, because of the compactness of its treatment of existential consciousness, is an account of why the real is so pertinaciously assumed to be somewhere "out there." What is at the existential *root* of the cognitive disorientation that Lonergan corrects from within the realm of cognitional theory? Why is it that we require *a conversion* to exorcise ourselves of our spontaneously assumed cognitional theory? The answer is that we are cognitively disoriented because, more radically, we are existentially disoriented, terrified, resourceless, impoverished, estranged from our genuine being. Cognitive disorientation is not our fundamental malaise; it is the consequence of an existential desperation that can be healed only by an existential agency. In fact, without this agency, a thorough-going cognitional analysis may even intensify the desperation of the existential subject. For the resolve to be an empirically, intellectually, and rationally conscious unity is not self-grounding. The refining fire of dialectic heals the mind only if it has first touched the heart. As Lonergan expresses it in his later writings, intellectual conversion follows upon religious and moral conversion, in the general case.[131] The foundational positions emerge only from an objectification of the full range of the dialectic process that grants to its existential dimension a position of primacy over the cognitional derivatives.

As we have said, even in *Insight*, the existential patterns assume their proper primacy, but only in an unthematic manner. For there Lonergan proposes to move the reader to a basic semantics of interdisciplinary collaboration by bringing him to conceive, affirm, and implement the ordered set of all heuristic notions. In this proposal there is latent the hinge-point from cognitional to theological foundations. Three kinds of operations must be employed in order to move from latent metaphysics to explicit metaphysics. First, one must understand, conceive, and formulate the integral heuristic structure of empirically, intelligently, and rationally known being. Second, one must affirm one's conception of this integral heuristic structure as correct. Third, one must implement what one has affirmed to be true.

When, then, is *implementation?* The operations involved in conceiving and affirming anything, including oneself, have already been set forth in the first thirteen chapters of *Insight*. Moreover, we have ourselves understood and affirmed these operations of understanding and affirming in the basic position on knowing. But unless one implements what one has affirmed to be true, one does not move to explicit metaphysics. But what operations are involved in implementing an understanding and formulation that one has come to affirm as true? Does implementing one's intelligence and reasonableness follow automatically from conceiving and affirming them or does it depend on other operations that are not accounted for by the affirmation of the position on intelligence and reasonableness? If implementation were the necessary and automatic consequence of understanding and affirmation, there would be no need to add a reference to "implementing" in an account of the movement from latent to explicit metaphysics. Explicit metaphysics would result automatically from correctly affirming the present state of the integral heuristic structure of what the human mind can know.

As every reader of *Insight* is well aware, however, nobody is automatically intelligent and reasonable. There is a flight from understanding, a desire not to know. *Insight* urges its readers to recognize this perversion with as much insistence and persuasiveness as it invites them to appropriate their intelligence and reasonableness. The invitation to appropriation, then, is the insistence that one must make one's intelligence and rationality *one's own*, despite the constant inclination to disown them, to abdicate, to be governed by other desire or by external circumstances. At the root of the pertinacity with which we cling to the myth that the real is somewhere out there and that I will finally find it if only I get myself into the position where I can see what I have been looking for is the inclination *to disown oneself*, to un-appropriate one's ownmost capacities. This inclination is counterpositional, not so much to the conception and affirmation of intelligence and rationality as to their *implementation*.

Therefore, the question remains: what, in the terms provided us by *Insight*, is involved in implementing a conception that is intelligent and an affirmation that is rational? What operations are involved in this procedure? Surely more is involved here than the operations that one affirms when one claims to be a knower. One is genuinely a knower only if one wants to be a knower. But what is it to *want?* Only by answering this question can we understand and affirm what it is to implement a knowledge that one knows is true. Only by facing the foundational domain in a new, existential fashion can we move from latent metaphysics to explicit metaphysics. Only by the appropriation of the operations of implementation can we understand why the self-affirmation of the knower is a *conversion.* The existential theoretic question has already been posed in *Insight.* But only in *Method in Theology* does there emerge the distinct heuristic notion of value that differentiates the field in which this problem can be resolved. And with an emerging heuristic notion there emerges of necessity a refinement of the integral heuristic structure of proportionate being.

The implementing self as objectified can approximate coincidence with the implementing self as conscious only if the self as objectified includes an account of the conscious operations involved in the implementing of a knowledge that one knows to be true. In this differentiated coincidence, alienation begins to be overcome. And the finality of the transcendence of alienation reaches its full extent when one discovers from the objectification of the operations of implementation that the good is not to be identified in an unqualified manner with being, or, to state the matter better, that there is a fourth element to the universe intended by our intentionality, an element that is not coincident with central or conjugate potency, form, or act,[132] except in so far as it is the possible term of the upwardly but indeterminately directed dynamism of the concrete universe to ever fuller being. Until the dynamism incrementally reaches *value,* value is not act, and to that extent, being is not good. And so there is grounded the condition of the possibility that we can approve of what does not exist and disapprove of what does. In such approval and disapproval are uncovered the foundations of the implementation of what one knows to be true in the cognitive and existential orders. In brief, the integral heuristic structure of proportionate being has been granted a more differentiated outline in *Method in Theology.* This new outline enables us to say what we mean by implementing in general. Such expanded self-knowledge opens a differentiated field for the implementation of the integral heuristic structure of proportionate being. And such implementation is the specific existential responsibility of the subject in the third stage of meaning, the subject who can assemble, conceive, and affirm, and so be prepared to implement, this integral heuristic structure.

8. The Theological Foundations of Interdisciplinary Collaboration.

The implementation of the integral heuristic structure of proportionate being--the latter supplemented by the recognition that the order of value is incomplete in that the good is not act, that existential consciousness is isomorphic with the good that is yet to be accomplished--will go forward not in an isolated consciousness, but in interdisciplinary collaboration. We are now prepared to discuss in a more expanded context what was introduced at the end of the previous chapter: the function of such collaboration will be to *specify, initiate, promote, and sustain* new ranges of schemes of recurrence in human cognitional and existential praxis. The schemes have taken generic form through the leap in being that is transcendental method. The foundational reality of such interdisciplinary collaboration is the functioning order of normative intentionality. Transcendental method has objectified this order. The objectification itself constitutes foundations. In Lonergan's terms, foundations articulates the order of interiority established by intellectual, moral, and religious conversion. From such an objectification can be derived objective correlatives of authentic subjectivity. That is, the integral heuristic structure of proportionate being can be conceived and affirmed. But because the articulation that constitutes foundations not only includes but highlights existential interiority as the fountain of objectivity, this heuristic structure can also be implemented. The human good can be promoted self-consciously. Positions can be explicitly developed and counter-positions explicitly reversed. Common sense can be reoriented. Science can be reoriented and integrated. The reorientation and integration can--indeed must--be a communal enterprise. It will advance the promotion of world-cultural humanity on the basis of the common ground on which men and women who intend to think and act on the level of history can meet. This ground is the leap in being that occurred when the development of the human mind reached the point where the operations of intentionality, precisely *as* intentional, could be applied to the operations of intentionality as conscious.

The implementation, of course, will not be confined to the theoretic order, for praxis is the foundational reality of theory, and praxis itself is pre-eminently existential. No reorientation of science and common sense through the explicit development of positions and the explicit reversal of counter-positions can remain in a purely theoretic domain. Science and common sense enjoy a symbiotic existence in modern culture, and together they generate the course of history. The reorientation of science and common sense will inevitably entail the reorientation of human history itself. If the reorientation of science occurs through the development of the positions and the reversal of the counter-positions, and if the reorientation of common sense promotes a dramatic artistry that is one with existential authenticity, the reorientation of history is in the direction of the concrete process, at once individual and social, that consists in the making of humanity, in the fulfilment of affectivity, in the advance of authenticity, and in the direction of human labor to goals that are truly worth while. The subject in the third stage of meaning has the existential responsibility not simply to think but also and foundationally to decide and act on the level of history. The cumulative effect of the community of men and women who meet on the common ground of the leap in being that is transcendental method will be the effective promotion of the human good. The *kairos* of our day appears precisely in the fact that no good will short of this leap in being will effectively promote the advance of human flourishing in history. The responsibility is grave. But the opportunity of meeting it is available, for the leap in being has occurred. It is up to each person individually to appropriate it. The authenticity of the individual who has kept up with the very substance of history lies in that dimension of religiousness that Whitehead captures when he defines religion in terms of what the individual does with his or her own solitariness. The specific determination by each individual of that generic existential category is the standard which measures the authenticity of one's responsibility to the intersubjective community, to the social order, to human history, to the concrete universe of proportionate being, and to the absolutely transcendent source of universal and historical order.

CHAPTER THREE

PSYCHOLOGY AND THE FOUNDATIONS OF INTERDISCIPLINARY COLLABORATION

OUTLINE

Introduction. The Problem: dramatic and practical control and direction of intellectual development; the neglected psyche and sociocultural deterioration.

1. The Longer Cycle of Decline. The root of decline. Shorter and longer cycles. Exigencies of reversal.
2. The Structure of the Human Good. The three ends of human action. Cultural infrastructure and suprastructure. Community and individual. Terminal values and originating values. The threefold structure of one's relation to community. Its common collapse into a twofold structure. Moral conversion and the human good.
3. The Neglected Psyche. The exigence for self-appropriation. Existential self-appropriation as narrative. The victimized psyche in the longer cycle. Lewis Mumford: post-historic and world-cultural humanity. The neglect of soul as constitutive of the longer cycle.
4. The Existential Differentiation and the Science of Psychology.
    - 4.1. Symbols and the Psychology of Orientations. The transcendental significance of the sensitive psyche. Feelings and orientation. Feelings and symbols. Interpreting symbols.
    - 4.2. Authentic Religion and Orientation. Universal willingness and the soteriological differentiation. Moral impotence and the gift of God's love.
    - 4.3. The Soteriological Foundation of the Transformation of Order. Redemptive experience and sustained authenticity. Reversing the neglect of the psyche. The disproportion of sensitivity and spiritual intentionality: the problem of temporality and the experience of unrestricted love. The soteriological base of epochal differentiations. Affective conversion.
    - 4.4. Methodical Psychology and the Third Stage of Meaning. The reorientation of psychology. The psychological complement to intentionality analysis.

According to our interpretation of Lonergan, theology's principal contribution to cognitive and existential praxis in the third stage of meaning will be to provide the very foundations of this praxis. It will do so by promoting the cognitive, moral, and religious self-appropriation that both elevates one onto the third stage and provides one with a new set of controls of meaning in terms of interiorly differentiated consciousness. In differentiated interiority one finds the basic terms and relations of a new science of humanity. This science takes the form of an evaluative hermeneutic of cultural meanings and values. It advances the positions and reverses the counter-positions in all of the developments and accomplishments of the human mind and heart, both past and present. Its foundations thus enable it to be a normative and critical, comprehensive and collaborative reflection on the full substance of history, where that substance is conceived, with Eric Voegelin, as the totality of the experiences and insights in which the mind and heart have gained an understanding of their humanity and of their limits. Moreover, the new set of controls of meaning through interiority provides a cumulatively assembled base from which the third-stage subject is equipped not only to understand history but to direct it. The community of self-appropriating subjects will contribute to the making of a world-cultural humanity by articulating the common transcultural exigencies of the normative order of the search for direction in the movement of life. Since a methodical theology makes a foundational contribution to this leap forward in human conscious evolution, it will perform both a disclosive and a transformative task. It will enable all of the historically available differentiations of the original experience to achieve a nuanced and dialectically mediated unity in the self-appropriating cognitional and existential interiority of the third-stage subject. But it will also provide the grounds for a series of new differentiations and integrations that will advance the realization of a transcultural human community.

In the first chapter we described the disclosive task of a methodical theology in sufficient detail for our present purposes. In this chapter we will study the way in which the performance of the transformative function reverses a process of social and personal disintegration. We will argue that decline occurred because the theoretic controls of the second stage of meaning were unable to achieve an integration with the organic and psychic spontaneities from which they dissociated themselves. They could not withstand the destruction that these lower spontaneities cause when they are not functioning in harmony with the advancing differentiations of theoretic consciousness. The mediating factor between theoretic intelligence and organic and psychic spontaneity should have been found in a dramatic and practical agency whose development kept pace with the advances of philosophic and scientific intelligence. And these advances should have been sublated into an existential authenticity that was at home in the various differentiations and that was able to move with ease from one differentiation to another, honoring the rightful claims of each but also preventing each from overextending its territorial demands in the economy, indeed the ecology, of interiority.

What has happened instead is just the opposite of this emergence of existential authenticity in dramatic and practical living. The dramatic and practical patterns of experience have not been stretched to the point where they would be in command of the intellectual development of humanity. As a result, they have distorted this development, pressing it into the service of an undeveloped and untransformed practical common sense. The distortion of theoretic intelligence, its surrender to the claims of biased practicality in the making of humanity, has been accompanied by a progressive neglect of the vital spontaneities of the organism, whose neural demands for psychic representation are conditioned by the situations constituted by practical intelligence. In modern times these situations have been less and less the product of an authentic interiority that would honor the self-transcendent dynamism of advancing differentiation. As the social situation deteriorates, the dialectic between the practical intelligence of the subject and the neural demands of the organism for integration in conscious living becomes an ever more distorted sequence of transactions between biased practicality and lower-order spontaneities. These spontaneities can achieve harmonious integration in conscious living only if sublated by an intentional consciousness authentically set on the course of differentiation and integration dictated by the normative order of the search for direction in the movement of life. As the exigencies of the normative order, which demand an existential-practical development capable of sublating and integrating theoretic development, are progressively neglected, the neural demands of the organism become progressively chaotic, disordered, disoriented, impulsive, and dissociated from their spontaneous and congruous ideational complements. The result is an unintegrated manifold of fragmented psychic complexes in the sensitive consciousness of the biased subject. As the ideational complements of these energic spontaneities become more and more incongruous, the danger increases that the organic and psychic darkness of the subject, which C. G. Jung calls the shadow, will vent its frustrated appeal for conscious integration in the form of "the compensating function of mischievous destruction."[1]

The establishment of foundations in interiorly differentiated consciousness, then, must meet not only the problems raised by the modern intellectual context. It must meet also the existential, psychological, and sociopolitical problems of a modernity that, despite its stupendous intellectual advances, has failed to achieve an existential-practical standpoint from which ever more comprehensive syntheses of the substance of history can be assembled as the context for further advance. In fact, what has happened, despite the scientific sophistication of modernity, has been a series of ever *less* comprehensive viewpoints for understanding and making human history. Speculative intelligence has surrendered its normative and critical functions; it has been conscripted into the service of an untransformed practicality that did not keep up with the theoretic differentiations. The long-term results of this centuries-long cumulative surrender are witnessed today in the cancerous expropriations of the human intellect for the narrowly conceived practical purposes of the two major political powers of our world: the totalitarian multinational corporation, which is the natural result of the uncritical liberal democratic myth of automatic progress and expansion, and the totalitarian communist state, which results from the equally uncritical myth that class conflict can resolve what is, in truth, the most keenly penetrating and extensively reaching dialectic affecting the human mind and heart: the dialectic of fidelity and infidelity to those normative exigencies of inquiry that lead humanity to the fulfilment of its search for direction in the movement of life. We need only witness what has happened to the University in both liberal democratic and communist societies in order to recognize the extent of the deeper aberration. The University has become a new monolithic entity dedicated to the uncritical service of "the useful as defined by society's demands."[2] Progressively disappearing from the academy's administrative and curricular policy-making and planning is any concern for the integrity of the search for direction in the movement of life that once was the hallmark of a liberating education, i.e., of an education that facilitated the organic assembling of an ever more comprehensive and integrated point of view.[3]

A large portion of this synopsis of my position is obviously dependent on Lonergan's analysis of the political component of history and more specifically of modernity. But the reader versed in Lonergan's writings will recognize that I have stressed a dimension whose inclusion is necessary both for understanding and for reversing the longer cycle of decline: the constitutive function and contribution of *the neglected psyche* in the process of sociocultural deterioration. In the course of this chapter, I hope to provide sufficient grounds for claiming that Lonergan's contribution to the foundations of the third stage of meaning on the basis of a mediation and therapy of intentionality must be complemented by an equally thoroughgoing mediation and therapy of the sensitive psyche. Otherwise we will be subject to a subtle form of alienation that, by its relative neglect of one constitutive dimension of interiority, would, however unobtrusively, gradually distort our movement into the third stage of meaning. I will set up my argument by interpreting, first, Lonergan's account of the longer cycle of decline and of the structure of the human good in which there emerges the existential authenticity that can reverse this longer cycle, and then Lewis Mumford's provocative suggestions regarding the aesthetic dimensions of sociocultural deterioration and world-cultural reversal. The final major section of the chapter sets the stage for a heuristic outline for integrating intentionality therapy and psychotherapy into a higher synthesis that can ground the collaborative cognitive and existential praxis needed to promote the advancing differentiation of a transcultural community of meanings and values.

1. The Longer Cycle of Decline.

The classical experience of reason, the existential and soteriological differentiations of the Gospel, and the integration of these and other advances in the theologies, first of Augustine, and then more systematically of Aquinas, culminated, in the latter's writings, in a briefly and narrowly flourishing medieval synthesis: a synthesis of reason and faith, of immanently generated differentiations and revelation, of freedom and grace, of the natural and supernatural dimensions of the transcendental field, of the secular experience of world- and self-constitution and the discovery of a grace-enabled opening to world-transcendent reality. For many reasons, this synthesis was to shatter before it ever was able to consolidate its achievement into a ground of further differentiating advance in the course of the history of modern science, historical scholarship, and philosophical interest in epistemology. These modern developments were not further advances upon the medieval integration: on the contrary, they proceeded by either ignoring or rejecting this synthesis. In the list of reasons for the breakdown of the medieval synthesis in terms of its effective history must be included its own inherent incompleteness and its blind spots, many of which were due to its classicist assumptions regarding science and culture. But, in addition, the medieval synthesis was neither thematic enough regarding cognitive interiority to spot the methodological flaw in subsequent conceptualist bickerings[4] nor persuasive enough to motivate human practicality to achieve a higher integration in the existential-practical order that could sublate the higher speculative synthesis into the world-constitutive agency of existential consciousness. It is this intellectual dialectic of biased practicality and theoretic differentiation that is accounted for by Lonergan in his treatment of the longer cycle of decline and that is in principle resolved in his heuristic outline of the structure of the human good.

The theological context of this dialectic and reversal emerges from a study of Lonergan's complete treatment of these issues. Decline begins because human subjects refuse to conduct their cognitive and existential praxis in accord with the normative exigencies of the empirical, intelligent, rational, existential, and religious levels of human consciousness. "As self-transcendence promotes progress, so the refusal of self-transcendence turns progress into cumulative decline."[5] This refusal is rooted in a state of unwillingness to submit oneself to the experiences and insights, the evidence and the moral exigencies, that would promote one's constitutive existential agency to the capacity for ever more refined and comprehensive contributions to the making of humanity. But there is a radical flaw in the immanent structure of human development itself: one cannot be persuaded to willingness until one is willing to be persuaded.[6] This flaw, which Lonergan calls moral impotence,[7] necessitates the higher integration in the being of the subject that I have called the soteriological differentiation and that Lonergan has outlined in his treatment of the heuristic structure of the absolutely supernatural, divine solution to the problem of evil.[8] Basic to Lonergan's understanding of *the acceptance of higher syntheses by the mind* is the need of *an antecedent higher integration of the very being* of the subject. This integration is the fruit of God's gift of his love, and it brings with it the willingness for that self-transcendence in the existential order that will permit the sublation of advances in the cognitive order. From this perspective, the refusal of self-transcendence in the existential rejection of cognitive advances is an instance of sin, "basic sin."[9]

Among the insights whose refusal generates decline are two sets of ideas that affect our practical and existential agency in the transformation of the human environment and of humanity itself. Although these two sets of ideas are related to one another in intricate ways, for the purposes of analysis we may follow Lonergan in discussing them separately. There are those ideas that remotely or proximately effect an equitable distribution of material goods to all groups in a social system, and there are those ideas that regard more ultimate issues and results, or that demand the solution of more theoretic issues, or that presuppose the adoption of a long-range point of view that is equivalent with the self-transcendent capacities of human intentionality for intelligibility, for truth, and for a hierarchically arranged set of values where the effective realization of the higher values conditions the harmonious establishment of the lower values.

The first set of ideas is practical in the usual and more immediate sense of the word. These ideas regard directly the social order that conditions the realization of vital values. Proximately, they regard technical or material improvements that would give to the disadvantaged a just share in the standard of living of a society, a culture, or a world; more remotely, they regard the economic adjustments and the modifications of political structure that would assure this equitable distribution of material advantages. The rejection of such ideas is partly constitutive of decline.[10]

The second set of ideas consists of the insights that arise from such pursuits as art and literature, science and philosophy, religion and theology. They regard the cultural, personal, and religious levels of value. They are not unrelated to the concerns that find expression in the first set of ideas, for, as we have seen, religious values condition personal authenticity, authenticity conditions the realization of genuine cultural meanings and values, and genuine cultural meanings and values condition the realization of a just social order, which in turn conditions the possibility of meeting the vital needs of every member of that social order.

The second set of ideas tends to be resisted and ridiculed by the practical common sense of *all* classes of people in society, be they successful or oppressed, so long as their practicality has not been transformed by the higher integration in their being that can sublate into existential agency the higher syntheses that would emerge from paying due respect to these ideas. The first set of ideas, on the other hand, is resisted, not by all classes, but only by that class that has found that its own exaggerated material well-being is at the expense of the oppressed, and that wants to keep it that way. Around this set of ideas regarding material and technical improvements, economic adjustments and political modifications, i.e., regarding the vital and social levels of value, there turns what Lonergan calls a shorter cycle in human relationships. That is to say, the practical ideas neglected or resisted by recalcitrant power sooner or later join with the frustrated sentiments of the oppressed to generate either social reform or revolution.[11] If the efforts at change succeed, the unjust supremacy of one group at the expense of another is brought to an end, though there is no guarantee that new forms of oppression and injustice will not flow from the new political and economic arrangements.

The neglect or rejection by all classes of the second set of ideas bearing upon religious, personal, and cultural values generates a longer cycle of decline in human affairs. It leads to the sequence of ever less comprehensive syntheses that has attended even the stupendous advances in science, scholarship, and philosophy that mark the centuries since the brief flourishing of the medieval synthesis. For the latter synthesis to have functioned in the history of ideas as a plateau from which further differentiating advances and consolidating integrations could have occurred in a genetic fashion, the synthesis would have had to develop a sophisticated account of cognitive interiority under the pressures of the scientific and scholarly advances of modernity. But it would also have needed to generate *the expansion of practicality into an existential authenticity* that could sublate the cognitive synthesis into the intellectual base for a world-constitutive agency. Neither of these developments occurred. The resulting decline was not limited to the intellectual order, where decadent scholasticism was counteracted by the alienating epistemologies of Descartes, Locke, Hume, and Kant. It affected as well the entire scale of values, reducing the order of the teleology of human action to vital values and the good of order. This reduction is classically represented in Machiavelli's *The Prince* and Hobbes' *Leviathan*. Through the series of ever less comprehensive syntheses that it generated, it ultimately produced the opposed totalitarianisms of the multinational corporations and of the communist state. In both the cognitive and existential orders, then, we find verification for the hypothesis that the cumulative neglect and refusal of the normative order of the search for direction in the movement of life generates a sequence of ever less comprehensive syntheses. At the root of the decline lies the general bias of untransformed practicality, refusing to reach for the existential equivalent that could have made operative in praxis the synthesis once achieved and so have provided the condition for that synthesis to undergo a process of cumulatively enriching and advancing transformations. Under the influence of biased practicality, not only the intellect but the social situation itself deteriorates. Eventually, even culture, morality, and religion surrender to and become allies with the social decline. And in the positivist phase of their decline they have reached the point of ruling themselves out of court, abandoning their critical and normative functions in the understanding and making of humanity.[12] Witness, again, the social function being fulfilled by the contemporary University, even by the contemporary Catholic or Christian University.

If the longer cycle is to be reversed before it is too late to do anything about it, it will be necessary, first, to develop the existential agency that, because of its allegiance to the scale of values dictated by the normative order of inquiry, is capable of pursuing, assenting to, and promoting a contemporary synthesis of the experiences and insights that constitute the substance of history, and, second, to ground this contemporary synthesis in the sophisticated set of controls of meaning that arise from the explanatory account of interiority which the medieval synthesis lacked. In the existential order, then, there is needed the promotion of an antecedent universal willingness to submit to the normative order of inquiry. In the intellectual order, there is needed the precise knowledge of the terms and relations that constitute that order. The willingness and the knowledge together generate self-appropriation; and, as we have been arguing, self-appropriation generates the theological foundations of the third stage of meaning. Humanity's present task is to allow itself to be elevated to this third stage and thus to become one.[13]

2. The Structure of the Human Good.

The foundations that Lonergan has discovered and slowly amplified into a transcendental or generalized empirical method are necessitated not simply by the movement of science from classicism to modernity; there emerges from the stage we have reached in the longer cycle of decline a need, a historical exigence, for a critical and normatively directive human science. In the previous chapter we saw how the foundations of this science follow from the reflexive technique of bringing the operations of consciousness as intentional to bear upon the operations of consciousness as conscious. But these foundations can be extended to include an account of the structure of the human good. This account would ground the existential perspective on history that could inform the praxis of a third-stage community concerned with reversing both the longer cycle of decline and the shorter cycle of oppression and revolution.

Central to this account of the human good is a threefold generic differentiation of the ends of human action: particular goods, the good of order, and terminal values. Existential consciousness is a notion of value. According to the normative scale of values that flows from the equation of authenticity with self-transcendence, value is only partially constituted by the particular goods that satisfy spontaneous desires and needs and by the good of order or social good that ensures for a given group the regular recurrence of particular goods. The notion of value enables these dimensions of the good to be related organically to other, and higher, conditioning dimensions in the areas of religious, personal, and cultural objectives. At our present historical juncture, the disengagement of the objective of terminal value as distinct from but including particular goods and the good of order is of utmost significance, for the neglect of this ulterior objective is what has generated the longer cycle of decline. Lonergan is not the only author to arrive at this conclusion. Ernest Becker has demonstrated with dramatic conclusiveness the unworthy conspiracy of confusion that results when the notion of value is not distinguished either from the urge to satisfaction on the level of vital desires and needs or from the cheap cultural heroics through which this urge is almost universally repressed in one form only to be satisfied in another.[14] And Eric Voegelin has traced the same confusion to Thomas Hobbes' neglect of the psychology of orientation, that is, of the immanent and normative order of the soul that was one touchstone of pre-modern Western cultural advance.[15] The masks of the artificial personhood that results from shortchanging the reach of the notion of value are quickly removed when Lonergan retrieves what is perhaps the most important and decisive insight in the history of at least pre-Christian Western humanity: "It is by appealing to value or values that we satisfy some appetites and do not satisfy others, that we approve some systems for achieving the good of order and disapprove of others, that we praise or blame human persons as good or evil and their actions as right or wrong."[16]

The existential differentiation, then, dictates that, in addition to the particular good that meets a spontaneously felt need or desire at a given place and time, and in addition to the good of order, the concrete set of "if-then" relationships by which human cooperation is organized in a given social system, there are terminal values that we settle on and pursue when the process of existential deliberation comes to term in decisions that honor the thrust of our liberty for real self-transcendence. Genuine terminal values promote "a good of order that is truly good and instances of the particular good that are truly good."[17] This means that to intend and to realize terminal values, existential consciousness must transcend the standpoint of common sense practicality's aversion to ultimate and long-term issues and results, and it must do so not simply in particular operations of choosing and deciding, but with a habitual antecedent willingness that enables one to move to good decisions without constant need of persuasion. In *Insight*'s terms, "the detached and disinterested desire extends its sphere of influence from the field of cognitional activities through the field of knowledge into the field of deliberate human acts," and thus sets up "an exigence for self-consistency in knowing and doing."[18] This exigence is the operator that promotes practical common sense beyond itself to authentic existential agency.

The liberty with which terminal values are chosen is exercised in a matrix of spontaneous intersubjective relationships that "normally are alive with feeling. There are common or opposed feelings about qualitative values and scales of preference. There are mutual feelings in which one responds to another as an ontic value or as just a source of satisfactions."[19] This spontaneous intersubjectivity constitutes in part the infrastructure of the social order, along with the set of schemes of recurrence that function, or malfunction, in the everyday economic and political institutions of the society; the suprastructure lies in the theoretical elaboration of meanings and reflective discernment of values that are found in any advanced culture.[20]

The recognition of the notion of value enables us to disengage a pursuit of community that is neither collapsed into the infrastructure of spontaneous intersubjectivity nor reduced to the group ethos that arises from the division of labor within a social order.[21] The pursuit is a process of achieving *common meanings and values*.[22] Moreover, we are enabled to understand the manner in which both the existential and cognitional *orientations* of the individuals within the community are constitutive of the orientation of the community itself. Both orientations are evaluated against the standard of the normative order of inquiry, which requires us to "advance in understanding, to judge truthfully, to respond to values."[23] As individual development is not inevitable,[24] so communities are subject to the dialectic of sequences of more or less comprehensive ranges of schemes of recurrence in the form of the good of order, to the extent that their common meanings and values result from their open fidelity to the normative order of inquiry. Just as persons are subject to the laws of progress and decline, depending on their fidelity to or neglect of the normative order of inquiry, so too communities realize a sequence of ranges of schemes of recurrence in the form of the good of order that is more or less comprehensive depending on the extent to which their members are faithful to the same order of inquiry. The discovery of foundations thus disengages the roots of progress and decline.

> Progress proceeds from originating value, from subjects being their true selves by observing the transcendental precepts, Be attentive, Be intelligent, Be reasonable, Be responsible. Being attentive includes attention to human affairs. Being intelligent includes a grasp of hitherto unnoticed or unrealized possibilities. Being reasonable includes the rejection of what probably would not work but also the acknowledgment of what probably would. Being responsible includes basing one's decisions and choices on an unbiased evaluation of short-term and long-term costs and benefits to oneself, to one's group, to other groups.[25]

Decline has an opposite principle of genesis and propulsion:

> Evaluation may be biased by an egoistic disregard of others, by a loyalty to one's own group matched by hostility to other groups, by concentrating on short-term benefits and overlooking long-term costs. Moreover, such aberrations are easy to maintain and difficult to correct. Egoists do not turn into altuists overnight. Hostile groups do not easily forget their grievances, drop their resentments, overcome their fears and

> suspicions. Common sense commonly feels itself omnicompetent in practical affairs, commonly is blind to long-term consequences of policies and courses of action, commonly is unaware of the admixture of common nonsense in its more cherished convictions and slogans.[26]

The extent of the aberrations dictates the breadth and pace of the social distortion. Not only is the course of progress compromised, but the very notion of progress is discredited.

> Corrupt minds have a flair for picking the mistaken solution and insisting that it alone is intelligent, reasonable, good. Imperceptibly the corruption spreads from the harsh sphere of material advantage and power to the mass media, the stylish journals, the literary movements, the educational process, the reigning philosophies. A civilization in decline digs its own grave with a relentless consistency. It cannot be argued out of its self-destructive ways, for argument has a theoretical major premiss, theoretical premisses are asked to conform to matters of fact, and the facts in the situation produced by decline more and more are the absurdities that proceed from inattention, oversight, unreasonableness and irresponsibility.[27]

The implications of the disengagement of the normative order of inquiry for a critical theory of society are that

> the basic form of alienation is man's disregard of the transcendental precepts, Be attentive, Be intelligent, Be reasonable, Be responsible. Again, the basic form of ideology is a doctrine that justifies such alienation. From these basic forms, all others can be derived. For the basic forms corrupt the social good. As self-transcendence promotes progress, so the refusal of self-transcendence turns progress into cumulative decline.[28]

Clearly, then, the movement to foundations has brought the notion of authenticity to center stage. Moreover, the centrality of personal value gives rise to a distinction between the terminal values that are decided upon by a self-transcending consciousness or community and the *originating values* that are identical with the authentic persons who so decide. Values "are terminal inasmuch as they are objects for possible choices, but they are originating inasmuch as directly and explicitly or indirectly and implicitly the fact that they are chosen modifies our habitual willingness, our effective orientation in the universe, and so our contribution to the dialectical process of progress or decline."[29] One becomes an originating value in this dialectical process by fidelity to the normative order of inquiry. Such fidelity elevates one's practical agency to existential authenticity. An antecedent universal willingness has promoted a higher integration in one's being.

The threefold order of ends generates a corresponding threefold structure in one's relationship to the human community. There is the spontaneous cooperativeness rooted in the immediacy of primordial intersubjectivity; there is the concrete manner in which cooperation is organized in the institutional frameworks that constitute the social order, dictating the inter-relationship between the development of one's skills and the institutional tasks that must be performed if the social order is to ensure a recurrence of instances of the particular good; and there is, in the authentic subject, a commitment to the establishment of a good of order that is truly just because conditioned by the effective realization of religious, personal, and cultural values. To limit the relations between the individual and the community to the first two levels of this structure, to the conspiracy between the orders of operation instituted by the two levels of the particular good and the good of order, is to promote Hobbes' Leviathan. The human subject is equipped with a principle of criticism that relentlessly goes to work on any finite scheme of recurrence, with a notion of value that raises the insistent questions, Is it worth while? Is it really good or only apparently good? Can we devise a more humane order? Only a subject alienated from the normative order of inquiry will find truly good a social order constituted by the neglect of the notion of value in favor of a pragmatic conspiracy of order and spontaneous desire. The restlessness of the human mind and heart, which will be quieted only in the discovery of a good beyond its powers of criticism, apprehends that "any course of individual or group action is only a finite good and, because only finite, it is open to criticism. It has its alternatives, its limitations, its risks, its drawbacks."[30]

Under the pressure of this insistent question, one can opt, more often than not at a great cost to oneself, for the long-range point of view and course of action, for what is better, for what, because it honors the thrust of liberty to religious, personal, and cultural values, will more effectively promote the human good. Such a decision is necessarily made in solitude and even in loneliness. One will be subject to misunderstanding and ridicule to the extent that one's social milieu has collapsed the order of ends to the conspiracy of the first two levels of value. But one will contribute incrementally to the realization of genuine terminal values, to the establishment of a good of order that is truly good and of instances of the particular good that are really worth while. We can transcend the calculus of pleasures and pains, the grid of passional motivations, the self-enclosed and self-defeating surrender of the normative order of inquiry that collapses the threefold structure of ends into the distortion of history that arises when only particular goods and the good of order are acknowledged. We can opt for self-transcendence. We can originate value in ourselves, in our milieu, in our community of meanings and values. Moreover, "since man can know and choose authenticity and self-transcendence, originating and terminating values can coincide. When each member of the community both wills authenticity in himself and, inasmuch as he can, promotes it in others, then the originating values that choose and the terminal values that are chosen overlap and interlace."[31] We can consciously execute the existential option to become the individual. We can free ourselves from the inauthentic, drop those satisfactions rooted in the illusion that the ends of human action are but twofold, transcend our fears of suffering and failure, discover value we had previously neglected or overlooked, and bring our spontaneous scale of preferences to accord with the objective scale that receives its very objectivity from the exigencies of subjectivity.[32] Then we have opted for moral self-transcendence.

Such an option is the fruit of a conversion which elevates one's practicality to an authentic base of existential agency. The criterion of what is good shifts away from the particular good or the good of order to the terminal values that are good precisely because they are consistent with the order of the search for direction in the movement of life. One chooses as the horizon of one's existential agency "the making of man, his advance in authenticity, the fulfilment of his affectivity, and the direction of his work to the particular goods and a good of order that are worth while."[33] To the extent that one sustains such an option for the human good, one has gained one's life, usually as a prize of war. To the extent that such an option is not made or sustained one has lost one's very being, even if one has gained the world.

3. *The Neglected Psyche.*

The existential option which we have just discussed is obviously not dependent upon one's entrance into the third stage of meaning, i.e., upon one's ability to give an explanatory account of the option one has made, an account in which terms and relations of interior process fix one another in the manner of existential self-appropriation. Lonergan's account of the genesis and reversal of the shorter and longer cycles of decline, his disengagement of the terms and relations that obtain in the order of existential subjectivity and its responsibility for history, for the human world, and for the character of the self, outlines heuristically the structure of such an explanatory account. But history provides myriad instances in which the one choosing did not, and could not, account for the option in such terms. Obviously, too, the option itself has proven to be far more significant than the ability to account for it in an explanatory fashion. And yet we have argued that a major contemporary exigence is for a critical and normative human science that can facilitate such self-appropriation. The exigence arises from the generative role of inauthenticity at the speculative level itself with regard to the longer cycle of decline. The disastrous historical consequences of counter-positions in human science and philosophy must be met by the construction of a human science and philosophy that are more than homespun, common-sense wisdom. They must be met on the level at which they arise, if the root of the malaise is to be attacked. It is not sufficient, though surely it is necessary, to be morally converted from biased practicality to existential willingness, if one wants to attack the root of the longer cycle of decline. One of the values to which one can respond with all of one's heart is that of constructing a human science which can advance the positions and reverse the counter-positions in those efforts at human science that ignore or neglect the explicit and normative order of inquiry. One can discover that normative order and make its self-appropriation the foundation of a transformative human science. This is precisely how we interpret Lonergan's two works, *Insight* and *Method in Theology*. They represent his contribution to the foundations of a critical and normative human science. Because these foundations are existential as well as cognitive, he refers to them not inappropriately as theological. And because the structure of the exigencies revealed by these foundations is transcultural, indeed universally human, the self-appropriation of these exigencies provides a basis for the unity of humanity across cultural boundaries and, consequently, for a leap forward on the part of humanity. The unity is based, not on the totalitarian exercise of power, but on the sharing and appropriation of the meanings discovered and the values responded to in different epochs and in different peoples' search for direction in the movement of life.

In his analysis of the genesis of the longer cycle, Lonergan has emphasized the neglect of the reach of the unrestricted desire to know. On the basis of his later existential differentiation, I have sublated this analysis of *Insight* into an account of the collapse of the order of value to an exclusive acknowledgment of vital values and of the social order and, consequently, to the neglect of the religious, personal, and cultural values that condition the possibility of a just social order. Discovering the existential core of the neglect enables us to attend to another aspect of human interiority whose imperious demands are overriden when the order of value is contracted into the schemes that arise from an exclusive conspiracy of the social order with recurring satisfactions. Moreover, the recovery of this other neglected dimension will enable existential self-appropriation to move beyond the heuristic outline of the structure of existential consciousness and of its correlative objective, the process of the human good. It will enable one to give an account of *one's own* participation in the dialectic of history, to *tell the story* of one's own discovery of and response to the objective scale of values. Existential self-appropriation in the concrete must be a narrative. The gaining or the losing of one's very being occurs in the dramatic pattern of experience in which one's life either becomes a work of art or, by succumbing to bias, renders one an *artiste manqué*. The self-appropriation of the dramatic will take the form of telling the story of one's search for direction in the movement of life.

This other neglected dimension to which I am referring is the human psyche--the sequence of sensations, memories, images, conations, emotions, bodily movements, and spontaneous intersubjective responses that attend and are sublated by our operations of inquiring and fleeing understanding, of reflecting and rejecting the truth, of existential evaluation and biased practicality. Concomitant with the failure to sublate practicality into the base of authentic existential agency, i.e., the failure that has generated the longer cycle of decline, has been a neglect of the transcendental aesthetic dimension of our subjectivity. In these later stages of the longer cycle of decline, this neglect is manifest in the appalling statistics of crime, drug addiction, alcoholism, suicide, mental breakdown, political torture, and international violence with its potential to destroy civilization. These phenomena have attended both the liberal democratic illusion of unlimited progress and the totalitarian illusion that class conflict will bring the social order into conformity with human subjectivity's normative demands. These evils afflict not only the obvious victims of these illusions, the masses oppressed under the domination of the multinational corporations and the communist states. The proponents and perpetrators of an illusion are even more its victims than are those on whom it is foisted. For they are directly subject to the charge of moral self-destruction. Nor is this a new insight, original with liberation theology and conscientization theories. It is quite plainly expressed in the Platonic dialogues and in the Scriptures of Israel and Christianity. But, in our time, when the longer cycle of decline is predicated upon the neglect of the reach of human interiority in its search for direction in the movement of life, the stories of the unwilling victims and the willful perpetrators of these illusions form series of chaotic and bizarre human tragedies. These are stories told by battered psyches. If we could reverse the neglect of the psyche that has attended the biased practicality of the truncated existential subject, we would come into contact with these stories, and so promote both existential authenticity and existential self-appropriation. The foundations of the third stage of meaning are decisively enriched by attending to and making one's own the story told by one's sensitive psyche concerning one's participation in the dialectic of progress and decline.

In Part Two I will explain the foundational role of a transcendental aesthetic in the constitution of the foundations of the third stage of meaning, and so in the guidance of the cognitive and existential praxis of the community of third-stage subjects. I will integrate the transcendental aesthetic with Lonergan's generalized empirical method. I will show how the third stage of meaning rests on the complementary mediations of intelligent, rational, and existential intentionality and of the sensitive psyche. And I will explain how that complementarity is established by the very structure of the existential differentiation itself. For the remainder of the present chapter, I will simply fasten attention on the psychic dimension of our being and on its constitutive function in promoting progress and offsetting decline or in generating decline and ridiculing progress. If beauty is the splendor of truth, we must attend to the notion of the beautiful before clarifying its self-appropriation.

I begin by turning to another author who has realized that the discovery of the unity of humanity across cultural boundaries is indispensable for a humane future. The cultural historian Lewis Mumford has projected two ideal types to help us imagine and understand alternative human futures: post-historic humanity and world-cultural humanity. The first, he says, is probably no more than a theoretic possibility, for it is likely that, if the conspiracy of confusion between totalitarian organization and human atavism cannot be reversed, we have begun the last act in the human tragedy.[34] This suicidal course can be reversed only on the one basic assumption that "the destiny of mankind, after its long preparatory period of separation and differentiation, is at last to become one."[35] The unity is to be realized in accord with the principles that no differentiations achieved in the past can be left behind and that none of them can enter world culture in the form that it took independently in an earlier period.[36] For these principles to be realized, there must be deliberately cultivated "another great historic transformation" in the evolution of human consciousness, the creation of a new self whose province is the world and whose task is to bring that world to "an organic unity, based upon the fullest utilisation of all the varied resources that both nature and history have revealed to modern man."[37] This new self will be interiorly constituted by an ecology of energies in the interest of wholeness--a wholeness that "is impossible to achieve . . . without giving primacy to the integrative elements within the personality: love, reason, the impulse to perfection and transcendence."[38]

I refer to Mumford at this point even though I find neither sufficient explanatory power in his analysis of the development of consciousness nor anything approaching an adequately trenchant critique of cognitive interiority in his analysis of scientific intelligence. On the latter point, I am perhaps spoiled by the first five chapters of Lonergan's *Insight*, which despite their extraordinary difficulty, manage to explain scientific authenticity with an exactness that makes possible the relevant distinctions that are necessary in any conscription of scientific intelligence into a higher and foundational synthesis. But Mumford's work has the merit of emphasizing another neglected dimension of our interiority that Lonergan leaves room for only in his later writings--a dimension, moreover, whose place in the needed critical human science Lonergan leaves to others to explore in explanatory fashion. This other dimension is the aesthetic, the affective, *the psyche's intentionality* toward the organic wholeness or integration of the person. Mumford's critique is similar to some of the oracular utterances about modernity of the psychologist C. G. Jung[39] and to the theological views of John Dunne, both of whom find in the modern experiment a neglect, not primarily of intelligence, but of the soul or the heart.[40] The neglect of soul is, for Jung and Dunne, more radical than the derailments of the spirit into an exclusive emphasis on instrumental reason or practical intelligence or positivistic methodology. In fact, it is *responsible for the cumulative process of these intellectual aberrations*. The implication is clear: attention to the psyche would alert one to intellectual inauthenticity, would provide a set of defensive circles safeguarding the authenticity of one's cognitive praxis,[41] would make possible the elevation of practical common sense to an existential authenticity that would both dictate and sublate into practical agency the operations in which we seek intelligibility and verification in a normative, intelligent, and critical manner.

The inauthentic surrender of intelligence to biased practicality affects the processes of the sensitive psyche. These effects manifest themselves in the spontaneous flow of sensitive consciousness itself, in a disharmonious and nonsequential, incongruous and nonrhythmic distortion of the flow of sensations, memories, images, emotions, conations, associations, bodily movements, and spontaneous intersubjective responses that we name the psyche. Attention to the sensitive malaise would point out the failure of self-transcendence in the realms of intellectual, rational, and existential inquiry. At the same time, the integration of the flow of sensitive consciousness would provide one with an indication that one's search for direction in the movement of life is in harmony with the normative order of that search. Inauthentic inquiry will have negative repercussions on the sensitive psyche; authentic inquiry will manifest itself in the integration of the movement of life itself with the order of one's inquiry. The movement is sensitively experienced. As such it permeates all intentional operations at the higher levels of consciousness; it is sublated by these operations; and it can be harmoniously sublated only by a praxis of these operations that is in keeping with the normative order of the search. If cognitive and existential praxis are inauthentic, there cannot but be a distortion of the sensitively experienced movement of life, for by inauthentic inquiry one will not find direction in this movement. When one is discovering direction, the sensitively experienced movement of life will make this clear; and when one is not finding direction, the same movement of life will be sensitively experienced as disharmonious, nonsequential, incongruous, and nonrhythmic, or, in Jung's terminology, as lacking *synchronicity* with the spiritual process of one's insights, judgments, and decisions.[42] Thus, because intellectual, rational, and existential inauthenticity is responsible for aesthetic disintegration and breakdown, attention to the latter would alert one to the former and would provide the materials one needs to reverse the process of one's own decline and of one's contribution to the decline of the social order. It is in this sense that we may speak of psychic process as providing a set of defensive circles for the integrity of the search.[43]

Mumford's principal concern, then, is with the effect that the liberal democratic and totalitarian myths have had on the neglected psyche of human subjects. Laissez-faire economics and totalitarian states have neglected the ancient insight, already articulated in the West in Greek tragedy and the ethics of Aristotle, that there are organic limits to expansion in every domain. In post-historic humanity, the neglect of the pole of aesthetic spontaneity in the service of life, in favor of the pole of practical intelligence in the service of power, would be complete. Neglect of the instinctual, the purposeful, and the organic would govern human responses not only to the realm of reality known by physics, but also to the realms of the biological, the psychological, and the social. The same canons of science that are applied to the physical world would be extended without remainder to the study of organisms, where the notion of organic development would be neglected, and to the study of the person, where subjectivity and teleology would be ignored.[44] But the result, already upon us, is that

> power and order, pushed to their final limit, lead to their self-destructive inversion: disorganisation, violence, mental aberration, subjective chaos, [and finally] the compensating function of mischievous destruction. . . . Since [man] cannot reinsert himself, as a fully autonomous being, into the mechanical process, he may become the sand in the works: if necessary, he will use the machine to destroy the society that has produced it.[45]

At a moment when such total destruction is a distinct possibility, Mumford finds, with Jung, a series of alternative images already prefigured and released by the deeper sources of life in the organism and the psyche, images of a "new self" and a "new culture," of a great transformation of the substance of history through which humanity can come to a spiritual and psychological unity by cultivating and enriching those very meanings and values that have been differentiated in the various cultural communities of history. The key to the new self is found in a conscious orientation on the part of the individual personality to wholeness and to an ecological balance of the energies of interiority. This orientation will involve recognizing, accepting, and redirecting aspects of the organic and psychic dimensions of the self that have been buried by the hypertrophic emphasis on instrumental reason or practical common sense. The role of the neglected psyche in the reconstitution of humanity is central. We might say that even now, at the tether of its exasperation with the blindness of biased practicality to its enriching potentialities, the psyche is projecting those very images that are needed for the insights, the judgments, and the decisions through which alone we can reverse the longer cycle of decline.

4. *The Existential Differentiation and the Science of Psychology.*

4.1. *Symbols and the Psychology of Orientations.*

Our task in the remainder of this chapter is to set up the argument for an integration of Lonergan's intentionality therapy with the healing of the neglected psyche. The integration will promote a synthesis of interiority that can ground the collaborative cognitive and existential praxis which would promote the advancing differentiations and integrations through which a transcultural community of meanings and values can be established. We begin by commenting further on the relocation of affectivity in Lonergan's thought that we highlighted toward the end of the last chapter.

When Lonergan acknowledges that terminal values are apprehended and aspired to in intentional feelings,[46] the differentiation of the existential fount of personal value has granted to the sensitive psyche of intentionally ordered human subjects a transcendental significance. Feelings mediate consciousness at its fullest, for existential deliberation begins with feelings. The original experience becomes acknowledged once again as the search for direction in the movement of life. It is not perverted into some variant of the typically modern reduction of intentionality's order to sensitive psychological determinants; the latter rather share once again in the order of humanity's basic and specifically differentiating quest through which a world is mediated and constituted by meaning. Through this share, the sensitive psyche receives its integration. The intelligibility of orientation, which is quite distinct from the passional motivation that takes over only to the extent that the psyche is neglected, is restored in principle to modern psychology when the transcendental significance of feelings is acknowledged.

For the most part, modern psychology has lost the notion of orientation because of the general modern collapse of the order of ends into particular goods and the good of order. Even when the notion of orientation is preserved, as in the Jungian teleology of individuation and in some of the "third force" psychologies, it lacks the normative context that would be afforded by an adequate heuristic structure of its intelligibility. This state of affairs is due in large measure to the oblivion into which modernity has cast the classical epochal differentiations of intelligence that appear in Plato and Aristotle and of existential consciousness as it is illuminated by Christianity. Without the recognition of the source of the soul and its order as well as of its world-transcendent finality, human desire all too easily is compacted into any of a variety of psychological pseudo-explanations that are caught in the conspiracy of confusion generated by neglect of the ulterior objectives of existential consciousness. When the order of ends is contracted to either the particular good or the good of order, or both, then all attempts at explanatory understanding of behavior will take the form of a psychology of passional motivations rather than of intentional orientations. General bias' neglect of the reach of intentionality is necessarily a neglect of the sensitive psyche. The reorientation of science that the leap in being of transcendental method makes possible includes (pre-eminently, as we shall see) an elaboration of the sensitive psyche that both verifies and promotes a deeper and broader appropriation of the methodical disengagement that appears in Lonergan's writings. The science of psychology is thereby placed on a new footing, for its foundations are seen to lie in the objectification of normative intentionality. And because it is psychology that is so reoriented, the key is provided for the reorientation also of common sense, of dramatic artistry and practical efficiency, through a maieutic that enables the appropriation of sensitive desire and its ordering in accord with the exigencies of normative inquiry.

Moreover, as it is with the momentum of affectivity that one participates existentially in the social and political drama of the human good, so the very structure of affective engagement provides one with the clue to one's orientation in the struggle. The apprehension of ends in feelings initiates the process of questions for deliberation that promotes the subject to existential consciousness. Thus the intelligent, reasonable, and responsible negotiation of one's feelings "makes it possible for one to know oneself, to uncover the inattention, obtuseness, silliness, irresponsibility that gave rise to the feeling one does not want, and to correct the aberrant attitude."[47] Moreover, the recognition and negotiation of the feelings that impel one's dramatic engagement in the dialectic of history is facilitated by the mutual relationship between *feelings and symbols*. A symbol is "an image of a real or imaginary object that evokes a feeling or is evoked by a feeling."[48] Affective development or aberration, measured against the scale of values determined by the normative order of inquiry, can be ascertained through the interpretation of one's radically spontaneous and intimately personal set of elemental symbols. Affective development therefore involves "a transvaluation and transformation of symbols. What before was moving no longer moves; what before did not move now is moving. So the symbols themselves change to express the new affective capacities and dispositions. . . . Inversely, symbols that do not submit to transvaluation and transformation seem to point to a block in development."[49]

The primary function of symbols, then, is intrasubjective. Symbols make available to the subject the possibility of *internal communication* between organic and psychic vitality on the one hand and cognitional and existential intentionality on the other.

> Organic and psychic vitality have to reveal themselves to intentional consciousness and, inversely, intentional consciousness has to secure the collaboration of organism and psyche. Again, our apprehensions of value occur in intentional responses, in feelings: here too it is necessary for feelings to reveal their objects and, inversely, for objects to awaken feelings. It is through symbols that mind and body, mind and heart, heart and body communicate.[50]

The understanding of elemental symbols, then, is achieved by appealing both to the dramatic engagement of the subject in the dialectic of history and to the context of internal communication: i.e., to the dialectic of the subject in the context of the dialectic of history. The reciprocal relation between symbols and the intentional feelings which provide the momentum of each person's engagement in the dialectic of history will provide us with our clue to advancing existential differentiation.

4.2. Authentic Religion and Orientation.

Despite the compacted treatment accorded existential consciousness in *Insight*, where its differentiation from cognitive operations is not as clearly acknowledged as it is in Lonergan's later writings, and where feelings are relegated to an insignificant place in the discussion of the responsibilities of rational self-consciousness, the book does offer a series of extremely important clues that may be exploited in the disengagement of the differentiation of the realm of transcendence and of its proximate finality in one's participation through cognitional and existential praxis in the divine solution to the problem of evil. For by the end of Lonergan's discussion of ethics, the course of evil in history is laid bare with a precision and depth of insight and feeling seldom matched in the history of human inquiry. There appear in clear light the radical moral impotence of the human subject when left to his or her own resources and the desperate exigencies of an integration of human living that requires more than a genetic unfolding of human potentialities. The key to the integration lies in the gift of *universal willingness*. The capacity for vertical self-transcendence raises the question of God. But only the soteriological differentiation of a graced solution, originated by God, to the victimization of humanity by evil answers the pure question that is the normative order of inquiry.

As we have seen, refusal of self-transcendence is rooted in a state of unwillingness. Until one is willing to act in accord with the normative order of the search for direction in the movement of life, one is not effectively free to promote genuine progress in the consistent fashion that not only takes its stand on the distinction between terminal values and satisfaction but that also arranges these values in accord with the hierarchy that flows from the equation of authenticity with self-transcendence. This state of antecedent and universal willingness can be reached only through a process of persuading oneself and submitting to the persuasion of others. Effective freedom can be won only by devoting time to this process. Until one devotes that time, one remains closed to certain dimensions of self-transcendent activity, if not because of dramatic, egoistic, or group bias, then because of the general bias against ultimate issues and results that necessarily afflicts one until one's intellectual and moral development has brought one beyond the standpoint of common sense. But, asks Lonergan, "how is one to be persuaded to genuineness and openness, when one is not yet open to persuasion?"[51] One's effective freedom is restricted not simply by external circumstance, not even simply by neurosis, but "in the profound fashion that follows from incomplete intellectual and volitional development."[52] There is a gap between one's actual effective freedom and that which one would possess if one had the necessary preparatory insights and if one were endowed with a universal antecedent willingness to follow the exigencies of the full and normative order of inquiry.

Lonergan calls this gap moral impotence. The gap differs in extent from one person to the next, and at different times in the life of any given person. It is not totally unconscious, for awareness of it is what prompts some people to profit by their failures and others to surrender to moral self-renunciation. It affects not only the individual conscience but, in a heightened manner, the common decisions that determine the course of events in the social sphere. The family, technology, the economy, and the political order are as subject to ethical transformation as is the development of the individual subject. Just as individual decisions are likely to suffer from individual bias so long as the standpoint of common sense is not transcended, so group decisions are likely to suffer from group bias under the same conditions. Moreover, all decisions, whether by the individual or by the group, are likely to suffer from general bias. Thus, beyond the conflicts between the individual and the group, among various groups within the state, and among states, there are the far more significant conflicts that emerge between the decisions that are demanded by the normative order of inquiry and those that are actually made, whether they be by individuals or by groups. When common sense screens alternative courses of action to eliminate those that are impractical to an undeveloped and biased intelligence, the social situation becomes a compound of the rational and the irrational. But there also develop philosophies that welcome the irrational components as proof of their views, demand the expansion of the social surd, and call for the elimination of whatever intelligibility still remains. Since the average person of common sense is unequipped to meet these philosophies on the level where they must be addressed, one easily repudiates the significance of the philosophic issues and settles for what common sense says is the most practical immediate course of action. In this way, "the civilization drifts through successive less comprehensive syntheses to the sterility of the objectively unintelligible situation and to the coercion of economic pressures, political forces, and psychological conditioning."[53] The development and implementation of the critical human science that could meet the longer cycle of decline seems at best ineffective, at worst impossible. "To whom does it bring the light? To how many? How clearly and how effectively? Are philosophers to be kings or kings to learn philosophy? Are they to rule in the name of wisdom subjects judged incapable of wisdom? Are all the members of our democracies to be philosophers? Is there to be a provisional dictatorship while they are learning philosophy?"[54]

Because of moral impotence, one is incapable of sustained development until one finds and introduces into living another source of development besides one's own intelligence, reasonableness, and willingness. This source must be not simply a higher viewpoint in the mind but, grounding the very possibility of such a higher viewpoint, a higher integration in life than can be arrived at through the immanent development of human intentionality. The very dynamic structure of cognitive and moral development has resulted in a paradox: one cannot be persuaded to willingness until one is willing to be persuaded. A source of universal willingness other than that discovered in the development from below upwards of one's intentional capacities is needed if the longer cycle of decline is to be reversed. It is at this point that immanent development must give way to religion. So, too, if we are to understand the higher integration, philosophy must give way to an explicitly theological point of view.

From this perspective, the refusal of self-transcendence that is rooted in unwillingness becomes "basic sin," and the cumulative decline that this refusal generates both in oneself and in the social sphere becomes "moral evil."[55] Basic sin is a failure to yield to the exigencies of the normative order of the search for direction in the movement of life. It is the root of the surd in human life. The higher integration that would transcend the effects of the surd and reverse the process that leads to its expansion must be capable of liberating the human subject from this basic sin. The introduction into human history of a higher integration takes on the aspect of a solution to the problem of evil. The discovery and reception into one's own conscious living of the divine solution to the problem of antecedent unwillingness and refusal constitutes what I have been calling the soteriological differentiation of consciousness. Lonergan speaks of it in terms of the absolutely supernatural conjugate forms of charity, hope, and faith[56] which constitute the fifth level of consciousness.[57]

Better differentiated in Lonergan's later works is the manner in which the solution takes effect in one's life: one's existential consciousness is invaded by an experience of unconditioned and unrestricted love that reorients the direction of one's development both from above and, consequently, from below. This experience corresponds to what in *Insight* is the absolutely supernatural conjugate form of charity. Against the theological extrinsicists, Lonergan maintains that there is an experience of being in love in an unrestricted fashion that is the proper fulfilment of the capacity for self-transcendence revealed in our unrestricted questioning. Against the immanentists, he maintains that this experience is not the product of our knowledge and choice, for it "dismantles and abolishes the horizon in which our knowing and choosing went on and . . . sets up a new horizon in which the love of God will transvalue our values and the eyes of that love will transform our knowing."[58] This experience brings to fulfilment the restlessness of the transcendental intention of value. It provides existential consciousness with a base of willingness that cannot be surpassed, a base in absolute transcendence. It makes one ready to deliberate, judge, and decide with the ease of one who is in love. Above all, it is the binding force of the higher integration of human living demanded by our moral impotence, by our incapacity for sustained development and for authentic engagement in the dialectic of history on the power of our own resources, by our inevitable tendency, without this experience, to contract the order of ends to the levels of the particular good and the good of order. This experience of divine love is radically affective; it is a conversion of affectivity to a self-transcendent differentiation of the order of its intentional responsiveness in accord with the objective scale of values. Fulfilment of the normative order of inquiry that, even in compacted consciousness, makes the human subject a pure question for the fullness of intelligibility, for the unconditioned, for the unqualified good, "brings a radical peace, the peace that the world cannot give."[59] The momentum of one's participation in the dialectic of history, in the making of humanity, is transformed in such a way that the fulfilment of one's conscious being that one is brought to by the gift of world-transcendent love "bears fruit in a love of one's neighbor that strives mightily to bring about the kingdom of God on this earth."[60]

4.3. *The Soteriological Foundation of the Transformation of Order.*

The higher integration in the being of the subject that occurs with the discovery of the bending of God in history toward the soul in grace, with the experience of a loving response on the part of the absolutely transcendent reality to the exigence of the normative order of inquiry for absolute intelligibility, unconditioned truth and being, and unqualified goodness, is the existential foundation of the concrete historical process of the human good. It introduces into the making of humanity the indispensable condition for transcending the personal and social determinisms that constitute moral impotence.[61] Without redemptive experience, an advance in authenticity cannot be sustained. The fulfilment of affectivity will be shortcircuited by dramatic bias to the satisfaction of passional motivation. The direction of human labor toward procuring the particular goods that are really worth while within the developing context of a sequence of ever more comprehensive series of ranges of schemes of recurrence in the organisation of human affairs will be impossible because of individual, group, and especially general bias.

Let us now relate this synthesis of the positions on religion in *Insight* and *Method in Theology* to our concern to reverse the neglect of the sensitive psyche. Authenticity, fulfilled affectivity, and nonalienated labor are impossible because of the breakdown of the creative tension between sensitivity and intentionality that is the principle of progress. Temporality is the radical horizon of sensitive receptivity; the notion of being, which is unrestricted by time,[62] is the very constitution of intentionality, and so is the measure of progress. Between the inner form of time and the intention of what can be intelligently grasped and reasonably affirmed, there is a radical disproportion. This disproportion is the ontological condition of evil in human affairs.[63] It is moral impotence. The originating principle of the human good is subjectivity in its native and normative orientation to the intelligible, the true and the real, and terminal values. The sustained participation of the individual subject in the process of effecting and enjoying the human good, however, demands the collaboration of organic and psychic vitality in the normative order of inquiry. Such collaboration is not possible without a conversion of human sensitivity's internal time-consciousness, which is its willingness, to taut participation in the unrestricted orientation of the notions of being and value. This participation is universal willingness. It alone transcends the contraction of the order of ends to exclusively short-term practical goals. The human subject must be healed of its condition of inner conflict, of splitness, of schizophrenia in the most literal sense of the word. The healing cannot obliterate either half of the duality, but must transform both aspects into operators of the cumulative promotion of internal communication, heading toward responsible praxis in the cognitive and existential orders. While the particularity and temporality of internal time-consciousness, the very form of human sensitivity, must be transformed so as to collaborate in the intentional pursuit of intelligibility and truth in cognitional praxis and of terminal value in existential praxis, the normative order of inquiry itself must be corrected of any pretensions to seek and find the human good by evading historical responsibility in historical time. Precisely because the normative order of inquiry is conjoined with a sensitivity whose inner form is temporality, pursuit of the human good will promote the development of individual and social reality in historical process. Advances in authenticity, fulfilment of affectivity, and the promotion of non-alienated human labor that is directed to what is truly worth while in a manner that is truly worth while, are radically historical tasks, precisely because temporality is the inner form of the sensitivity which is in irretrievable, if conflictual, symbiosis with the normative order of inquiry.

The Protean commingling of opposites that is human interiority achieves an unsurpassable base of foundational praxis only in the experience of being in love in an unrestricted fashion. Then intentionality and sensitivity are satisfied in a manner that can only be enriched and heightened and deepened but never surpassed. They are reconciled with each other when they become the place of conscious encounter between radically finite, historically conscious proportionate being and absolutely transcendent intelligibility, reality, truth, and value. Without that redemptive experience, the disproportion of sensitivity and intentionality is not advanced to creative tension. On the contrary, from the disharmony of our being there emerge only manic-depressive oscillations of interiority that distort *both* the internal time-consciousness of sensitivity *and* the intentional exigencies to be intelligent, reasonable, and responsible. The internal time-consciousness of sensitivity is distorted into depressive or guilt-laden denials of the future, on the one hand, and into anxious delusions of historically rootless infinity, on the other. The normative order of inquiry is deflected away from the field of cognitional and existential praxis, either through a neglect of the questions for intelligibility, truth, and value due to the insistence of sensitive desire or through a Zarathrustrian narcissistic inflation of intellectual consciousness that immanentizes the world-transcendent source, sustainment, and destiny of intentionality and of the sensitivity that collaborates with inquiry in the authentic making of history. The soteriological mediation of unrestricted goodness to the intentional quest of the human subject is therefore the foundational reality of authentic historical cognitional and existential praxis. Such praxis is the proximate base of the human good, the originating value through which the making of humanity becomes an advance in authenticity, a fulfilment of affectivity, and the direction of human labor to what is worth while.

From these general principles of a theology of redemptive history, we turn to our present drama. The epochal moments in human history coincide with those points at which the advance of human authenticity cannot occur without a leap in being. The leap in being is always a matter of a new differentiation of human consciousness without which the course of history will run down a blind alley. A distinction must be drawn, however, between the proximate generation of epochal changes by the normative order of inquiry itself and the roots of epochal change in the noetic or redemptive experience of world-transcendent reality.

The epochal change that is the individual and cultural drama of our day, without which the course of human history could suffer an irretrievable breakdown, is the transformation in human being that will bring us into the third stage of meaning. The third stage rests on the explanatory self-objectification of the subject. When the operations through which the normative order of inquiry is satisfied are brought to bear as intentional upon these same operations as conscious, the order of interiority gains a base of cognitional and existential praxis that will make possible a new series of ranges of schemes of recurrence in human living. The proximate foundations of the leap in being are found in intellectual conversion, which is the irreversible self-affirmation of a consciousness that at once is empirical, intelligent, and reasonable.

We have already discussed at some length the existential determinants of authentic *cognitional praxis*. The argument holds with equal and, indeed, even greater force for the *cognitional self-appropriation* that is the strict meaning of intellectual conversion, entitling this conversion to be called the proximate foundation of a third stage of meaning.[64] Without a *decision* in favor of the value of self-transcendent praxis in general, the knower will neither be intelligent and rational nor affirm his or her own intelligence and rationality in the pure, disinterested, and explanatory fashion to which we are invited in the epochal eleventh chapter of *Insight*. In the present context, however, we must push our analysis to the point where we can at least glimpse the remote but indispensable soteriological foundations of the existential factors that make intellectual conversion possible. As we do so, we must bear in mind that intellectual conversion in the strict, philosophic sense is but the beginning--the indispensable consolidation--of the leap in being that is achieving ever further refinement as intellectually self-appropriating subjects advance in their cumulative assembling of a full position on the human subject. Short of a theory of history generated from both the upper blade of transcendental method and the lower blade of the experiences through which the development of the human mind and heart has occurred, these remote soteriological foundations of intellectual conversion can only be glimpsed and set forth in the transcendental fashion of an argument that establishes conditions of the possibility of facts and events. Despite their limitations, such arguments are nonetheless valid, and their validity is sufficient to establish our point.

We begin by noting that religious conversion, in the sense not simply of noetic fidelity to the transcendent exigence but of the experience of unrestricted and unsurpassable love, is in part affective conversion.[65] It is, in an expression which Lonergan once used orally, the blossoming of eros into agape.[66] As such, it is the consolidated advancement of sensitivity to taut participation in the unrestricted reach of the normative order of inquiry, and so the establishment of a creative tension in the duality of human consciousness. From that love is born a knowledge that without that love one could not have. This knowledge is called faith.[67] Faith sustains the hopeful advance of intentionality's history toward the fullness of life in the Kingdom of God, in the face-to-face knowledge and love of the world-transcendent source and destiny of inquiry.[68]

This advance, of course, occurs through questioning in a normative fashion. It is the creative movement from below upwards by which one advances "from experience to growing understanding, from growing understanding to balanced judgment, from balanced judgment to fruitful courses of action, and from fruitful courses of action to the new situations that call forth further understanding, profounder judgment, richer courses of action."[69] Until the disproportion that is the moral impotence of human consciousness is healed, however, creative development from below upwards is not possible, because of the schizophrenic oscillations between depression and inflation on the levels both of sensitivity and intentionality. Until human sensitivity and the normative order of inquiry are reconciled to one another in a manner that obliterates neither and fulfills both, individual and social history move in the direction of a sequence of ever less comprehensive series of ranges of schemes of recurrence in the making of humanity. But the reconciliation occurs only through the experience of falling in love in an unrestricted fashion, only in the discovery of a base that can be enriched and deepened and heightened but not surpassed, only in the affective fulfilment of being in love with the world-transcendent source, sustainment, and destiny of the normative order of inquiry. This redemptive experience, then, is the foundational condition of the possibility of the existential determinants of authentic cognitional praxis. *A fortiori*, it is the foundational condition of the possibility of the self-appropriation that begins in intellectual or philosophic conversion. And because this intellectual conversion is the consolidation of the emergent leap in being into the third stage of meaning, redemptive experience is the foundational condition of the possibility of world-cultural humanity. Only a divine love that orients sensitivity in the cosmos effects the transformation of internal time-consciousness into the proximate condition of participation in a historical order whose generating principle of progress is the normativity of the intentional quest. Internal time-consciousness becomes universal willingness through a detachment of sensitivity that matches the unrestricted character of the notions of being and value. Without affective conversion, the measure of authentic praxis in the normative order of inquiry is too great a burden for the internal time-consciousness of human sensitivity. The horizon of intentionality is then restricted to the limits imposed by concerns that can only be called shortsighted, because sensitivity itself is ordered to participation in the unrestricted quest. These limited concerns contract the finality of existential consciousness to particular goods and the good of order.

Since affective conversion through redemptive experience is the condition of the possibility of the third stage of meaning, it obviously occurs outside of and prior to the third stage. History clearly demonstrates that such is the case. What must concern us now, however, is the peculiarly third-stage manner of sensitive participation in the unrestricted quest.

4.4. Methodical Psychology and the Third Stage of Meaning.

The existential differentiation presented in Lonergan's later work decisively shifts the significance that is to be attributed to the sensitive psyche within the context of the normative order of inquiry. When existential bewilderment is thought to find its resolution in the self-affirmation of the knower, as in *Insight*, the psyche is said to reach "the wealth and fullness of its apprehensions and responses under the higher integration of human intelligence."[70] But when the human good is differentiated from the intelligent and reasonable, when it is understood to be a concrete process in which human knowing and human feeling are integrated with one another in the authentic pursuit of a sequence of ever more comprehensive series of ranges of schemes of recurrence in the making of humanity, then existential consciousness itself, not rationality, is the dimension of subjectivity in which the sensitive psyche receives its integration. What integrates the cognitive and affective dimensions of the subject is good decision, faithfully executed according to the exigencies of the notion of value as these are concretely specified in any one person's unique vocation within the emergent probability of historical process. Discovery and pursuit of that vocation bring psychic integration under the form of the love that is universal willingness. Not only is the psyche a constitutive feature of existential consciousness--because there is a *normative* order of inquiry, *all* levels of consciousness unfold *dramatically*--but also the psyche reaches the wealth and fullness of its apprehensions and responses in the self-transcendent decisions of the world-constitutive existential agent.

I have insisted that the consolidating step in the emergent leap in being that is transcendental method occurred in the eleventh chapter of *Insight*. But I have also indicated that, because this step enabled the establishment of a new series of ranges of schemes of recurrence in conscious being, the irreversible explanatory self-knowledge that is achieved in the self-affirmation of a consciousness that is at once empirical, intelligent, and rational is capable of further extension and refinement. Not only is Lonergan's own existential differentiation in his later works a major example of such further development, but, because this differentiation clears, in a manner not achieved by the great psychologists of the twentieth century, the context in human life within which the sensitive psyche assumes its deepest subjective significance, the possibility is established of erecting the heuristic structure of a science of psychology in a manner that respects the specifically human ontological differentiation that lies in the normative order of the search for direction in the movement of life. Thus the development in Lonergan's thought affects not only transcendental method, where the significance of the psyche shifts from a position in which psychic apprehension is integrated by cognitive praxis to an understanding of the subject that assigns the integrative function to existential consciousness. Beyond this development within method, the clearing of the adequate heuristic structure of psychic intelligibility enables the reorientation of an entire area of modern science. We are able to make critically grounded statements explanatory of psychic process, of the flow of sensitive spontaneity. The critical ground of a methodical psychology enables the development of the positions and the reversal of the counter-positions in the various modern psychologies of passional motivation, and it does so in such a way that the singular contributions of these psychologies to the understanding of humanity are integrated into a psychology of orientations. At the same time, psychology becomes, not a theory in the manner of the second stage of meaning, but, because its concern is with the order of interiority, an explanatory contribution to the third stage of meaning. That is, it becomes a theory in the manner of explanatory self-knowledge rather than in the manner of a natural science whose canon of selection limits its statements to the data of external sense observation.[71] Since the data of psychology lie within the realm of interiority, the science of psychology is a distinctly third-stage science, just as much as the science of intentionality that Lonergan has developed in transcendental method. And because the key to third-stage science is the disengagement of the normative order of inquiry, psychology does not receive critical grounding short of this emergent leap in being. To put the matter simply and bluntly: if one wishes to study psychology, one must arrive at the explanatory self-knowledge of theological foundations that will allow one to develop the positions and reverse the counter-positions that have evolved in the period during which psychology was misconceived as a theory in the mode of the second stage of meaning. More often than not, what is taught in university departments of psychology is only coincidentally relevant to the human psyche, because the human psyche has not found its proper context of intelligibility in the leap into the third stage of meaning. Without that leap and its existential differentiation, adequate explicit heuristic techniques of psychological study are simply not available.

Psychology as science, then, is foundationally a matter of psychic self-appropriation within the context of the normative order of inquiry. But the relationship is reciprocal: as the discovery of this order makes possible an explanatory science of psychology, so the science of psychology complements and develops the disengagement of the order of inquiry. The theory of interiority makes possible the understanding of the drama of authenticity, but an appropriation of the drama enriches the theory. Psychic self-appropriation is a further refinement of the existential differentiation. Moreover, because of the existential determinants of cognitional praxis, psychic self-knowledge enriches the methodical disengagement of the entire normative order of inquiry.

Part Two of this book will be devoted to establishing the mutual influence between theological foundations and a properly conceived science of sensitive psychology. The final result may be anticipated now: the existential differentiation advances in self-appropriation in an explanatory mode when the upper blade of the differentiated notion of value meets the lower blade of elemental symbolism through which a person's subjective dialectic within the dialectic of history becomes a story that can be *identified*, *told*, and *constituted* by the authentic dramatic artist whose subjectivity has successfully negotiated the emergent leap in being into the third stage of meaning. Moral being and religious experience are cumulatively retrieved from compactness as the symbols that indicate the dialectic of willingness and unwillingness in the apprehension and pursuit of value are negotiated. Such a framework provides the science of depth psychology with the higher integration that is required if this science is to contribute coherently to the complete science of humanity; and the science of humanity, grounded in theological foundations, receives a differentiating advance which enables its articulation of the existential differentiation to proceed in third-stage genuineness. The conscious tension of limitation and transcendence approximates the self-transparency that is intended when, through bringing one's conscious operations as intentional to bear upon one's conscious operations as conscious, one joins the collaborative enterprise of assembling the full position on the human subject.

4.5. Psychology and the Theological Foundations of Interdisciplinary Collaboration.

A transcendentally methodical psychology is dependent on the differentiation of the normative order of inquiry. Therefore, it must await the elaboration of theological foundations in the form of an explanatory account of cognitional and existential praxis. But such a psychology is also a further exploration of the normative order of inquiry itself, and in this sense its position within the *scienza nuova* of third-stage interdisciplinary collaboration in the interests of the promotion of the human good cannot strictly speaking be called derivative. Rather, it must be granted a foundational position and acknowledged as part of theological foundations. For what is known in such a psychology is the dramatic significance of both the normative order of inquiry itself and its function as criterion of personal value, of authenticity. Because the mediations of intentionality and psyche are complementary, each of them is foundational, despite the relative dependence of the mediation of psyche on the differentiation of the specifically human normative order of interiority.

A third-stage science of humanity, then, finds its foundations in the explanatory account of the data of intentional and psychic interiority. Because of this grounding, the derivative accounts of social, cultural, political, and economic order can employ categories at once experiential and explanatory. The basic conjugates of human science are at once pure and experiential.[72] In Eugene Gendlin's words, we are enabled "to devise a social and scientific vocabulary that can interact with experiencing"[73] in a quite direct manner, because the theological foundations which provide this vocabulary lie in the objectification of the cognitive and existential constituents of concrete human praxis.

This understanding of foundations offers a solution to a methodological problem of major significance in the social sciences. The solution is at once scientifically respectable, because it is mindful of the explanatory intention of all genuine science, and existentially pertinent, because it keeps scientific explanation bound to the world as it is and hence verifiable in concrete experience. The methodological problem of which I speak is the determinination of the relation of scientific categories to the everyday common-sense symbols that fire the loyalties, inspire the commitments, inform the slogans, and describe the results, of dramatic and practical activity.[74] Once the explanatory account of all symbolizing is rendered possible by reason of the understanding of the relations that obtain between symbols and the normative order of inquiry, social scientists are provided with a foundational base that enables them to account for common-sense symbols in a scientific manner. Without that foundational base, the scientific account is only coincidentally related to the social reality that one is attempting to explain.

Moreoever, when the disengagement of the normative order of inquiry generates a methodically explanatory account of the mythopoetic core of imagination, a dialectical analysis of common-sense cultural and political symbols is possible that relates them critically to the dialectic of history itself. When transcendental method reorients the science of depth psychology into an elucidation of the drama of the authenticity of the search for direction in the movement of life, it simultaneously achieves the standpoint from which a critical theory of society can be begun. The objectification of the structural dynamics of interiority in a patterned set of judgments about cognitional and existential praxis founds a comprehensive reflection on the human condition, an evaluative cultural hermeneutic. This means that theological foundations would ground authentic social and cultural, economic and political praxis, in both the cognitive and the existential orders, on the part of an emerging world-cultural community.

The evaluative cultural hermeneutic grounded in theological foundations exhibits the same eightfold structure of functional specialties that Lonergan has assigned to its complete theological component. But, strictly speaking, it is not to be called theology. It includes, in its first phase, research into cultural anthropology, economic and political history, and philosophic, literary, and religious texts; and, in its second phase, positions, systematic constructions, policies, planning, and execution of programs that relate directly to the orders of cultural, social, and vital values as well as to those of religious and personal values. For example, from the foundations there will be derived *in oratione recta* a new economic and political theory that represents a viewpoint beyond those of the liberal democratic and Marxist systems and that integrates classical political wisdom with uniquely contemporary concerns for conscientization and the liberation of oppressed peoples and of oppressors. But the foundations of this higher synthesis of the liberal thesis and the Marxist antithesis will lie in the self-appropriation of the tension of limitation and transcendence that is constitutive of authentic consciousness. In that self-appropriation will be found the basic categories of political and economic theory, as well as the locus of ultimate verification of political and economic judgments and decisions.

4.6. The Notion of the Beautiful.

The sublation of psychology by the differentiation of the normative order of inquiry will make of psychology a transcendental aesthetic. To integrate psychic and neural energy into the normative unfolding of the pure question of the human spirit by exploiting the relocation of the psychic dimensions of subjectivity in Lonergan's existential differentiation is a first, because still foundational, step in the implementation of the integral heuristic structure of proportionate being that is the existential responsibility of the subject in the third stage of meaning. Such an integration completes the therapeutic intention of the leap in being that is transcendental method to effect a mediated return to the immediacy of concrete experience on the part of the cognitive and existential subject. Before this integration, the heuristic structure of foundations is still incomplete, for the *drama* of cognitive and existential praxis remains incompletely mediated. But without the drama, without the aesthetic participation of sensitive consciousness in the differentiation of interiority, the subject does not return to himself or herself. The finality of the emergent leap into the third stage of meaning is therapeutic. The neglect of the Greek anthropological and transcendent noetic differentiations, of the Yahwistic historical-theological differentiation, and of the Christian soteriological differentiation leaves contemporaries on the receiving end of a series of ever less comprehensive ranges of schemes of recurrence in the organization of human affairs. As a result, we are left with the task of healing an entire planet.[75] The healing can begin only when the subject returns to himself or herself through the explanatory mediation of cognitive and existential praxis. This mediation is foundational therapy. But from its cumulative articulation there is progressively derived the capacity to generate the theoretical and yet directly experiential categories that will inform the therapeutic praxis of third-stage genuineness in the social and cultural, economic and political domains.

The mediation of psychic sensitivity complements the normative elements of the transcendental infrastructure of human experience that Lonergan has uncovered. It retrieves the dimension of experience that was left relatively undifferentiated by Western humanity in its previous leap in being to theoretical expertise, to *logos*. Sensitive spontaneity, the aesthetic component that permeates the normative order of inquiry, has not been the Western concern. Its differentiation and refinement mark much more the achievements of the great Eastern religions. The Western anthropological, transcendent noetic, Yahwistic historical, and soteriological differentiations have surrendered to the egophanic desire for the practical mastery and domination of nature and even of humanity. The contemplative resources of receptive aesthetic appreciation have been left unintegrated in the mainstream of the Western evolution of consciousness. In fact, with the derailment of the theoretical achievement of the medieval synthesis into the modern truncation of the normative order of inquiry, aesthetic sensitivity has not only been left undeveloped but has been mishandled and mauled by such aberrations of intentionality as the concern with mechanical technique rather than with existential praxis, the neglect of the existential determinants of cognitional praxis, and the compacting of the order of finality into the twofold differentiation of the particular good and the good of order. The sensitive psychological sickness of contemporary Western men and women is a result of an aberration of intentionality that has overtaken Western culture and that could push us headlong into a brief but immeasurably wretched post-historic age. Intentionality goes astray when it severs its own capacities for transcendence from the counterbalance imposed upon human ambition by the countervailing dimension of limitation that makes itself known in our spontaneous sensitivity. Oddly enough, we will find that attention to limitation *prevents* intentionality from succumbing to short-sighted practicality, whereas neglect of limitation is precisely what *limits* the human spirit from adopting the long-range point of view. For the key to the long-range fruitfulness of praxis is found in *integrity*, and integrity means the genuineness that is constituted by the creative tension of limitation and transcendence in the cognitive and existential praxis of the subject.

The Kafkaesque organization of human affairs that is our daily experience as we teeter on the border of a post-historic age is nothing other than the unreconciled disproportion of transcendence and limitation writ large. The danger was inherent in the theoretical breakthrough of our cultural forebears, for theory is that peculiar variety of human knowledge that transcends imaginal representation.[76] But the positive gains of the theoretical differentiation can be consolidated, it seems, only if the subject in whom such capacities become differentiated retains respect for the imaginally represented processes of his own sensitivity, without which theoretical insight is impossible. Without that sensitivity, the aesthetic order is neglected and violated. Moreover, because the first level in the normative order of inquiry is an internally and externally sensitive empirical consciousness that is not obliterated but only sublated by the further steps in cognitional and existential praxis, the destruction of aesthetic subjectivity means the destruction of humanity itself. To retrieve, as Lonergan does, the cognitional praxis of intelligence and reason and the existential praxis of deliberation and decision, is to lead consciousness decisively forward to the retrieval of self that is the therapeutic finality of the emergent leap in being. But even transcendental method is shortcircuited until there is developed and refined for our use a maieutic of that sensitive consciousness without which intelligence, reason, and decision become not only inhuman but satanic. Only with the recovery of the transcendental aesthetic component of all conscious subjectivity does the emergent leap come full circle. Only then is the heuristic structure of theological foundations complete. And only with the completion of this heuristic structure is it time to move to the functional specialties of positions, systems, and execution within the evaluative cultural hermeneutic that is the comprehensive reflection on the human condition proper to humanity in the third stage of meaning.

To speak, then, of *psychic conversion* is to retrieve in the mode of interiorly differentiated consciousness an option not chosen by our Greek predecessors when they decisively opted for logos over psyche. But it is also to vindicate their decision. For without theory, there are no data on human inquiry to warrant a differentiation of its normative order; and without the differentiation of the normative order of inquiry, the significance of psychic spontaneity does not emerge. Lonergan has made it possible to retrieve in the way of interior differentiation the option that lies behind the history of Western civilization. His own work can now be complemented by another retrieval, in the same order of interiority and dependent on the differentiation of this order's normative structure--a retrieval of the sensitive and imaginal base in aesthetic consciousness out of which there emerge all inquiry, insight, conceptualization, formulation, reflection, affirmation of the virtually unconditioned, deliberation, and decision.

Nor is this complement outside the subjective foundations of the transcendental field. The medievals did not limit the transcendental field to the intelligible, the true, the real, and the good; they included as well the beautiful, the objective of human aesthetic intentionality. Now that sensitive consciousness is seen to receive its proper integration, not through the higher integrations effected by intelligence and rationality, but in the good decisions that promote the making of humanity, its advance in authenticity, the fulfilment of its affectivity, and the direction of its labor to particular goods and a good of order that are truly worth while, the context is established within which it makes sense to attempt, in the way of methodical interior self-differentiation, a statement of the relation of the sensitive intention of the beautiful to the intelligent intention of meaning, the rational intention of truth, and the existential intention of value. That existential self-transcendence is integrative of cognition and feeling indicates that there are existential determinants not only of intelligent and rational praxis but also of aesthetic orientations. Sensitive consciousness itself is intentional; nor is its intentionality superseded by that of the spiritual dimensions of our conscious being. It is, rather, sublated into the pursuit of meaning, truth, and value. As there is a transcendental notion of the intelligible, of the true, of the real, and of the good, so there is a transcendental notion of the beautiful. As the former are heuristically anticipated by the unfolding of the normative order of inquiry, so the latter reveals itself in the intentional feelings that give to the intention of meaning, the reflective grasp of truth, and the existential orientation to value their momentum, their drive, their satisfaction, and their specifically human drama. One's story is a matter of the satisfaction or frustration of one's desire for meaning, truth, reality, and value. That the story is so human is a function of the specifically differentiating normative order of inquiry. But that it is a story at all is a function of the transcendental notion of the beautiful. This intention resides in a sensitive consciousness that cannot be left behind in any human exercise of intelligence, reason, and deliberation.

PART TWO

PSYCHIC CONVERSION

In Part One, we articulated a program for a contemporary methodical theology. We disengaged the extratheological responsibilities of such a theology by offering the judgment that Christian theological foundations are to ground the collaborative interdisciplinary construction of a disclosive and transformative human science whose basic terms and relations are to be found in the realm of interiorly differentiated consciousness. This new human science will implement the integral heuristic structure of proportionate being by reorienting contemporary practical common sense through the elevation of practicality to a base of authentic existential agency in harmony with the objective scale of values; and by reorienting and integrating contemporary scientific knowledge through the development of the positions and the reversal of the counter-positions that have issued respectively from the authentic or inauthentic cognitional praxis of modern and contemporary scientists. These foundations will enable us to reverse the longer cycle of decline. The explicit foundations of this third-stage science of humanity are located in the explanatory self-appropriation of the structure of authentic existential and cognitive praxis. This self-appropriation is a recovery of the original experience of the search for direction in the movement of life. It is a mediated return to immediacy[1] that is effected by bringing the operations of conscious intentionality as intentional to bear upon the operations and states of conscious intentionality as conscious. Chapter One set the context of our discussion. Evidence was provided in Chapter Two that the development of Bernard Lonergan's thought supports such an interpretation of the situation and responsibility of a methodical theology at the present juncture in human history. Chapter Three called attention to the aesthetic dimension of interiority and suggested that the foundational quest is fulfilled only when this psychic locus of verification for the authenticity of cognitive and existential praxis is itself submitted to explanatory differentiation in the mode of interiority. It is in this aesthetic dimension that the struggle of willingness and unwillingness is conducted; it is to this aesthetic dimension in its existential qualification that the divine solution to the problem of evil is most immediately offered; and this radical gift of God's love, effecting antecedent willingness, is to be acknowledged as the condition of the possibility of the self-appropriation of cognitive and existential praxis that constitutes the foundational quest itself. Explanatory differentiation of the aesthetic transforms the science of psychology, which, because its domain is the realm of interiority, is an intrinsic constituent of theological foundations.

Our task in the second part of this book is to explain in heuristic fashion the reflective praxis in the mode of the third stage of meaning that will enable the self-appropriation of the aesthetic dimension and, through this self-appropriation, the elevation of practicality to a base of authentic existential agency capable of directing participation in the reversal of the longer cycle of decline. How do we recover the story in which is verified the authenticity or inauthenticity both of our judgments of value and of our consequent cognitional praxis? How do we move from this recovery to assume our distinct historical responsibility for the concrete process of the human good? In answering these questions, we shall be offering not only the key to the reorientation of common sense, but also an instance of the reorientation and integration of the science of depth psychology. That is to say, we will be actually engaged in implementing the integral heuristic structure of proportionate being. Finally, because we are dialectically engaged with a science that has to do with the realm of interiority, our implementation will be foundational; and because the dimension of the realm of interiority with which we are engaged establishes a set of defensive circles for the authenticity of those dimensions that sublate it into higher integrations, we will be bringing full circle the foundational quest that received its first and indispensable consolidation in the eleventh chapter of Bernard Lonergan's *Insight*.

CHAPTER FOUR

SOUL-MAKING AND THE OPPOSITES

OUTLINE

1. Transcendence and Limitation. Limitation and the long-range point of view.
2. The Basic Notion of Psychic Conversion. The clue. An initial approximation. Reorienting scientific psychology and common sense.
3. The Notion of Experience. Experience as coextensive with consciousness. Patterns of experience and their existential determinants.
4. Psychic Conversion and Affective Conversion. Psychic conversion as interiorly differentiated consciousness.
5. The Psyche and the Opposites. Spirit and matter. The psyche as mediating their integration. Soul and soul-making. The difficulty of soul-making, historically and ontologically viewed.

1. *Transcendence and Limitation.*

In this chapter our task is to specify the function of the aesthetic dimension of interiority in reconciling the duality of human subjectivity. We had called attention to this dimension in the last chapter, concluding that the general bias of practical common sense against ultimate issues and results, with its time-distorting contraction of the reach of existential consciousness to the realms of the good of order and the particular good, has effected, in the course of the history of the longer cycle of decline, a cumulative neglect of the human psyche. To neglect this aesthetic dimension is to *attempt* to leave it behind. The tendency is built into the notion of being, which is not restricted to time. But because the very constitution of our being dictates that the aesthetic dimension cannot be left behind, this dimension wreaks its vengeance sooner or later upon the inauthentically inquiring, reflecting, and deliberating subject, by effecting, as we have said, a distortion of the movement of life itself. It thus contributes to praxis that is unintelligent, irrational, and irresponsible, i.e., praxis that neglects the historicality of the concrete process of the human good. The neglect of the order of value is inevitably a neglect of the sensitive psyche, for values are apprehended in feelings before they are ever pursued by deliberation and decision. To neglect the sensitive psyche is to distort time, to introduce a surd into history. To contract the order of values into its two lower levels of the particular good and the good of order is to cripple the participation of the sensitive psyche in the search for direction in the movement of life. Under these conditions it is impossible to discover direction. This movement of life is itself experienced precisely by the sensitive psyche. Therefore, to neglect the constitutive participation of the psyche in the search for direction in its own most intimate sphere is to distort that sphere itself, to render the movement itself a chaotic series of fragmented, unrelated, dissociated, and bizarre complexes of affects and representations. Paradoxically, then, to neglect the *long-range* point of view is to neglect the organic and psychic root of *limitation;* conversely, to neglect limitation is to refuse to adopt the long-range point of view. The long-range point of view is honored only when integrity is pursued for its own sake, and to pursue integrity is to act from the tense unity of transcendence and limitation. This unity is displaced when attention to pragmatic results is granted priority over the *doing* of authentic knowing and valuing, when getting things done becomes more important than doing the truth and incarnating the good.

Cognitive and existential authenticity is, in Lonergan's terms, a matter of the integrity of limitation and transcendence in one's development. To neglect one of these two poles of the duality is necessarily to distort, to short-change, to corrupt the other. By virtue of our cognitive and existential self-transcendence, we are obliged to ask questions about ultimate issues and long-range results; the very constitution of our sensitive limitations, in our capacity to apprehend religious, personal, and cultural as well as social and vital values, is oriented to supporting us to our efforts to meet this obligation. To neglect the need of our sensitivity for an ordered response to values is to deny transcendence and to cripple limitation. Values themselves are constituted by the dialectic of transcendence and limitation. Therefore, when the order of values is compacted into the social and particular goods, transcendence is distorted into a megalomanic drive to power and domination. Such an abrupt over-reaching of transcendence is simultaneously a neglect of limitation, which, if it were attended to as it aspires toward an ordered response to values, would at once humble transcendence by grounding it in limitation and, paradoxically, stretch it to the full capacity of its intentional reach, rendering it responsive to ultimate issues and long-term results. Only by maintaining integrity with our bodily and psychic limitations can we be genuinely transcendent. A transcendence that neglects these limitations by *over*extending its reach is actually unduly *limiting* itself to short-term consequences and crippling the inherent limitations that could sustain genuine self-transcendence. To deny limitation is to be destroyed by limitation; to affirm and respect limitation is to achieve transcendence. "Any activity which fails to recognize a self-limiting principle is of the devil."[1] Furthermore, the failure to recognize the self-limiting principle prevents the activity from being really transcendent. Under the illusion of unlimited transcendence, we invite the destructiveness of the neglected limitation, which has been rendered destructive precisely by the neglect. Conversely, to grant free range to the full reach of transcendence is to promote the flourishing of limitation.

We are convinced, then, that the neglect of the limiting psyche is a constitutive element in the genesis of the longer cycle of decline and that redressing the injury by attending to the pain of the neglected psyche is a constitutive element in reversing the same longer cycle. Attending to the psyche will enable us to discover not only the story of the decline but also the elements that are still available for reversing the course of that story. Attending to the psyche will enable us to assemble these restorative elements into a story of our own making--the story of our self-conscious constitution of a human world in which authenticity is advanced, affectivity fulfilled, and labor non-alienated because directed to social and particular ends that are really worth while from the objective standpoint of religious, personal, and cultural values. The recovery of intentionality is not adequate until it includes the telling and the making of *the story of intentionality.* This means that the recovery of intentionality must extend, in an explicit manner, to the mediation of the immediacy of aesthetic consciousness. Then and only then does the emergent leap into the third stage of meaning land on adequate foundations, on foundations that can support it and can prevent it from breaking down. It is not enough to recover the spiritual intention of meaning, truth, and value, for these objectives have no home except in the movement of life. That movement itself must be just as subject to explanatory mediation in the realm of interiorly differentiated consciousness as are the intentions of meaning, truth, and value without which the movement has no direction. There is no integral movement without direction; but there is nowhere to go if direction is not embodied in the movement of life. Disembodied meaning, truth, and value--i.e., insights, judgments, and decisions without an aesthetic component--are a human impossibility. To retrieve the intentions of meaning, truth, and value is a task that is not complete without the recovery of that aesthetic component, a task that, for all the brilliance of its execution, will suffer the same unfortunate fate as did the medieval synthesis unless it is brought full circle by bringing it home. And the exigencies of our current historical crisis are such that we cannot afford to let that happen if we want to bequeath to future generations a spiritual, psychic, and organic environment in which their humanity can genuinely flourish.

2. *The Basic Notion of Psychic Conversion.*

The clue that led me to try to bring transcendental method home by completing its set of foundations was found in Lonergan's existential differentiation, in the disengagement of the notion of value as distinct from, determinative of, and sublating the notions of the intelligible and the real that propel the subject under the dominance of the desire to know through the process that will lead to correct understanding. This notion of value is endowed, as we have seen, with a complex structure that unfolds as the subject moves from the intentional feelings through which potential values are apprehended, through questions for deliberation, to the judgments of value and the decisions that either ratify or negate the original affective apprehensions. Since the drive and momentum of existential consciousness derive from the apprehending feelings, the affective development of sensitive consciousness becomes central in the account of the flourishing of existential authenticity. Because existential consciousness is determinative of the authenticity of cognitional praxis, these same feelings permeate also the search for intelligibility and truth. And these feelings are in a reciprocal relationship with symbols, for feelings both evoke and are evoked by symbols. Just as it is because of feelings that the intentional quest is a drama, so it is through the symbols linked with these feelings in an elemental fashion that the drama can be disengaged. These symbols, then, provide the materials for existential self-appropriation. Correct interpretation of the elemental symbols of one's being permits the most accurate narrative of the story of the search for direction in the movement of life. Thus, it is through the twofold relation of feelings, first to existential or evaluative consciousness and secondly to elemental symbols, that we arrive at the notion of psychic conversion. We need now to explicate this notion.

Psychic conversion, initially, is the acquisition of the capacity to disengage and interpret correctly the elemental symbols of one's being and to form or transform one's existential and cognitive praxis on the basis of such a recovery of the story of one's search for direction in the movement of life. Psychic conversion aids the telling and the making of the story of one's engagement in the specifically human responsibility of advancing the human good by authentic performance at all levels of intentional consciousness. The notion of psychic conversion, framed as it is within the context of transcendental method, will permit us to develop the positions and to reverse the counter-positions that appear in the writings of the great twentieth-century architects of the science of depth psychology. In this manner we can responsibly take up the task of consciousness in the third stage of meaning, which is to implement the integral heuristic structure of proportionate being by reorienting contemporary common sense and science. Because psychic conversion is both a scientific notion and a key to appropriating the dramatic and practical patterns of experience, or, better, the story of cognitive and existential experience, the implementation in this case is a reorientation *simultaneously* both of science and of common sense. As a reorientation of science, it dialectically integrates the discoveries of depth psychology into the theological foundations of interdisciplinary collaboration laid by transcendental method. As a reorientation of common sense, it elevates dramatic and practical common sense beyond themselves and into the existential quest of value on the part of the subject in the third stage of meaning. Finally, psychic conversion is the key to the completion of the finality of the task of transcendental method itself. With psychic conversion, the therapeutic intention of the foundational quest comes full circle. For this advance in interior differentiation establishes a set of defensive circles that safeguard the schemes established by the leap in being to interiorly differentiating consciousness and prevent the intentional subject from falling victim to a fundamental and sustained lapse into alienation and ideology. Therefore, we must call further attention to the dimension of consciousness that becomes transparent through psychic conversion.

3. *The Notion of Experience.*

"Experience" is Lonergan's term for the first, or empirical, level of consciousness. The operations that occur on this level include acts of external sensation and internal operations of registering, imagining, associating, and remembering. Such acts always occur in conjunction with some experientially *felt* condition or state of conation and emotion. The interior complex of sensations and feelings perdures as one moves beyond these empirical operations to intellectual, rational, and existential operations. Feeling especially is the empirical dynamism that permeates the entire intentional context that unites a manifold of contents and of acts at the various levels of consciousness. It is primarily because of feelings that we can speak of *experience* of the data of consciousness, even when these data consist of operations that occur not on the empirical level, but on higher levels of consciousness. These operations sublate the empirical level of consciousness into participation in their own most intimate concerns. Participant feeling makes inquiry, insight, reflection, judgment, and deliberation a matter of consciously experienced drama. For

Lonergan, then, experience is coextensive with consciousness itself.

All operations and feelings that constitute experience as such have a bodily base. The acts and states of empirical consciousness "never occur in isolation both from one another and from all other events. On the contrary, they have a bodily basis; they are functionally related to bodily movements; and they occur in some dynamic context that somehow unifies a manifold of sensed contents and of acts of sensing."[2] The context that unifies is described by Lonergan as an "organizing control" that results from "a factor variously named conation, interest, attention, purpose. We speak of consciousness as a stream, but the stream involves not only the temporal succession of different contents but also direction, striving, effort. Moreover, this direction of the stream is variable."[3] The variations of direction are what determine different dynamic *patterns of experience:* biological, artistic, intellectual, dramatic, practical, sexual, scholarly, religious, mystical, existential, introspective.

The operations and states that constitute experience can function as an operational definition of the term, psyche. Lonergan agrees with this point, for in *Insight* psychic development is referred to and defined as "a sequence of increasingly differentiated and integrated sets of capacities for perceptiveness, for aggressive or affective response, for memory, for imaginative projects, and for skillfully and economically executed performance."[4] The various elements that entered into the implicit definition of a pattern of experience also figure in this definition of psychic development: sensitive perception, emotion, memory, imagination, and a variety of directions.

To speak, then, of empirical consciousness in an anthropological context is really an abstraction, as Kant recognized in his otherwise unfortunate account of *Anschauung*. In a context quite beyond the Kantian horizon, the empirical, understood as "a set of intelligible relations that link together sequences of sensations, memories, images, conations, emotions, and bodily movements,"[5] always receives the direction of its intentionality from the same *existential* determinants that set intelligent and rational consciousness upon their course, whether it be the intention of being or the flight from understanding, the intention of value or the capitulation to the confines that contract the order of the ends of human action. There are, of course, exceptions to this existential determination, and Lonergan treats them under the rubric of the biological pattern of experience. The exceptions are moments in human experience when, without any personal existential determination, the sequences of sensations, memories, images, conations, emotions, associations, bodily movements, and spontaneous intersubjective responses "converge upon terminal activities of intussusception or reproduction or, when negative in scope, self-preservation."[6] But except for such dimensions of conditioning and determinism, one's pattern of sensitive experience is under the relative dominance of existentially directed orientations and so can be variously dramatic, intellectual, artistic, mystical, practical, sexual, scholarly, or (as in the present case) interiorly differentiating. In all such instances, experience does not function in isolation from the orientation of one's existential willingness and, consequently, of one's intelligence and rationality. It is rather their substratum, their infrastructure, and is sublated by them in different ways into various higher integrations in the various patterns of experience. Empirical sensitivity, then, is not independent of the drama established by the spiritual exigencies for the intelligible, the true, and the good that constitute the normative order of the search for direction in the movement of life. Moreover, as we indicated at the end of Chapter Three, transcendental intentionality includes this empirical level of consciousness and prescribes that a sensitive psyche that is sublated into higher integrations by a spiritual intention of meaning, truth, and value should have its own distinctive finality, a finality that is realized when empirical consciousness is harmoniously integrated by the authentic intention of the ends of the higher levels. This distinctive finality is the beautiful, which is the sensible splendor of truth. The finality of the empirical level is not realized in isolation from the finality of the various existentially determined patterns of experience. Rather, the harmony and peace of empirical consciousness is a function of the authentic self-transcendent performance of intelligence, reason, and responsibility in the various existentially determined patterns of experience. For this reason there are aesthetic concomitants, even criteria, of authentic performance in these various patterns, since the aesthetic finality of empirical consciousness is sublated by the respective finalities of intelligent, rational, and existential consciousness. It is on this basis, for example, that Christian spiritual theology has maintained that fundamental, sustained, and unsurpassable peace can legitimately be assumed to be a criterion of discernment for decision on the part of a poised, open, detached consciousness intent on discovering the will of God.

4. *Psychic Conversion and Affective Conversion.*

Such peace and harmony of affectivity, though, are not what is meant by psychic conversion. They are a function rather of moral and religious conversion, and they testify to the affective conversion of sensitivity itself to participation in the normatively human in any stage of meaning. The term, psychic conversion, is used in a quite technical sense to refer to *a specifically third-stage development of subjectivity*, in the same sense as intellectual conversion when the latter term is used to denote not simply the authentic functioning of intelligence and rationality, but the self-appropriation that results from the explanatory self-affirmation of the knower and from the positions on being and objectivity. Psychic conversion is a further agent of interiorly differentiated consciousness. That its cumulative outcome may eventuate in a third-stage variant of the happy conscience in the self-transcendent person does not mean that this outcome is to be identified as its immanent intelligibility. For that lies elsewhere--in the gaining of the capacity to disengage the primal, elemental symbolic ciphers of one's participation in the search for direction in the movement of life. Only those whose development demands and makes possible the leap into the third stage of meaning need psychic conversion in order to satisfy the sensitive demand for participation. But the third stage of meaning is the cultural drama of our time, and for those whose development brings them this far, psychic conversion is truly necessary if they are to bring to term the foundational finality of the leap in being. Without psychic conversion, intellectual conversion itself risks causing in incipient third-stage subjectivity an alienation of intelligence and rationality from sensitivity, an inflation of the human spirit, a schizoid split, a failure to come home.

The aesthetic finality of sensitive empirical consciousness, then, may be realized in any sufficiently differentiated consciousness that is *de facto* faithful to the normative exigencies of the intentional quest. Psychic conversion differentiates this aesthetic finality in the mode of interiority and in an explanatory fashion. As such, psychic conversion is dependent upon the intellectual conversion of the self-affirmation of the knower with which the leap into the third stage of meaning itself began. For with the self-affirmation of the knower one begins the process of explanatory interior self-appropriation. One learns the art of a new differentiation of consciousness. Psychic conversion develops this art still further, extending its maieutic capacity to the realm of the elemental symbols through which the sensitive psyche expresses its experience of the drama of the search for direction in the movement of life.

5. The Psyche and the Opposites.

We have referred already to a dialectic of transcendence and limitation in the unfolding of authentic intentionality, and we have indicated that due respect to each pole of this dialectic is the condition of the possibility of the genuine satisfaction of the other pole. Transcendence and limitation, however, are the conscious representatives of a more basic opposition in the human person--a conscious integration that may be anatomically based in the two hemispheres of the brain. Ontologically, the more radical opposition is the duality of spirit and matter.[7]

It is important to conceive the opposites correctly. Ernest Becker finds that "in recent times every psychologist who has done vital work" has taken the problem of the opposites as the main focus of reflection.[8] Becker himself calls the opposites self and body. But this nomenclature immediately establishes an exaggerated and quite Cartesian dualism that Becker never manages to transcend in his reflections on the human condition. In fact, he maintains that the dualism is inescapable and that any attempt to transcend it is futile. It is a hopeless existential dilemma. Our only recourse is to find the most creative illusion, and Becker finds this solution in Kierkegaardian faith.

Among the psychologists whom Becker credits with having done vital work is Carl Jung, and I have found that Jung points us beyond the opposites. For the moment, I limit myself to mentioning one happy use of language that is found in the Jungian corpus. Much of Jung's language is imprecise,[9] but on one particular matter he is quite helpful.[10] Jung reserves the term "self" for the totality beyond the opposites. Thus he includes "body" in "self." Moreover, perhaps Jung's most important insight is that the psyche--however ill-conceived this may be in his thought--mediates between the opposites of spirit and matter. The individuating negotiation of psychic process thus becomes the way of reconciling the opposites of spirit and matter in a cumulative and conscious unification of the totality that is the self.[11] With the help of Lonergan, we may say that this cumulative unification assumes conscious representation and integration in the form of the conditional and analogous law of genuineness, where the tension of limitation and transcendence is admitted into consciousness in either a spontaneous or a reflectively recovered and self-appropriating manner, depending on the stage of meaning into which one's development has brought one.[12]

The radical ontological duality of the human subject, then, is that of spirit and matter. The operator of their progressive integration is the psyche, i.e., the sequence of sensations, memories, images, emotions, conations, associations, bodily movements, and spontaneous intersubjective responses that constitutes the empirical level of consciousness that is sublated by the spiritual intention of meaning, of truth, and of value. It is in the realm of the aesthetic that the human subject achieves a conscious integration of the opposites, under the form of transcendence and limitation. The psychic, the sensitive, the empirical, the aesthetic--these four terms refer to the same dimension of human interiority, that dimension whose intentional finality is the beautiful as the splendor of the truth of genuineness.

In recent thought influenced by Jung, this dimension has also been referred to as the "soul."[13] The term is not used to refer to the spiritual central form of the human subject, as in Aristotelian and Thomist thought, but in a sense that captures a significance that has been lost in our modern usage of the original Greek word, psyche. Modern psychology has emptied the psyche of soul. That is, it has lost the perspective that "mediates events and makes differences between ourselves and everything that happens," that deepens events and makes them experiences, that converts reality into symbol and metaphor,[14] and that places the subject in primordial relatedness to other persons, to the whole of nature, and to God. "It is as though the life of the soul is the middle ground between the life of the body and the life of the mind, as though self without soul is divided between body and mind. To suffer through the conflict of one's passions, to suffer through the split between body and mind may be the way to recovery."[15]

I shall follow this terminology and shall speak with James Hillman of "soul-making." But by this term, I shall mean attentiveness to the sequence of sensations, memories, images, emotions, conations, associations, bodily movements, and spontaneous intersubjective responses that constitutes the human sensitive psyche: existentially directed attentiveness to the movement of life itself, to that movement in which direction is discovered by intelligent inquiry, reasonable reflection, and responsible deliberation. Soul-making results from attentiveness to the sensitively experienced movement of life. In the third stage of meaning, soul-making *brings home* the self-appropriating disengagement of the normative order of inquiry; it roots that order in the very movement of life in which one finds direction by remaining faithful to that order. Soul-making is a matter of bringing the operations of intelligent, rational, and responsible consciousness as intentional to bear upon the operations and states of psychic, sensitive, empirical, aesthetic consciousness as conscious. It is a matter of conscripting into the intentional quest of the human good that dimension of consciousness where the movement of life is most intimately experienced, and it does so precisely by bringing the intentional quest home to the movement in which it is responsible for discovering direction. The term "soul-making" is analogous. I use it especially to refer to the third-stage differentiation and integration of the mediating ground between the radical opposites of spiritual conjugates on the one hand and physical, chemical, botanical, and zoological conjugates on the other hand. Soul-making, then, is the explicit, self-appropriating constitution and development of sensitive psychological conjugates that unite *in consciousness* the purely spiritual and the purely material conjugates due to whose opposition the Greek philosophers not without reason defined the human person as the rational animal.

The neglect of the sensitive psyche during the longer cycle of decline has transformed the potential operator of human integration into a defective operator of human disintegration. By seeking our own lives, we have lost our soul. That is to say, by reducing the order of the ends of human activity to some conspiracy of confusion between the particular good and the good of order, we have lost the possibility for the integration of consciousness in the tense unity of transcendence and limitation. In order to restore this possibility of integration, we must attend to the task of differentiating and appropriating, and thereby healing, the sensitive, aesthetic dimension of our conscious being, which is presently distorted and crippled. The task is not easy. It represents the final moment in the establishment of the foundations for reversing the longer cycle of decline, and it is every bit as arduous and complex as the struggle to arrive at the self-affirmation of the knower and as the effort to disengage from this intellectual self-possession the existential differentiation that places intelligence and reason in their proper place in the service of life. The reasons for the difficulty are both historical and ontological.

Historically, the neglect of the psyche, which is partly constitutive of the longer cycle of decline, has made the meeting-place of spirit and matter, of intentionality and body, into something of a dense jungle, or a cavernous pit, or a volcano: that is, a series of dissociated and fragmented complexes whose phenomenology would reveal a disharmony and incongruity in the very movement of life itself. The depths of our malaise reach to the order of physical conjugates. Victimized and oppressed, the modern psyche must be approached with utmost care. It is every bit as angry as are the awakening minds and hearts of the oppressed peoples of the earth, and just as ready to perpetrate a violent revolution overthrowing its intrasubjective oppressor as the wretched of the earth are to destroy the social and economic systems that have enslaved them. In fact, these social and economic systems are nothing other than the intrasubjective neglect of the movement of life writ large and, as it were, "projected" into the dialectic of history. But the psychotic revolution of the sensitive psyche would be, likewise, only the last stage in the intrasubjective implications of the longer cycle of decline, just as the replacement of the egophanic myth of automatic progress and expansion by the Marxist myth that the solution to the shorter cycle will generate sustained progress, is the ultimate stage in the same longer cycle as it affects the dialectic of history. The approach to the psyche, as to the poor, must be grounded in an acknowledgment and avowal of injustice, in a genuine readiness not only to change but also to learn, in a reverence for that dimension of human reality where God makes known and most directly effective his own historical but absolutely supernatural solution to the problem of evil. For there are instruments of renewal present in the neglected sensitive psyche, but only the appropriate attitude will enable their discovery and implementation.

Ontologically, as the meeting-ground of matter and spirit, the human sensitive psyche shares in both, and so the aesthetic dimension of transcendental subjectivity is simultaneously both transparent and opaque to itself. The point of psychic conversion is to render the soul transparent to itself with a retrieved or recovered immediacy, in a manner analogous to that in which Lonergan's cognitional analysis and its resultant philosophic conversion render human intelligence and rationality self-transparent and effect a mediated return of the self-appropriating subject to the cognitive immediacy of that subject's search for meaning and truth.

Yet the task of psychic conversion is, if anything, even more difficult than that of philosophic or intellectual conversion. Not only is the modern psyche an extremely fragmented stream of sensitive impressions due to the neglect with which it has been treated during the centuries that measure the longer cycle of decline. Even without this distortion of the dialectic of the subject, the task would be difficult enough, due to the mixed nature of the human sensitive psyche, its share in both the spiritual and material dimensions of the one human subject. Sensitive consciousness shares in something of the transparency of the spiritual--it *is* consciousness--but it also participates in the opaqueness of the material, in the darkness of the physical, the chemical, the botanical, the zoological. It is, to use Carl Jung's suggestive term, the shadow. It is very close to that set of aggregates of aggregates of aggregates, etc., which, without the light of human intelligence and rationality, "unheard, unseen, silently eating, giving birth, dying, heads nodding through hundreds of millions of years, . . . would have gone on in the profoundest night of non-being down to its unknown end."[16] Sensitive consciousness, the home of the aesthetic, is the link between intelligent and nonintelligent emergent probability. It is in immediate contact with both, and it participates in both. It can integrate the two in a synchronistic process of world-constitution; that is, it can integrate the prime potency that is energy[17] under the higher conjugate forms of insights, judgments, and decisions. But when, through neglect, it becomes a fragmented and dissociated series of incongruous and nonrhythmic complexes, as it has in the course of the longer cycle of decline, it can and will contribute to the non-coincidence of spirit and matter not only in the individual subject but in the relations between history and nature.

The ontological reason for the difficulty of psychic conversion can be further elucidated. The intention of being that is human spirituality is not restricted to the horizon of space or even to that of time, whereas the horizons of space and time constitute the field of that dimension of being whose immanent intelligibility is nonintelligent emergent probability. Nonintelligent emergent probability is the immanent intelligibility in concrete extensions and concrete durations.[18] But the intellectual and rational desire to know intends an objective named being, which as such is neither within space nor within time. To conceive being as within space and time represents an illegitimate intrusion of imagination into the interpretation of being.

> 'To be' cannot mean 'to be in space' or 'to be in time.' If that were so, and space is or time is, then space would be in space and time would be in time. The further space and time, if real, would also be, and so would demand a still further space and time. The argument could be repeated indefinitely to yield an infinity of spaces and times. 'To be' then is just 'to be.' Space and time, if real, are determinations within being; and if they are determinations within being, then they are not the containers but the contained.[19]

The sensitive psyche, then, insofar as it shares in the properties of both matter and spirit, is invested with a native and radical *disproportion* that is independent of any particular historical vicissitudes such as that which it has experienced during the longer cycle of decline. It participates in, and is a higher integration of, the aggregates of aggregates of aggregates whose immanent intelligiblity is an emergent probability *within* the field of space-time. But it also participates in, and is to be integrated on a yet higher level by, a spiritual intention of intelligibility, being, and value whose objective is an unrestricted domain which encompasses the field of space-time and its intelligible emergent probability, but is not restricted to these. Sensitive consciousness, the human psyche, the realm of the aesthetic, is simultaneously restricted and not restricted to the field of space and the field of time. Not only does its synchronizing mediation of nonintelligent and intelligent emergent probability become a far more complicated task than it would be without this disproportion, but also the reflective task of psychic conversion, through which sensitive consciousness is elevated to a higher level of transparency, shows that this radical disproportion produces a gap in human intellectual and moral development. The gap is moral impotence; that is, it is the very condition of the possibility of basic sin and moral evil. Psychic conversion does not negate or overcome the disproportion, but simply exposes it.

The Jungian school of depth psychology implicitly joins forces with the Heideggerian reduction of the notion of being that is *Dasein* to the horizon of time instituted by the human imagination (*Einbildungskraft*, the art of forming into one [picture]). Both schools surrender the intention of being to the rhythms and processes of unintelligent nature, and so they constitute romantic agony. But the opposite aberration of neglecting the rhythms and processes of nature in favor of the transcendence of intelligence constitutes the egophanic reduction of the order of human teleology to the practical good of an efficient, highly centralized, mechanical social order. The synchronicity of the unrestricted intention of being and value in the constitution of the world with the rhythms and processes of the nonintelligent universe that are *within* being can be effected only by the tense unity of limitation and transcendence. This unity not only constitutes human authenticity but also conditions self-transcendence by attentiveness to limitation and conditions the flourishing of limitation by the fidelity of consciousness to the self-transcendent norms of inquiry. The tension of limitation and transcendence is not only established *between* intelligent, rational, and responsible intentionality *and* the sensitive psyche. More radically, it is *felt in* the sensitive psyche itself. For the sensitive psyche is at once the higher integration of coincidental manifolds at the pole of limitation, i.e., of physical, chemical, botanical, and zoological conjugates, and the potency for the higher conjugate forms at the pole of transcendence, i.e., for insights, judgments, and decisions. The higher conjugates, in spite of their extrinsic dependence on sensitive representation, are intrinsically independent of the energic prime potency that constitutes the residue from which insight abstracts, with whose brute facticity the rational factualness of the unconditioned stands in stark contrast, and from whose subjection to laws the legislative function of existential insight, reflection, and decision differentiates itself by the exercise of freedom. The synchronizing function of the sensitive psyche is fulfilled only when the sensitive psyche achieves a *detachment* from its own sensitivity--a detachment that is not a neglect, a disowning, an apathy, or an indifference, but the *willingness* to perform its unique function within the concrete universe of being. The antecedent universal willingness is the fruit of the divine solution to the problem of evil, and it is the condition of the possibility of the conscious integration of limitation and transcendence through which the sensitive psyche establishes the synchronicity in history of spirit and matter. The aesthetic is the radical domain of the reconciliation of opposites.

Soul-making, then, is the differentiation and integral constitution of the genuine tension of limitation and transcendence in aesthetic consciousness. I once referred to soul-making as "the subtlest of all human arts."[20] Why this is the case is clear from the foregoing explanation of the inherent ontological difficulty of rendering the sensitive psyche transparent to itself through psychic conversion. From this explanation, moreover, there emerges in yet another key the crucial theme of the differentiation of existential intentionality out of the cognitive compactness into which it was contracted in Lonergan's *Insight*. For the existential differentiation displays the authentic realization of the tension of limitation and transcendence in the *intentional feelings*--the reader is asked to catch the tension in the phrase--in which values are aspired to in an objectively ordered scale of preference.

CHAPTER FIVE

THE COMPLEMENTARITY OF INTENTIONALITY ANALYSIS AND PSYCHIC ANALYSIS

OUTLINE

1. Intentionality and Dramatic Art. Existential authenticity and dramatic artistry.
2. The Meaning of Psychotherapy. The constitution of true healing. Psychotherapy and soul-making.
3. Second Immediacy: Beyond Criticism and Therapy. Two modes of immediacy to the world mediated by meaning. Primordial immediacy and second immediacy.
4. Toward a Transcendental Aesthetic. Existential self-appropriation and the mediation of the aesthetic by psychic conversion.
    - 4.1. The Primacy of the Dramatic Pattern of Experience. The intellectual and dramatic patterns. The structure of the dramatic pattern.
    - 4.2. The Dramatic Pattern in the Third Stage of Meaning. The complementarity of intentional and psychic differentiation; of intentional and psychic self-appropriation.
    - 4.3. The Neglect of Narrative. Metz's "Apology of Narrative." Instrumental reason and the neglect of narrative. Narrative and criticism.
    - 4.4. Recovering the Story. Depth psychology and explanatory narrative.
        - 4.4.1. The Need for Reconstruction in Depth Psychology. The dialectic of depth psychology.
        - 4.4.2. Limitation and Transcendence in the Dramatic Pattern. *Insight* on dreams: the context.
        - 4.4.3. Dreams and Dramatic Artistry. Internal communication. A correction of Lonergan. The dialectic of the subject. The dialectic of history.
        - 4.4.4. Sublations. Sublating the dream by waking intentionality.
        - 4.4.5. Healing and Creating. Genuineness and psychic conversion. Psychic conversion as creating: aiding cognitive, moral, and religious self-transcendence. Psychic conversion as healing: a function of religious, moral, and intellectual conversion.

1. Intentionality and Dramatic Art.

Existential differentiation within intentionality analysis has opened the possibility for a psychology of orientations. There must be a way, then, to understand the subtle art of soul-making that will provide us with an interiorly differentiated self-knowledge that can be integrated with the disclosures that arise from intentionality analysis. For the conjunction of intentional feeling with existential consciousness in its native orientation to a normative scale of values would render soul-making in the third stage of meaning the self-owning of the subject as evaluating, deliberating, deciding, and acting. Intentional inquiry into the deliverances of the neglected psyche would thus institute the existential appropriation of the responsibility to reverse the longer cycle of decline and to initiate the coming of world-cultural humanity. Moreover, as the self-owning of the intelligent and rational subject gives rise to that portion of theological foundations in which there is articulated the horizon-shift on knowledge that is intellectual or philosophic conversion, so soul-making in the third stage of meaning would ground the articulation of the two other horizon-shifts of a methodical theology's foundational reality: moral conversion and religious conversion. The psychic analysis *by* intentional consciousness *of* aesthetic consciousness would be as foundational as the intentionality analysis *by* intentional consciousness *of* intelligent, rational, and existential consciousness. It would, in fact, complement the latter because aesthetic consciousness is implicated not only in all evaluative activity, but in every intelligent inquiry, every insight, every act of conceptualizing, formulating, hypothesizing, checking, marshalling and weighing of evidence, grasping the unconditioned, and affirming or denying. Psychic analysis is, strictly speaking, not a second variant of foundational-constructive activity, but the completion of the one movement of foundational subjectivity taking possession of its own domain as self-transcendent arbiter of intelligibility, truth, and value. In Heidegger's pregnant and suggestive terminology, *Verstehen* and *Befindlichkeit* are *equi*primordial constitutive ways of being the "there" of Being.[1] To appropriate either is to call for the appropriation of the other. Lonergan has effected the mediation of *Verstehen*. I am now proposing the mediation of *Bekindlichkeit*, a mediation that would be an *equi*primordial dimension of theological foundations.

While the direct link to the complementarity of intentionality and psyche is revealed in the existential differentiation of the reach of human feeling in its aspiration for value, the complementarity itself is obviously present throughout the structural advance of intentional consciousness from experience through insight and judgment to decision. Insight always features in one's dramatic intersubjectivity, but there is also something quite dramatic about insight. Insight is never a boring event. Even if it were, it would not cease to be dramatic, for boredom, too, is a modality of the human story. The ontological root of this mutual implication, of course, is the tension of the human subject in whose consciousness the sensitively and imaginatively empirical is necessarily sublated by the intellectual, the empirical and the intellectual by the rational, and the empirical, the intellectual, and the rational by the existential. In the latter sublation there is manifested a resurgence of the direct intentional significance of the sensitively empirical in the aspiration of intentional feeling to values. To attend by intentional consciousness to aesthetic consciousness, then, is not only to recover the existential base of one's morals and religion in one's intentional feelings, but to retrieve and narrate one's story of insight, conceptualization, formulation, reflection, and commitment to what is true. As we have said, the story is so human because we are intelligent, rational, and existential; but there is a story at all only because we are sensitive, aesthetic subjects. The permeation of intentional consciousness by aesthetic constituents establishes a coincidence between insight, judgment, and decision, on the one hand, and the constitution of one's life as a work of art, on the other. To follow the way of insight, rational commitment, moral decision, and religious love is to make one's life a work of art. To be genuinely transcendent is to assure the flourishing of limitation. To be inauthentic in one's inquiry, reflection, and evaluation is to be a failed artist. Insight, judgment, and decision have their home in the movement of life, in the aggregates of aggregates of aggregates of physical, chemical, botanical, and zoological conjugates that find their higher integration in psychic sensitivity. Through insight, judgment, and decision, we find direction in that movement. By finding and following the direction disclosed by insight, reasonable judgment, moral decision, and religious love, we mold the aggregates of aggregates of aggregates of lower order conjugates into a work of art. We make the movement of life a work of art. By neglecting insight, rational judgment, and authentic existential response we distort and corrupt the aggregates of aggregates of aggregates of lower order conjugates. We make the movement of life into a series of dissociated and nonsequential complexes.

2. *The Meaning of Psychotherapy.*

To speak of the fragmentation and dissociation of the movement of life and of the conscious representations of these distortions in sensitive, aesthetic consciousness is to suggest that soul-making in the third stage of meaning will have something to do with what we have come to know as the profession of psychotherapy. Viewed against the backdrop of the longer cycle of decline, psychotherapy may be understood as the principal manner in which the twentieth-century began, however coincidentally, to make amends for the centuries of neglect suffered by the sensitive psyche. Any real healing of the sensitive psyche would have to involve, then, a transformation of the sequence of sensations, memories, images, emotions, conations, associations, bodily movements, and spontaneous intersubjective responses from a condition of fragmentation, incongruity, and directionless wandering into a condition of harmonious participation in the normative order of inquiry through whose consistent application direction is discovered and pursued. No genuine psychotherapeutic theory or praxis, then, can be grounded in a psychology of passional motivations. To the contrary, a psychology of passional motivations must be integrated dialectically into a psychology of orientations that takes its stand on the aesthetic finality of sensitive consciousness as the home of the concrete process of the human good. It is clear that the disengagement of the normative order of inquiry gives rise to a new conception of the psychotherapeutic phenomenon, a reorientation of the praxis of psychotherapy on the basis of an adequate objectification of the psychic dimensions of human consciousness.

Even if a praxis of psychological healing is correctly conceived and pursued, however, it is no more than the beginning of what we mean by soul-making in the third stage of meaning. For a time, the therapeutic process will be the most frequent starting-place for the recovery of the movement of life. But soul-making does not take place in the therapist's conference room. Rather, it occurs in the dramatic events of life itself: in human relationships and in the passages of the subject from one stage of life to another. When correctly conceived and pursued the movement of psychotherapy can enable the subject to retrieve a story that was already going forward but could not be told. It can free the subject to identify, accept, and negotiate complexes of affect and representation that were previously fragmented and incongruous. It can help one catch up with the story about not only the years or decades of one's own life, but the centuries during which the conditions of the distortion of the aggregates of aggregates of aggregates of one's own physical, chemical, botanical, and zoological conjugates were being laid. It can retrieve roots. But it cannot nurture the newly discovered movement of life. That nurturing occurs only as one begins to *create* the story of one's search by authentic inquiry in harmony with the normative demands of one's interiority poised between the opposites. By retrieving the story of past years, decades, and centuries, one recaptures on the plane of realism what Hegel attempted to bring to absolute and final synthesis in the idealism of *Geist*'s self-alienation and self-recovery. But, on the plane of realism, there is no absolute synthesis within the domain of emergent probability. There is only the set of alternatives of being cumulatively dragged through life because one is negligent of the normative order and of its aesthetic home, or of finding the foundations on which one can walk through life upright because one has recovered the story of the past and is creating the story of the future.[2] Soul-making is only inchoatively a matter of psychotherapy. Most contemporary variants of psychotherapy, in fact, are not even the beginning of soul-making, for a psychology of passional motivations is in touch neither with the normative order of inquiry nor with its home in aesthetic consciousness.

3. Second Immediacy: Beyond Criticism and Therapy.

There is a duality of conscious immediacy to the world. Language, as spoken and heard, and as written and read, makes the world to which consciousness is immediate a world itself mediated by meaning.[3] Strictly speaking, that to which linguistically capable consciousness is immediate is the set of meanings by which the world is mediated to consciousness. Consciousness operates immediately with regard to the symbols, words, and images that mean, and mediately with respect to what is meant by these symbols, words, and images.[4] The basic distinction governing the differentiation of consciousness, then, is that between the world of immediacy and the world mediated by meaning.

When we enter the world mediated by meaning, we do not leave immediacy behind. There remains the immediacy of sight, hearing, touch, taste, and smell that is indicative of the here-and-now of egocentric particulars. But there also is an immediacy of mediating operations and of concomitant affective states to the words, images, and symbols through which the world is mediated by meaning. This immediacy of mediating operations and of concomitant states is the twofold immediacy of consciousness to mediating meaning. The operations are those that constitute the normative order of inquiry. The states are the feelings that permeate all operations of understanding, judging, and deciding. While it is through the operations that we discover direction in the movement of life, it is through the affective states that we experience a movement in which direction is to be found.

In order to develop the transcendental method that allows consciousness to disengage in explanatory and structural fashion both the operations and the movement itself, we have by necessity resorted to separating these two poles of immediacy for the sake of analysis. But in the actual course of the search for direction in the movement of life the two modalities of immediacy are not separate from one another. When psychic analysis is acknowledged to be an indispensable complement to intentionality analysis if we wish to bring full circle the mediation of immediacy, we are able heuristically to identify the end-result of this foundational process. If the two modalities of immediacy are themselves conjunctive, so too must be the two mediations. They meet in the self-appropriating recovery of the tension of limitation and transcendence that constitutes genuineness in the third stage of meaning.

Let us speak, then, of a primordial infrastructure of human consciousness, constituted by the immediacy of mediating operations and concomitant states to the media of words, images, and symbols through which the world is meant. Let us call this infrastructure primordial immediacy. It is an immediacy to the media of the world, an immediacy of inquiry, of understanding, of conceptualization, of formulation, of reflection, of judgment, of evaluation, of deliberation, of decision, and of the feelings that permeate these mediating operations and give them their drive and momentum. This immediacy is primordial, i.e., it is spontaneous, ingenuous, and unmediated. It also may be either authentic or inauthentic, depending on the *de facto* harmony between the mediating operations, with their concomitant feelings, and the normative order of inquiry.

This immediacy, however, can itself be mediated. This is precisely what happens in the foundational process of transcendental method. The operations of conscious intentionality are brought to bear as intentional on the operations and states of conscious intentionality as conscious. Through this process, the immediacy of mediating operations and of their concomitant states is mediated by meaning in such a way as to give rise to the explanatory self-appropriation of conscious intentionality in both of its dimensions, the operational and the aesthetic. Because this process results in self-owning, operational intentionality and affective intentionality become transparent to themselves, or, better, the one intentionality that is both operational and affective becomes transparent to itself. This transparency is a mediated immediacy of the mediation process itself. It is *second immediacy.* It is a retrieved spontaneity, a recovered ingenuousness, and an authenticity strengthened against the possibility of capitulation to alienation and ideology by the self-appropriating differentiation of authenticity and unauthenticity as they function respectively in the search for direction and in the flight from understanding, truth, and the really worth while. As a mediated immediacy of cognitional operations, second immediacy is a post-critical naiveté. As a mediated immediacy of aesthetic momentum and appreciation, second immediacy is a post-therapeutic naiveté. Criticism and therapy have performed the mediation of immediacy. But the end result is beyond both. It is a mediated return to immediacy, the asymptotic goal of the third stage of meaning.

4. *Toward a Transcendental Aesthetic.*

The direct link between the two mediations of immediacy is, of course, found in the existential disengagement of the relationship of feelings to the objective scale of values whose objectivity derives from the normative order of inquiry. We can best appreciate the significance of the mediation of aesthetic consciousness when we focus on the question of what constitutes self-appropriation at the fourth level of conscious intentionality--the level of evaluation, deliberation, decision, and action. The relevance of aesthetic mediation to cognitive self-appropriation depends on the existential determination of cognitive authenticity. Therefore, our most direct way to articulate the mediation of the aesthetic is to address ourselves to existential self-appropriation. Although we could not formulate the question in this manner without the existential disengagement itself, without the heuristic outlines of a scale of values and of the concrete process of the human good, and so without the existential sublation of *Insight*'s discussion of the longer cycle of decline, we can at the moment presuppose all of these developments and proceed to explicate the central thesis of psychic conversion: the self-appropriation in narrative form of existential consciousness depends on a maieutic of consciousness distinct from but intrinsically complementary to that proposed by Lonergan, a second mediation of immediacy, the mediation not of the inquiry that provides direction in the movement of life, but of the movement of life itself in which the direction is discovered by remaining faithful to the normative order of inquiry. While aesthetic mediation, then, is an objectification of a dimension of the whole of conscious intentionality, its special importance emerges only when we seek that access to the data of interiority that will allow self-appropriation at the fourth level to be as complete, as thorough, and as explanatory as that which Lonergan renders possible at the levels of intelligent and rational cognitive praxis.

Building upon these developments, then, and including in the existential disengagement the relation of intentional feelings to values and to symbols, the first step that we must take is to identify that pattern of experience, i.e., of sensitive or empirical or aesthetic consciousness, of the *movement* of life, that is operative when the human subject moves to existential praxis through questions for deliberation. The relevant pattern is that which Lonergan discusses in the first chapter on common sense in *Insight:* the dramatic pattern of experience. The aesthetic-empirical component of existential consciousness is dramatic. Conversely, empirical consciousness, when sublated by existential questioning, inevitably assumes a dramatic pattern: it becomes a sequence of sensations, memories, images, emotions, conations, associations, bodily movements, and spontaneous intersubjective responses organized by the guiding intention of dramatic artistry.

4.1. The Primacy of the Dramatic Pattern of Experience.

The treatment of patterns of experience in *Insight* differentiates four quite distinct dynamic directions in which the sensitive stream can be oriented: the biological, the artistic, the intellectual, and the dramatic patterns of experience. Within the overall context of the entire book Lonergan's primary concern is obviously with the intellectual pattern. But in the section dealing with the general notion of patterns of experience, the dramatic pattern receives the lengthiest and most involved treatment. This is because this topic falls in the first chapter on common sense, among whose concerns is the dramatic artistry involved in spontaneous intersubjectivity and in stamping one's life with a style that gives it a human dignity. Nonetheless, the overall impression one gains from the book is that the intellectual pattern of experience has a primacy over all other patterns. Not only is it through the intellectual pattern that the very notion of patterns of experience can be discussed and that the various patterns can be distinguished and related to one another, but also, as we have seen, the self-affirmation of the knower is portrayed as a solution to the native bewilderment of the existential subject. Thus the impression is conveyed that the position on knowing will resolve the dilemma of the dramatic subject.

With the advance in the differentiation of the normative order of inquiry that occurs with Lonergan's disengagement of a notion of value that is distinct from, determinative of, and sublating the notions of intelligibility and being, the relative primacy of the various patterns of aesthetic participation and direction undergoes a decisive shift. If existential authenticity is foundational of cognitive praxis, and if the latter is for the sake of the former, then not only does existential consciousness assume a primacy over intellectual and rational consciousness in the development of a full position on the human subject, but also the intellectual pattern of aesthetic orientation now becomes subordinate to existential direction. The *drama* of knowing, of seeking and fleeing understanding, becomes determinative of authentic cognitive praxis. The concern of existential intentionality for authenticity links up with the psychic pattern of the dramatic subject. Dramatic artistry is the sensitive psychic correlative of existential authenticity. As cognitive praxis is for the sake of existential authenticity, so the intellectual pattern of the sensitive stream is for the sake of a work of art: to make of one's life and of the human world a work of art. There is, then, a dramatic pattern of experience, organized by one's concern to stamp one's life with a style that is one's own, with grace, with freedom, with dignity.

This dramatic pattern operates in a preconscious manner, as imagination and intelligence collaborate in supplying consciousness with the materials one will employ in structuring the contours of one's work of art. These materials emerge into consciousness in the form of images and accompanying affects. The images meet the demands of underlying neural manifolds for conscious representation and integration. From a pre-psychological point of view, these underlying manifolds are purely coincidental. They find no systematization at the physical, chemical, and botanical levels. They are a function of energy-become-psychic, a surplus energy whose formal intelligibility can be understood not by laws of physics, chemistry, botany, or zoology, but only by irreducibly psychological understanding. The images and affects which systematize this surplus of energy emerge into consciousness at the empirical, sensitive, aesthetic, psychic level. But the agent of their emergence is the preconscious collaboration of intelligence and imagination, which reaches into the aggregates of aggregates of aggregates of physical, chemical, and botanical conjugates for the coincidental energic manifold that will yield images for the weaving of the pattern and the shaping of the contours of one's work of dramatic art.[5]

The intelligence and imagination that cooperate in a preconscious manner to select images for conscious attention, insight, judgment, and decision may or may not be authentic. To the extent that they are authentic, they are open to and even will into consciousness the images that are *needed* for the insightful, truthful, and loving construction of the human world and concomitantly of oneself as a work of dramatic art. They are free to admit to conscious negotiation the complexes of affect and image that are really one's own, however much in need of healing and integration these complexes may be. To the extent that they are inauthentic, they are the instruments of an unwilling existential intentionality that is not open to receive the energic complexes that constitute one's own aesthetic stream of sensitive consciousness. They then function as a repressive censor. Repression violates the demand of lower-order conjugates for integration in consciousness. When the demand is cumulatively violated because one does not want the images one needs if one's insight is to suggest courses of action that would correct and revise one's current viewpoints and behavior, the affects become cumulatively dissociated from their proper imaginative schemata and associated with other and incongruous schemata through which, at least, they may find their way into some sort of conscious representation and psychic integration. But in that case the complexes that emerge into consciousness support and sustain the biased unwillingness that admitted them in their incongruous form. The repressive censorship of unwilling dramatic consciousness conspires with distorted psychic conjugates. In the limit, the result is psychotic breakdown. Short of that, there are the endless varieties of neurosis, of failed artistry, that bring varying degrees of anguish to their abnormal subject.[6]

Lonergan's acknowledgment of the primacy of existential intentionality entails a sublation of the intellectual pattern of experience by the dramatic pattern. The intellectually patterned sequence of psychic conjugates that subjects the sensitive stream to the organizing control of a concern for explanatory understanding cannot be granted primacy in the relations among the various patterns of experience. If the existential sublates intelligence and rationality, the dramatic pattern of experience sublates the intellectual pattern of experience. The latter is at the service of the construction of the human world as a work of art. To state the matter more fully, we can say that the dramatic pattern of experience, as the psychological concomitant of existential intentionality, must integrate at the level of sensations, images, memories, emotions, conations, associations, bodily movements, and spontaneous intersubjective responses the interplay of all other patterns of experience, including the intellectual. If one is psychically differentiated to operate in the intellectual pattern, this pattern as well as all others in which one can operate is sublated by the concerns of the dramatic artist/existential subject. So, too, from the standpoint of self-appropriation, the self-affirmation of the knower is sublated by the self-affirmation of the intention of the human good that is the notion of value. Because the psychic correlative of the notion of value is the dramatic pattern of sensitive consciousness, an appropriation of this pattern is a knowing of the notion of value. It renders possible the sublation of the knowledge of knowledge by the knowledge of existential intentionality. It aids the self-objectification of one's own moral and religious consciousness. It contributes substantively to the developing position on the subject that constitutes theological foundations.

4.2. The Dramatic Pattern in the Third Stage of Meaning.

The more differentiated one's consciousness, the more complex becomes the task of dramatic artistry, for the more subtle must become the flexibility of one's sensitivity. Just as it is the existential subject who shifts from one differentiation of consciousness or realm of meaning to another--from common sense to theory to art to scholarship to transcendence to interiority--by shifting the procedures and direction of conscious intentionality, so it is the dramatic artist who transposes the sensitive stream from one pattern to another, depending on the intention that is operative and determinative of one's orientation as a subject at any given time. Intentional shifts are accompanied by a concomitant adaptation of the stream of sensations, memories, images, emotions, conations, associations, bodily movements, and spontaneous intersubjective responses, under the direction of the dramatic artist. One does not employ the intellectual pattern to cross a busy street. It is the task of dramatic artistry to govern the interplay of the various patterns of experience. Thus, the psyche of an intentionally more differentiated consciousness will be a more differentiated psyche. Differentiation in the various realms of meaning is joined with differentiation in the patterns of psychic experience that are organized and controlled by these realms of meaning. Intentional and psychic differentiation are mutually complementary. Indeed, it may be argued that psychic differentiation guarantees the objectivity, the self-transcendence, of the intentional differentiation. It integrates the latter as sensitive spontaneity adapts to the new capacity. New differentiations are usually accompanied by an outburst of enthusiastic emotion. But the outburst is not yet the integration of the person equipped with the new differentiation, which becomes habitual as the sensitive psyche adapts to it. As long as the sensitive psychological concomitant of the new differentiation remains at a relatively primitive emotional stage, the new differentiation is even disruptive of one's inner being. One must gain the new sensitive psychological flexibility that permits one to operate in the new realm of meaning with the matter-of-factness of mature detachment. One must come to be at home in the new realm of meaning, if one's discovery is not to be derailed into ideology and alienation. Intentional differentiation without psychic differentiation can be a contributing factor to decline. A critical-social analysis of modern scientific and technological developments could well be based on this statement of what happens when psychological differentiations fail to catch up with cognitive differentiations.

Not only is it true, however, that new differentiations in the intentional order demand correspondingly new psychic flexibilities and adaptations. It is also true that an appropriation in the realm of interiority of the various intentional differentiations demands an appropriation in the same realm of the concomitant psychological stream of sensitive consciousness. *Insight* is a set of exercises by which one enters upon differentiation in the realm of interiority. Such differentiation is self-appropriation, which ushers one not only into a realm of meaning but into a new stage of meaning. At this stage, meaning is controlled neither by practical common sense nor by theory but by the terms and relations that obtain in the order of interiority. But with this advance, one's dramatic pattern of experience must also undergo differentiation. It has to become a sequence of sensations, memories, images, emotions, conations, associations, bodily movements, and spontaneous intersubjective responses that are permeated by the same transparency that affects one's intentional operations. There must be extended to the psyche explicit differentiation in the realm and stage of interiority.

The need for such a development appears inchoatively even in *Insight*, where, intrinsic to the self-appropriation of the normative order of cognitive consciousness, is the recognition of the sensitive detachment or willingness without which the pure desire to know that pursues the objectives of intelligent and rational consciousness is distorted into the misuse of intelligence that constitutes bias. Moreover, if it is true that existential intentionality is determinative of knowing, and that right decision is the ulterior goal of all four levels of human intentionality, it is also true that willingness will primarily affect the existential level before it permeates cognitive praxis. Therefore, the self-appropriation of existential intentionality includes explanatory disengagement of the sensitive psychological concomitant of the intention of value. Its role in this intention is heuristically specified by the correlations between feelings and values and between feelings and symbols. But beyond this heuristic specification and within the framework that it establishes, there is a need for the concrete disengagement of the terms and relations that obtain both in one's own dynamic sequence of feelings and in the symbolic system that is reciprocally related with these feelings. Only then is the dramatic psychological dimension of one's *Existenz* clarified and illuminated in its concreteness.

With respect to the concrete order of human living, then, we must say that Lonergan has only begun the task of showing the way to existential self-appropriation. He has outlined its heuristic structure. He has clarified the notion of value that is the final meaning of conscious intentionality. But he has not provided the maieutic that will allow self-appropriation of the fourth level of intentional consciousness to approximate the concreteness that his analyses of the notion of being achieve in the domain of cognitive praxis. Where are we to go for the set of five-finger exercises that will facilitate the self-appropriation of existential subjectivity? Where is the workbook that will aid the self-possession of soul? Is there a reflexive technique for the control of value-intention that matches the subtlety and completeness of detail that the maieutic of cognitive consciousness facilitates? Has there emerged in modernity an as yet coincidental and thus still potential source of existential self-appropriation? Does the heuristic framework of value-intention that Lonergan provides enable this coincidental contribution to be integrated into an explanatory maieutic of third-stage consciousness? Can we recover the neglected psyche on the basis of our recovery of neglected intentionality? Can we find a maieutic that promotes existential authenticity in the third stage of meaning? It is clear from what we have seen that to appropriate a dramatic pattern of experience is to retrieve a story. Existential self-appropriation will express itself in narrative form. Since everything existential is dramatic, everything existential is a story. The appropriation of existential consciousness expresses itself when one tells one's story, when one tells it as it is. But how do I know that I am not just covering up? We must investigate the general notion of story and its role in theology before answering these questions.

4.3. The Neglect of Narrative.

Johann Baptist Metz has found it necessary to write "a short apology of narrative,"[7] in order to restore to theology a dimension of language and understanding that had been neglected in modern times. Theology has outlawed narrative as precritical. The content of the original experience of faith has been preserved only in ritual, dogmatic, or metaphysical language. But theology, says Metz,

> is above all concerned with direct experiences expressed in narrative language. . . . Reasoning is not the original form of theological expression. . . . If reason is closed to the narrative exchange of experiences of what is new and completely breaks off that exchange for the sake of its own critical nature and its autonomy, it will inevitably exhaust itself in reconstructions and become no more than a technique.[8]

The narrative form of communication is not unenlightened about its own performative function. It is not "ideologically unconscious of the interest that governs it. It presents this interest and 'tries it out' in the narrative process. It verifies or falsifies itself and does not simply leave this to discussion about the story which lies outside the narrative process."[9] The story is sacramental: it is an effective sign united with its practical effect. The reality to which it bears witness is not just reflected by the story, but continues to live in it. Christians are not primarily an argumentative and reasoning community, but a story-telling community. Yet theology has suppressed the narrative language of faith. It is

> no longer able to narrate with a practical and socially critical effect and with a dangerous and liberating potential. . . . Freedom and enlightenment, the transition from dependence to coming of age, are not achieved simply by giving up narrative language in favour of the art of reasoning possessed by those who are enlightened and those who claim it as their privilege.[10]

Metz's point is not simply to extol the pastoral and political aspect of narrative, but to insist that narrative is essential to the structure of theology itself. It is inseparably connected with theological argument, which must mediate between the history of suffering and the proclamation of redemption and reconciliation in Jesus Christ. Metz finds that the central question of systematic theology in our day is this: "Can this theological mediation exist without becoming reconciled in too ambitious and ultimately too speculative and too self-deceiving a way with this history of suffering or without salvation-history being suspended in view of this history of suffering?"[11] The question can*not* be answered by a theology that would completely negate the strictly theological role of narrative. Such a theology will either reduce history to historicity, thus withdrawing from the experience of suffering non-identity to a transcendental identity of the ego, or it will keep salvation itself ever at stake, projected into the future, employed as a heuristic utopian device, or it will cancel out the non-identity of suffering in a conceptualistically dialectical account of the history of salvation. The question *can* be answered only by a memorative and narrative theology that enables "salvation in history, which is, of course, a history of suffering, to be expressed without either salvation or history being diminished."[12] The narrative memory of redemption in Christ is not to be reduced to a preliminary mythological stage in the Christian logos that is theology. "A purely argumentative theology which conceals its origin and does not make this present again and again in narrative memory inevitably leads, in the history of human suffering, to those many modifications in reasoning which result in the extinction of the identifiable content of Christian salvation."[13] The function of argument in theology is "to protect the narrative memory of salvation in a scientific world, to allow it to be at stake and to prepare a way for a renewal of this narrative, without which the experience of salvation is silenced."[14] Stated in the terms which we have used in this volume, the appropriation of the soteriological differentiation will take narrative form. In this form, then, will be realized the objectification of specifically Christian conversion that Lonergan still leaves in too generic a form in his talk of religious conversion.

I would suggest that the neglect of narrative, not only by modern theology but by modern reason in general, is but a function of the neglect of the psyche that stems from the reduction of the order of the ends of human action to the particular good and the good of order. In other words, the exclusively instrumental reason that neglects ultimate issues and results and refuses heed to the warning voice of sensitive psychic limitation is also an exclusively *argumentative* reason preoccupied with an inflated image of its own capacities. Stories that are effectively liberating cannot be told to an exclusively instrumental reason preoccupied with its own transcendence of limitation. To what other aspect of ourselves and of our world is the memory of Jesus *dangerous* except to that dimension that has given rise to the longer cycle of decline? Liberating narrative is dangerous only to a reason that does not want to be liberated, that does not wish to acknowledge the sensitive aesthetic dimension which could free it to be genuinely rational. Narrative appeals precisely to that sensitive aesthetic dimension and awakens it to its constitutive function in the tension of opposites that structures the genuinely human. A reason that has rejected this tension is a reason that has become *both* purely instrumental *and* exclusively argumentative. It resorts to the exclusivity of argumentation in order to defend its exclusively instrumental practicality. To a sensitively conscious opposite pole that protests against its pretensions it replies, "Don't tell me stories; give me reasons." And of course aesthetic consciousness neither can give reasons, nor must it. Its effective witness lies in the story it tells, the story of the havoc wrought by an intelligence and rationality that, inflated with a sense of their own power and mastery, have become thoroughly stupid and silly and, as an unfortunate consequence, have become impervious to the liberating and transformative force of the story told by aesthetic consciousness.

This is not to say, however, that there is not also a legitimate hesitation on the part of a genuinely critical reason, when confronted with this insistence on story. How can an emphasis on narrative be reconciled with the genuine advances of modernity in historical criticism and hermeneutics, in the philosophy of interiority, in the science of politics? It is not sufficient to argue, as Metz does, that narrative is a constitutive dimension of critical reason itself, as that reason has been advanced to a critique of criticism by the *Frankfurter Schule*. The retrieval of narrative must display and utilize the very advances in reason that criticism has made possible. It is not to be a regression to pre-critical consciousness, but an advance forward beyond the critique of cognitive consciousness to the critique of existential consciousness and of its concomitant dramatic-aesthetic component of psychic sensitivity. It is to take place by bringing the operations of consciousness as intentional, which have been retrieved by the movement of criticism beyond epistemology to the more radical questions of cognitional analysis, to bear upon *the operations and states of dramatic sensitivity as existentially conscious.*

4.4. Recovering the Story.

The appropriation of existential consciousness achieves objectification when one tells one's story as it is, and in explanatory fashion. In order to find the as yet coincidental maieutic for an *explanatory narrative*, we are to turn to *the science and praxis of depth psychology*. This praxis disengages the terms and relations that obtain in dramatic sensitivity: between feelings and what one values, between feelings and elemental symbols, between elemental symbols and what one values, and among elemental symbols themselves as indicative of feelings and of what one values. The science of depth psychology is the as yet coincidental but nonetheless potential source of existential appropriation. It is coincidental because as a theory and as a praxis it has not yet been integrated by the framework provided by a correct cognitional theory, an adequate epistemology, an all-inclusive metaphysics of the structure of proportionate being and of the human person, and an account of existential intentionality that would enable it to be based on orientations rather than on passional motivations. This framework, however, is now available through the disengagement of the normative order of inquiry into the direction to be found in the movement of life. Depth psychology finds the higher integration that can consolidate it as human science precisely by bringing the operations that constitute the search for direction to bear upon the movement of life in which direction is discovered by those operations. This is the reflexive praxis of appropriating and promoting value-orientation. It is as concrete and thorough as Lonergan's reflexive praxis of appropriating and promoting cognitive authenticity.

This new and complementary reflexive praxis affords to third-stage intentionality informed by thoroughgoing criticism the maieutic for recovering its own story in the explanatory fashion that fixes terms and relations by one another. Narrative and criticism thus will join as complementary features of the one process of mediating our cognitive and aesthetic immediacy to the mediating vehicles of the world.

4.4.1. The Need for Reconstruction in Depth Psychology.

The merely coincidental character of the science of depth psychology in its present state accounts for the fact that the praxis of the various psychotherapeutic techniques discovered since the publication of Freud's *Traumdeutung* has resulted in genuine psychological healing only to the extent that there has entered into the praxis of these therapies elements not accounted for in the theories of the architects of the various depth psychological systems. Paul Ricoeur has demonstrated the intrusion of such factors into psychoanalytic praxis.[15] It can be shown that something similar happens in Jungian analysis. The fact of the matter, moreover, is that ordinarily these therapeutic endeavors have *not* been successful, and their lack of success is due to the dominance of metascientific errors in the exercise of the psychotherapeutic profession--unless, of course, one considers the Freudian resignation to misery or the Jungian romantic agony a genuine embodiment of a flourishing sensitivity. I locate dramatic artistry elsewhere, and the task that remains in this book is to indicate precisely what I conceive such artistry to be.

The interpretation of the work of the major architects of the science of depth psychology is a weighty responsibility. For one thing, the interpreter will soon discover the dialectical differences that appear not only among the great depth psychologists themselves, but also between each of them and the positions on aesthetic sensitivity established by the disengagement of the normative order of the search for direction in the movement of life. At least two factors prevented the major architects of depth psychology from offering a coherent account of the sensitive psyche. First, none of them possessed either sufficient philosophical expertise or enough respect for the classical and Christian advances in differentiation to provide them with a broad enough horizon adequately to interpret their own findings. Second, and even more important at least from a proximate point of view, an adequate systematic contribution to the science of humanity is impossible when one's primary source of data consists of the many forms of aberration to which human interiority is prone. Depth psychology arose by studying those whose sensitive psyche was sick, and it is therefore no wonder that it has been largely a psychology of passional motivation rather than one of orientations.[16]

Transcendental method, on the other hand, provides an explanatory account of what makes for genuine human flourishing. It is an account that is in harmony with the great advances in differentiation that occurred in classical Greece, in Israel, and in Christian revelation. But it is also a further leap in being, a new advance in differentiation, the clearing of a realm of meaning, of a sphere of being, through which the axial advances are preserved but transformed so as to contribute to world-cultural humanity. Fidelity to the normative order of inquiry that transcendental method uncovers in explanatory fashion is the key to human well-being. Only within the framework established by an irreversible position on *what makes human beings well* can a science of the stream of sensitive psychological consciousness be undertaken that would both be accurate and contribute to human well-being.

The methodologist who wishes, then, to bring full circle the leap in being that is transcendental method by integrating its discrimination of the normative order of intentionality with the disclosures of elemental symbolic consciousness in the movement of life itself is confronted with a clear case of dialectic. In addition to stating in the form of methodological positions what one holds to be true about the human subject's sensitive psychological consciousness, one must eventually interpret the works of Freud, Jung, Adler, Rank, and others, and dialectically engage their respective views both with one another and with the positions that emerge from attempting to construct a science of the psyche within the context provided by the knowledge of the normative order of the search for direction in the movement of life. It will suffice here to disengage the adequate heuristic structure of a methodologically coherent account of the sensitive stream of empirical consciousness and to integrate this development with Lonergan's contribution to the laying of the theological foundations of interdisciplinary collaboration in the third stage of meaning.

4.4.2. Limitation and Transcendence in the Dramatic Pattern.

The clue to the reconstruction is found in the correct understanding of limitation and transcendence as they function tensively in the operations of the flourishing triple compound of spirit, psyche, and organism. To explain their proper functioning, let us begin with the affirmation that existential self-appropriation is a matter of explanatory narrative. The narrative unfolds as one disengages, interprets, affirms, and evaluates the elemental symbols that appear spontaneously especially in one's dreams. Let us review *Insight*'s discussion of such symbols and of dreams.

The overall context for this discussion is the effort to retrieve the role of insight in common sense. More precisely, the context is the changing, developing subjective field of common sense as intelligent. The subject operates in different dynamic patterns of experience, one of which is the dramatic pattern that is concerned to stamp life with a certain style and grace that is one's own. Our first work of art is our own living. Our own bodies and their actions provide the underlying materials for our work of dramatic art. Aggregates of aggregates of aggregates of physical, chemical, and botanical conjugates impose on our work of art constraining exigencies that limit the flexibility and the range of dramatic artistry. We cannot ignore the biological limitations of our bodily nature and still hope to succeed in our work of dramatic artistry. But we can, within limits, transform these limiting demands, and the first step in doing so is to grant them psychic representation and conscious integration by admitting into consciousness the higher synthesis of energic compositions and distributions at the level of the sensitive psyche. Neural process is subordinated to psychic determination, in that there is a surplus of energy that remains purely coincidental at the levels of lower conjugates but is systematized by conscious emergence at the sensitive level. There is a certain detachment or flexibility of neural process vis-à-vis the conative, sensitive, and emotional integration that releases and directs this underlying process. To be sure, neural process makes demands upon and limits the variability of psychic control. "Memory and imagination, conation and emotion, pleasure and pain, all have their counterparts in corresponding neural processes and originate from their specific demands."[17] But these demands are not unconditional. The emerging sensitive psychological experience is determined not only by neural processes, but also by the pattern in which neural demands are met. The elements enter consciousness already within a given pattern that is formed preconsciously by the influence and collaboration of intentionality and imagination. "The dramatic pattern of experience penetrates below the surface of consciousness to exercise its own domination and control and to effect, prior to conscious discrimination, its own selections and arrangements."[18] Thus the generic requirements of the underlying neural manifold for conscious integration through psychic representation can be met in a variety of specific ways, as long as this psychic flexibility does not exceed the neural exigence for an appropriate conscious complement. "To violate that exigence is to invite the anguish of abnormality."[19]

A second factor of limitation in the dramatic pattern of sensitive consciousness is found in the social context of our dramatic artistry. The task of making our lives into works of art is not achieved by a solo flight of virtuosity. Dramatic artistry performs its task in the presence of others, who also are actors in life's drama. More specifically,

> if aesthetic values, realized in one's own living, yield one the satisfaction of good performance, still it is well to have the objectivity of that satisfaction confirmed by the admiration of others; it is better to be united with others by winning their approval; it is best to be bound to them by deserving and obtaining their respect and even their affection.[20]

The limitations imposed by intersubjectivity and social organization also admit of a certain flexibility, for the network of human relationships finds its ground in "aesthetic liberation and artistic creativity, where the artistry is limited by biological exigence, inspired by example and emulation, confirmed by admiration and approval, sustained by respect and affection."[21]

Because of the social context of dramatic artistry, the intrasubjective dialectic of neural process and psychic representation is under the relative dominance of the dialectic of community, which "gives rise to the situations that stimulate neural demands" and "moulds the orientation of intelligence" that preconsciously operates to admit or reject imaginal materials for dramatic insight, reflection, and deliberation.[22] Thus, the limiting context of dramatic artistry is set in part by the situation of the subject vis-à-vis the shorter cycles of social injustice and political reform or revolution and the longer cycle of decline. Our elemental symbols will necessarily be conditioned by such historical factors. Moreover, the orientation of our selective intelligence will either be under the influence of the group and general bias that generate respectively the shorter and longer cycles or will have transcended these distorting influences by the elevation of practicality to a base of authentic existential agency. In either case, what images we admit into consciousness will be a function of our antecedent willingness or unwillingness to accept the insights that are needed if we are authentically to constitute the human world and ourselves within the parameters set by the historical process. Not only do we have no choice about becoming stamped with some character, but also "there is no deliberation about the fact that our past behaviour determines our present habitual attitudes; nor is there any appreciable effect from our present good resolutions upon our future spontaneity."[23] A number of limiting factors conspire to restrict the materials upon which inquiry, reflection, and deliberation can go to work in the shaping of our work of art.

A psychic analysis that would achieve an integration with intentionality analysis, and so become a transcendental aesthetic, must therefore concentrate upon the prior collaboration of imagination and intelligence in representing imaginally possible courses of action. In this prior collaboration the dramatic pattern of sensitive consciousness is already at work, "outlining how we might behave before others and charging the outline with an artistic transformation of a more elementary aggressivity and affectivity."[24] In the drama of life, we do not first learn a role and then develop in ourselves the feelings appropriate for performing in that role. We do not first assemble the materials and then impose upon them an artistic pattern. "There are not first the materials and then the pattern, nor first the role and then the feelings. On the contrary, the materials that emerge in consciousness are already patterned, and the pattern is already charged emotionally and conatively."[25] The patterning is done by the preconscious exercise of a constructive or repressive *censorship* on the part of imagination and intelligence. They determine whether the subject will advance to dramatic artistry or decline into existential breakdown. For they dictate the materials and the imaginal pattern which will be consciously available for the subject to negotiate. The censorship of imagination and intelligence is either willing or unwilling to admit the images that are needed for one to advance in one's work of dramatic art. If they are dominated by an antecedent existential unwillingness, they are prevented by some blend of the biases from admitting the requisite images. Since the biases are cured only by conversion, the inauthentic preconscious censorship needs to come under the influence of the multiform conversion process, for by this means alone can it overcome its closed and hardened obstinacy, its intransigence to insight and truth, its resistance to the materials that are required if insight and truth are to be achieved. The conversion process must reach into the preconscious domain of our being.

Such a penetration of the preconscious patterning censorship of imagination and intelligence by the process of conversion can and does occur with relative frequency in a nonthematic manner to subjects in the first and second stages of meaning. But the conversion process can go further. It can institute the philosophic conversion that promotes one to the self-affirmation of the knower and to further explanatory self-appropriation in the mode of interiority. Then, however, as we have seen, one's dramatic pattern of experience has to become self-transparent in this same mode, so as to include the sensitive sequence instituted by explanatory interior self-objectification. One must be brought by a further extension of the conversion process to a third-stage dramatic pattern of experience that, precisely as sensitive experience, is yet reflexively in control of other patterns of sensitive experience and sublates them into its supremely integrating intentionality. This third-stage pattern is provided when one gains a capacity for internal symbolic communication. It is precisely this capacity that is released by psychic conversion.

4.4.3. *Dreams and Dramatic Artistry.*

Internal communication occurs when one responsibly negotiates the images for insight, reflection, and decision that are admitted into consciousness in the dramatic pattern of experience. But because biased unwillingness extends its reach to repress the images that are really needed for authentic existential agency, one must locate a domain of imaginal production where images are released unhindered by the guardianship of waking consciousness under the dominance of the biases. This domain is the dream. The key to psychic conversion lies in the dream, which tells the story of intentionality in the language of the sensitive integration of underlying neural manifolds. Dream symbols are that language. They reflect the relations that obtain in the dialectic of the subject. They mediate to the interpreting subject in narrative form the condition of the tension between intentional transcendence, authentic or inauthentic, and neurophysiological limitation, between spirit and matter. The dream is a cipher of both authenticity and its immanent sanctions. In the dream, the distorted censorship of unwilling imaginative and intelligent collaboration is not active. Therefore, neural demand functions can and do find their real conscious complements in psychic images that, were they to be understood by the waking subject, would provide the materials that one needs for the ongoing structure of one's work of dramatic art. In dreams, the complexes of energic composition and distribution speak as they are. What preponderates in the dream is not the collaborative censorship of imagination and intelligence, willing or unwilling, but the energic demand functions of the underlying coincidental neural manifold and the complexes in which these demand functions are systematized.

Lonergan has treated the dream in *Insight* in precisely the same context of the dramatic pattern that we find ourselves in at present.[26] But he relies on the Freudian distinction between the dream's manifest and latent content, where the manifest content is purposely deceptive. Much of Lonergan's discussion remains valid, but we must qualify what he says on this point. In waking life, biased understanding and distorted censorship do prevent the emergence into consciousness of the images that would give rise to the insights necessary for correcting one's current viewpoints and behavior. Inauthentic censorship thus fragments the sensitive energic stream into incongruous complexes of affect and ideation. But in the dream these complexes, however distorted and incongruous they may be, appear precisely as they are. In a person under the dominance of an antecedent universal willingness because of the influence of the fifth-level assent to the divine solution to the problem of evil, neural demand functions are granted waking entrance into consciousness in an unrepressed and undistorted manner, but in a person fleeing the insights that are needed for authentic existential agency these neural demand functions are repressed from conscious representation. As this happens, the affective components of these functions or complexes are displaced. They become associated with other images in connection with which they can enter consciousness, however bizarrely this may be in the severely neurotic or psychotic subject. In the dreams of such a subject, the story of the dissociation and fragmentation that gives rise to these incongruities is told as it occurs. The repressed images, the dissociated affects, and the repressing and dissociating dramatic subject emerge as they are. The affects that spontaneously belong to repressed images are not disguised in the dream. They speak of their plight quite plainly and reveal their helplessly distorted object-relations.

The dream, then, is a blunt statement of the quality of one's dramatic artistry and existential agency. It evidences the extent to which the waking dramatic subject is or is not allowing needed imaginative schemata to emerge. The dreams of the biased subject, then, will be quite alien to the conscious performer; they may even interfere with sleep. On the other hand, dreams will be increasingly an ally, a complement, of the waking intentionality that is open to insight. Lonergan correctly describes the basic physiological function of the dream: it meets neural demands for conscious integration that have been neglected in the wear and tear of conscious living. Thus dreams will always provide imaginative schemata which waking consciousness may negotiate in such a way that neural demand functions will be met in a harmonious, integrated, and aesthetically congruous fashion. The dream is a natural energic phenomenon that displays the current linkage of image and affect. If one's subterranean life has been made the unwilling victim of one's own repression of conscious insight, the dream will display the plight, the crippled condition, the anger, the violence , the perversion, the helplessness of the oppressed.

Dreams, then, release symbols for internal communication that are not only unhindered by the possible biases of waking consciousness, but also revelatory of these biases and of their ensuing dialectical distortions. The dream indicates the openness or opposition of the existential agent to the materials that could give rise to insight into one's constitutive authenticity or inauthenticity. The dream tells the intimate story of one's world- and self-constitution. It reflects in a psychic mediation the ongoing relationship between the transcendence of intentional consciousness and the limitations of neural process in the task of the art of living. One creates a work of dramatic art to the extent that neural demand functions are harmoniously integrated with conscious orientation. The integration would take place by the admission into consciousness of appropriate imaginative schemata. When these schemata are not admitted, the dream will reflect, and in no disguised fashion, the inhibitions that a distorted and biased dramatic pattern has placed on neural demand functions, the violence that the flight from understanding has perpetrated upon the neural undertow of the movement of life. When such schemata are admitted by waking consciousness, this too will be reflected in the dream, which will exhibit a continuity and complementarity with one's conscious dramatic artistry and confirm its authenticity. The dreams of the biased subject will be discontinuous with and compensatory to the defective attitude of waking consciousness. But even this discontinuity is in the interests of the upwardly but indeterminately directed dynamism of energic process. It could provide a corrective to the conscious attitude. It could inform one about one's biases and oversights and about the sanctions of one's moral blindness. But if one continues to disregard the compensatory warning, the disharmonious quality of the dream's relation to waking consciousness will become, in the limit, the bizarre destructiveness of the insane psyche. Dream process depends on conscious attitude. But to one who has, more will be given. The dream is likely to be attended to only by one who wants needed insights, even if they revise current viewpoints and behavior. The dreams of this subject will reflect, even if through prolonged struggle and crisis at key turning-points in one's development, an increasingly capable artistic creativity in dramatic living, whereas the neglected dreams of the subject fleeing insight will manifest the violence done by such a subject to the underlying manifolds that constitute the movement of life. The dreams of one who wants the harsh light of truth will be increasingly themselves works of art, the splendor of truth in the beautiful. The dreams of one who loves the darkness of bias will be increasingly bizarre and incongruous. But in neither case will the dream be a deception. There is no opposition of manifest and latent content in either set of dreams. Incongruity is not deception. It is a perfectly clear, if desperate, cry for help on the part of the sensitively experienced movement of life itself.

One further point is to be made. Since the individual dialectic of the subject is dependent on the social dialectic of history, the dream will provide materials for understanding not only the spontaneously intersubjective aspect of one's dramatic artistry, but also its historical and political significance. Because the question of authenticity links up with a pattern of experience that is dramatic, the dreams of an existentially capable adult are a cipher precisely of one's existential participation in the promotion, obstruction, or decline of the human good. This relationship between the dialectic of the subject and the dialectic of history also reminds us once again of the complexity that must be taken into account in the interpretation of the dream. As we have indicated, failed artistry and inauthenticity are at times functions more of victimization than of unwillingness. As a civilization nears "the catalytic trifle that will reveal to a surprised world the end of a once brilliant day,"[27] i.e., as the longer cycle of decline moves toward the day of reckoning, the reversal of personal decline becomes more improbable, and the need for and, God help us, availability of an absolutely transcendent remedy more obvious.[28]

4.4.4. *Sublation*

Psychic conversion is a matter of explicitly, thematically extending to dreaming consciousness the relations of sublation that obtain among the levels of consciousness in the structure of the normative order of inquiry. Such an extension restores this order to its home in the movement of life. The extension is in the direction, not upwards from the order of cognitional praxis to that of existential praxis, but downwards, from the full order of praxis to the coincidental neural manifold whose conscious representation is our sensitive participation in energic process. The dream is a conscious state at the most rudimentary level of awareness. It occurs prior to our functioning on the levels of waking sensitivity, inquiry and insight, reflection and judgment, and deliberation and decision. Nonetheless, because our dreams are the dreams of an intelligent, rational, and existential subject, and because all of the lower levels of our conscious performance are contingent upon existential determinants of subjective orientation, the dream can be and is the unfolding story of our intentional mediation of the world by meaning and of our intentional constitution of both the world and the self through insight, judgment, and decision, or through the rejection of understanding, truth, and responsibility. Sensitive consciousness permeates the entire immanent and normative order of inquiry. The dream is the story of that participation, a story told in the elemental symbols that are the language of life emergent into consciousness.

We are familiar with the relations of sublation that constitute the normative order of inquiry. The experiential level of presentations is sublated through questions for intelligence by the level of insight, conceptualization, and formulation; this second level of intentional consciousness is sublated through questions for reflection to give rise to judgment; and the entire order of cognitive praxis is sublated by the intention of the good that manifests itself in questions for deliberation. Now, if sensitive consciousness undergoes this series of sublations, then permeating the entire reach of this spiritual self-transcendence for the intelligible, the true and the real, and the good, is the sensitive sequence of sensations, memories, images, emotions, conations, associations, bodily movements, and spontaneous intersubjective responses. These constitute what we call the psyche. Because it is bounded by the horizon of time and gives rise to a "psychological present,"[29] it stands in a condition of possible dynamic equilibrium and creative tension with the spiritual reaches of human insight, judgment, and free choice. But there is also the possibility of conflict, disruption, and imbalance of opposites due to a displacement of the tension of limitation and transcendence. This possibility is heightened by the absolute disproportion between the sensitive horizon of time and the unrestricted notions of complete intelligibility, being, and the good. While genuineness is the conscious creative tension of the opposites in the developing person, the realization of such a creative tension is anything but automatic. It is for this reason that continuous growth is so rare. But more, it is for this reason that the condition of the possibility of moral evil is constitutive of the very structure of the process of human development.

The resolution of the disproportion between a psychological present that is constituted by the time-bound character of human sensitivity and the spiritual intentionality that is not restricted by the horizon of time is located, as we have seen, in the gift of *universal willingness* that enables one to participate authentically in the dialectic of history. History is the scene for the resolution of the dialectic of the subject. As sensitivity participates in the dialectic of the subject, so the subject participates in the dialectic of history. Each participation partly constitutes its respective dialectic. Moreover, the relationships are reciprocal, in that sensitivity is partly constituted by the dialectic of the subject, and the dialectic of the subject is partly constituted by the dialectic of history.

The sublation of dreaming consciousness by the levels of waking attentiveness, intelligence, rationality, and existential responsibility reveals the story of the interplay of the various reciprocal constitutive relationships that make the human world a thoroughly dialectical reality. To sublate the dream is, first, to listen to it, to let it speak to waking intentionality, to receive it, to let it present itself; second, to interpret it, to have insight into the relationships it discloses, and by such insight to fix the terms that are meant by the symbolic indicators of the dream by the relations that constitute the structure of the narrative being told by the dream; third, to judge the validity of the interpretation by the self-correcting process of learning that occurs as one tests the interpretation by living it forward; and fourth, to act on the self-knowledge gained through this maieutic of psychic complexes. Through psychic conversion, the subject comes into touch with his or her own story, and does so in the explanatory fashion that links terms and relations by one another in the unfolding dialectic of one's subjective participation in the more dominant dialectic of history.[30]

As the operators of the sublations of empirical by intelligent consciousness, of empirical and intelligent by rational consciousness, and of empirical, intelligent, and rational by existential consciousness are, respectively, our questions for intelligence, for reflection, and for deliberation, so the operator of the sublation of the dream into waking intentionality is the collaboration of imagination and intelligence in the dramatic pattern of experience, seeking images for insight, judgment, and decision; or what in *Insight*, adapting Freud's meaning, is called the censorship.[31] Psychic conversion is the opening of the censorship upon the symbolically systematized manifold of neural demand functions so that these can be received into the order of inquiry, interpreted, and acted upon. It is the acquisition of the capacity for internal symbolic communication among spirit, psyche, and organism on the part of the self-appropriating subject already intent on religious, moral, and cognitive self-transcendence in the pursuit of the human good. *As conversion*, the sublation affects the lower reaches of our conscious being. The preconscious collaboration of imagination and intelligence comes to participate in the universal willingness that is the fruit of the divine solution to the problem of evil. Because of psychic conversion, the censorship is open and receptive to the images that are needed for an insightful, truthful, responsible, and loving construction of a work of art. But as effecting self-appropriation, psychic conversion is also relevant to the fourth level of consciousness, for the story it tells is an exposition of the existential determinants of our conscious being.

4.4.5. Healing and Creating.

The reorientation of the preconscious collaboration of intelligence and imagination to the exercise of a constructive rather than repressive censorship is quite complex, due to the interrelationships of the dramatic, individual, group, and general biases that render one unwilling. Religious, moral, and intellectual conversion are conditions of the possibility of psychic conversion, for they are needed to aid one in the struggle against bias. In effect, the operations of religiously, morally, and intellectually converted consciousness establish a series of ranges of schemes of recurrence for which psychic conversion is a defensive circle set up to prevent the sustained interference of bias in the exercise of intentional operations. Psychic conversion, then, is both a function of and an aid to religious, moral, and intellectual self-transcendence. We can understand this reciprocal relation between psychic conversion and the other three conversions if we reflect, first, on Lonergan's account of genuineness and, second, on his treatment of healing and creating in history.

Lonergan speaks of a conditional and analogous law of genuineness, to the effect that the self as it is and the self as it is understood to be, the real possibilities of the subject and the conscious intentional projects of the same subject, must operate from the same base along the same route to the same goal. All subjective systems--spiritual, psychic, and organic--are to work together for the same ends. The law of genuineness is conditional in that it arises only in as much as development is conscious. It is analogous in that in some cases it can be spontaneous and in other cases it can be operative only if one overcomes a displacement of the tension of limitation and transcendence.

In other words, if a development is conscious, its success demands correct apprehensions of its starting-point, its process, and its goal. The correct apprehension is sometimes minimal and sometimes quite extensive. The apprehensions are minimal when "they involve little more than the succession of fragmentary and separate acts needed to carry out the successive steps of the development with advertence, intelligence, and reasonableness." But they are extensive to the extent that "one begins to delve into the background, the context, the premises, the interrelations of the minimal series of conscious acts, and to subsume this understanding of himself under empirical laws and philosophic theories of development."[32] Genuineness results to the extent that the subject avoids conflict between the self as it is and the self as it apprehends itself to be. Whether the apprehensions be minimal or extensive, the ultimate root of error lies in the tension between limitation and transcendence that is constitutive of development: between the subject as functioning more or less successfully in a flexible circle of ranges of schemes of recurrence and the subject as a higher system on the move, between the subject as integrator and the subject as operator. The genuine subject admits that tension into consciousness as the necessary condition of the harmonious collaboration of potentiality and project. In the more extensive instances, the genuine subject tells his or her story as it is.

> Genuineness . . . is a habit of intrasubjective communication that does not brush questions aside, smother doubts, push problems down, escape to activity, to chatter, to passive entertainment, to sleep, to narcotics. It confronts issues, inspects them, studies their many aspects, works out their various implications, contemplates their concrete consequences in one's own life and in the lives of others. If it respects inertial tendencies as necessary conservative forces, it does not conclude that a defective routine is to be maintained because one has grown accustomed to it. Though it fears the cold plunge into becoming other than one is, it does not dodge the issue, nor pretend bravery, nor act out of bravado. It is capable of assurance and confidence, not only in what has been tried and found successful, but also in what is yet to be tried. It grows weary with the perpetual renewal of further questions to be faced, it longs for rest, it falters and it fails, but it knows its weakness and its failures and it does not try to rationalize them.[33]

One fails in genuineness by displacing the tension between limitation and transcendence. The displacement can be in either direction. In whatever direction, it is the root of "the dialectical phenomena of scotosis in the individual, of the bias of common sense, of basic philosophical differences, and of their prolongation in natural and human science, in morals and religion, in educational theory and history."[34] The radical dialectical significance of the retrieval of aesthetic consciousness, where the actual state of the relation between the opposites is consciously disclosed, could not be more obvious. And such retrieval is precisely what occurs through psychic conversion.

In the third stage of meaning, then, the conscious representation of the tension between oneself as one is and oneself as one tends to think one is will be mediated by the explanatory maieutic of one's transcendental subjectivity. This maieutic is the condition of genuineness in the third stage of meaning. It provides the kind of clarity about the duality of one's being that enables one to name with precision not only what one is doing when one is knowing, but what one is doing *each time* that one is knowing, each time that one is evaluating courses of action, each time that one is relating to the transcendent mystery, each time that one is seeking to respond appropriately in a dramatic, intersubjective situation. Through intentionality analysis and the philosophic conversion that it effects, one disengages the intentional dimension of one's interiority in its heading toward meaning, toward truth, toward the good. Through psychic conversion, one disengages the aesthetic movement in which these intentional operations discover authentic direction, as this aesthetic movement of life is energically woven into the oneiric narrative of one's cognitive and existential history. The narrative displays the actual relations that obtain, here and now, between the opposites of spiritual and energic potency in one's constitution of one's own work of dramatic art. Then, after both of these third-stage conversions, one is ready for dialectic, ready to confront the issues constituted by scotosis and bias, by philosophic differences, and by scientific, ethical, religious, educational, and historical conflicts. These were the issues that initiated one's foundational quest. When the quest comes home to the movement in which the issues arose, after discovering the control of meaning for resolving the issues, one is ready to assume one's part in the interdisciplinary confronting of the issues both cognitively and existentially.

The foundational quest brings one to a position on the originating fount of existential and cognitive objectivity. This fount is the religious, the existential, the intelligent and rational, the sensitively psychic subject. At each level one can be authentic or inauthentic. Religious conversion effects authenticity at the fifth level of intentional consciousness; moral conversion at the fourth, existential level; intellectual conversion at the second and third, intelligent and rational levels; and psychic conversion at the first level. The objectification of the authenticity of subjectivity entails a position on each of these four conversions. As the positions are assembled, the general heuristic structure of the foundations for confronting the issues of dialectic is established. The objectification is the condition of the possibility of genuineness in the third stage of meaning. But it also reinforces such genuineness, the harmony between the self as it is and self as it is known. For intellectual conversion in the third stage is the decisive, personal act of the self-affirmation of the knower; and psychic conversion is the readiness to confront the images that display the dramatic question of one's own existential authenticity or inauthenticity. As such, it helps one appropriate one's own moral and religious consciousness. It is thus an aid to religious, moral, and intellectual self-transcendence.

We have indicated, however, that in addition to aiding the other three conversions, psychic conversion is *a function of* these conversions. It depends on an antecedent willingness to change, to be healed, and so to become an originating value in human collaboration with the divine solution in the pursuit of the human good. Besides a consideration of the creativity of genuineness, then, we need to reflect upon the structure of healing. Only in this way can we understand the relations between psychic conversion and the other three conversions.

In any stage of meaning, and thus in more or less differentiated or compact forms, healing occurs in human life to the extent that the gift of God's love, however named, initiates a movement downward in subjectivity, awakening in consciousness an openness to all value at the existential level, an appreciation of the specific values of truth and complete intelligibility at the spiritual levels of cognitional consciousness, and finally a willingness for the appropriate images for insight. The movement from above downwards, from religious conversion to moral conversion and from moral conversion to an analogous realization of intellectual and psychic genuineness, constitutes one vector in development. Let us call it the therapeutic vector. The creative vector from below upwards depends on the therapeutic action that incites us to an ever precarious state of converted subjectivity. The creative vector moves from the deliverances of psychic representations through the operations of human questioning, first to insight, conceptualization, and formulation, next to critical reflection, grasp of the virtually unconditioned, and judgment, and finally to evaluation, decision, and execution of one's decisions.

The therapeutic significance of the third stage of meaning arises from the susceptibility of an immature modernity to "the up-to-date myth of ideology and the hypnotic, highly effective magic of thought-control."[35]

> As long as one is content to be guided by one's common sense, to disregard the pundits of every class whether scientific or cultural or religious, one need not learn what goes on in one's black box. But when one moves beyond the limits of commonsense competence, when one wishes to have an opinion of one's own on larger issues, then one had best know just what one is doing. Otherwise one too easily will be duped and too readily be exploited. Then explicit intellectual self-transcendence becomes a real need.[36]

The reciprocal movement of healing and creating is operative in any stage of meaning, and it is the condition of the analogous possibility of genuineness. But the specific task at the present juncture in human self-understanding and self-transformation is to objectify the patterns of these two vectors of development. The objectification is itself a change in the subject, an explicit conversion at both the intellectual and psychic levels. Transcendental method is itself both therapeutic and creative. But, as we saw in our discussion of "the soteriological foundations of the transformation of order" (chapter 3, section 4.3), transcendental method is therapeutic *before* it is creative. The conversions promote attentive psychic receptivity, explicit intelligence and rationality, and responsibility for reversing the longer cycle of decline. Therefore, the ulterior objective of the therapeutic function of transcendental method is the creative promotion of the making of humanity according to the structure of the human good. The methodical exigence[37] is really a therapeutic exigence, and transcendental method as intellectual and psychic self-appropriation is at root a work of responsible love.[38] The therapeutic and creative vectors that operate analogously--with compactness or more or less differentiation--at various stages of human development are not just objectified in transcendental method. The objectification is itself a function of their active influence, for transcendental method is an instrument of the healing of the subject, an aid to the consequent explicit self-transcendence of cognitional and existential praxis.

Psychic conversion as explicit appropriation is a result of the therapeutic movement from above downwards in the third stage of meaning. Intellectual self-appropriation calls for psychic self-appropriation in order to bring its own movement full circle, and so that intellectual conversion can be sublated by the moral and religious conversions in which the affectivity of the subject is of such great moment. Psychic conversion allows moral and religious conversion to be transposed into the post-critical context of self-appropriation and thus to be mediated to the subject in the realm of interiority.

But because it makes possible a recurrent scheme of collaboration between neural demand functions or psychic complexes and conscious discrimination, psychic conversion aids in the creative development of the subject from below upwards. Without the other three conversions, one is biased against the emergence of materials for insight, and so psychic conversion is a function of religious, moral, and intellectual conversion. But it also aids in the growth and development of the other three conversions, for it provides an antecedently willing intentionality with the materials needed if the insights are to occur that are required to offset both the shorter and the longer cycles of decline. It is thus the defensive circle set up by a triply converted intentionality to prevent the systematic interference of bias in one's knowing and deciding.

4.4.6. Attentiveness.

Psychic conversion affects the first level of consciousness, where imagination and intelligence collaborate to present psychic representations that will function as the material for insight, judgment, and decision. It enables us to clarify what is meant by the transcendental precept governing authentic performance on this level: Be attentive. Attentiveness is a function of one's willingness for insight, truth, and the assumption of constitutive responsibility. This willingness extends to the censorship, that is, to the prior collaboration of intelligence and imagination in the admission of images needed for a sustained and creative development of one's being as a cognitional and existential subject. One becomes watchful, vigilant, expectant, contemplative, sensitively free and composed. Only on the basis of such composure at the lower levels of consciousness can the intelligible emergent probability that is the immanent intelligibility even of neural process become recurrently and not just coincidentally an intelligent, truthful, responsible emergent probability. This occurs by the sublation into intentional consciousness of the aesthetic experience of the movement of life, by the recovery of the story told by the movement itself as it participates in the drama in which we find or miss the direction.

4.4.7. Universal Willingness.

As a conversion, psychic conversion affects, as we have seen, the lower reaches of our conscious being. It opens the censorship to constructive rather than repressive functioning in the admission of images to consciousness. It thus honors the finality, the upwardly but indeterminately directed dynamism, of corresponding underlying neural manifolds. As this finality for conscious integration is honored, there can develop in the subject a sensitive or affective self-transcendence that matches, accompanies, permeates, and sustains the detachment of intelligence, judgment, and decision. This affective self-transcendence comes to correspond to the objective scale of values dictated by the normative order of inquiry. Such correspondence is, again, both a function and a condition of the sustained possibility of authentic consciousness. It is "universal willingness," the divinely originated remedy for moral impotence.

We resist the purification of our sensitivity, even if it is also the flourishing of the psyche and the organism. The resistance is due to the disproportion between time-bound sensitivity and the unrestricted quality of spiritual desire. Who wants to be but one item in a universe of being? Who is content to admit that his or her own desires and fears are "but infinitesimal components in the history of mankind?"[39] Time-bound sensitivity lives in a habitat, an environment. Spiritual desire lives in a world constituted by a universal order.

> The self, as perceiving and feeling, as enjoying and suffering, functions as an animal in an environment, as a self-attached and self-interested centre within its own narrow world of stimuli and responses. But the same self, as inquiring and reflecting, as conceiving intelligently and judging reasonably, is carried by its own higher spontaneity to quite a different mode of operation with the opposite attributes of detachment and disinterestedness. It is confronted with a universe of being in which it finds itself, not the centre of reference, but an object co-ordinated with other objects and, with them, subordinated to some destiny to be discovered or invented, approved or disdained, accepted or repudiated.[40]

Who wants *that?* What is it to *want?*

The opposites in the constitution of the person constitute a dialectic of desire. Like the opposites, the dialectic can find its cumulative and progressive reconciliation only in the aesthetic mediation that shares in both poles of the opposition. Appropriation of this medium through psychic conversion reveals the complementary flourishing of sensitive and spiritual desire under the dominance of the divinely originated gift of universal willingness.

Through psychic conversion, the aesthetic mediation of spirit and matter is appropriated. The appropriation, as therapeutic, promotes the creative harmony of desire in world- and self-constituting cognitional and existential praxis. A portion of this activity of psychic conversion consists in instituting a self-possessed detachment in the realm of sensitive and affective spontaneity. Allowing the neural demand functions to receive their conscious complement in psychic representations promotes their detachment from the world of immediacy that is their natural habitat. Letting sensitive desire manifest itself to spiritual intentionality is the first step in its purification and participation in the spiritual desire for intelligibility, truth, and the good. What is good, is good for the whole person, and not simply for the upper reaches of consciousness. The lower manifolds are themselves energically, indeterminately, heading for the same good that higher conjugates understand, affirm, and choose. An intentionality open to things as they are is receptively instrumental in the flourishing of psyche and organism. The whole of creation groans in expectation of the liberation of the children of God. Sustained fidelity to the task of psychic conversion will make the story it releases "a mystery that is at once symbol of the uncomprehended and sign of what is grasped and psychic force that sweeps living human bodies, linked in charity, to the joyful, courageous, wholehearted, yet intelligently controlled performance of the tasks set by a world order in which the problem of evil is not suppressed but transcended."[41] Willingness becomes universal when it reaches into and transforms the unconscious itself, the aggregates of aggregates of aggregates of physical, chemical, and botanical conjugates that constitute the movement of life. Then the divine solution to the problem of evil is truly a harmonious continuation of the emergent probability of world process. The story of this harmony can be retrieved in the task of elaborating theological foundations. With the discovery and telling of this story, the heuristic intent of the foundational quest has come full circle in that retrieved, second immediacy wherein lies the therapeutic finality of the exigence for self-appropriation. This exigence found its essential moment of systematization in the self-affirmation of the knower. But it has undergone a series of higher viewpoints in moving, first, to the acknowledgment of the distinct reality of existential and religious levels of consciousness, then to the articulation of the reciprocal vectors of development, and finally to the completion of the heuristic structure of the foundational enterprise in psychic conversion. This second immediacy is the goal of the explanatory retrieval of the subject's religious, moral, intellectual, and affective being that is transcendental method. This asymptotically mediated immediacy of intentional operations and of feelings on the part of the adult whose world is mediated by meaning is a new stage of differentiation of the original and universal human experience of the cognitive and existential search for direction in the movement of life. The explicit articulation of psychic conversion completes the heuristic structure of foundations, and the foundations, although theological, ground not only the second phase of theology but the cognitive and existential interdisciplinary praxis that would mediate in a critical manner our movement from the present into the future.

The manner in which psychic conversion brings the foundational quest full circle, i.e., to its heuristic completion, is twofold. The first aspect has to do with the levels of consciousness; the second has to do with the interrelationship of the various conversions within one and the same conscious subject.

First, then, as we have already seen briefly, psychic conversion is the self-appropriation of the empirical level of intentional consciousness and the key to the story that would be the self-appropriation of existential and religious consciousness. The arguments for both claims should be clear by now. Through psychic conversion, the sequence of sensations, memories, images, emotions, conations, associations, bodily movements, and spontaneous intersubjective responses that constitutes empirical consciousness is mediated to the intelligent, reflective, existential, religious subject. But this very sequence itself, by reason of the relations of sublation that obtain among the levels of consciousness, becomes, through intentional feelings, the opening onto existential and religious awareness, and so a maieutic of sensitive spontaneity is just as pertinent to the self-appropriation of the upper levels of consciousness as it is to that of the lower. Moreover, intentional feelings evoke and are evoked by symbols, and so a familiarity with the elemental symbolizing of the psyche in dreams moves one significantly forward in one's ability to retrieve and tell the story of one's subjectivity, and so in one's existential and religious self-appropriation. Consequently, psychic conversion completes the movement of the self-appropriation begun in intellectual conversion, which had advanced the intelligent and rational levels of consciousness to self-appropriation. With intellectual and psychic conversion in their third-stage sense, the heuristic structure of the full order of self-appropriation is complete.

Second, however, in addition to intellectual and psychic conversion, there are the conversions that Lonergan calls religious and moral. They generally precede the conversions that are required to move into the third stage of meaning--intellectual conversion--and to integrate this differentiation through existential self-knowledge--psychic conversion. And yet moral conversion and religious conversion are said to sublate the advances of intellectual conversion into their own openness to all value and to the world-transcendent source and destiny of cognitive and existential operations. When intellectual conversion is understood in its third-stage sense, however, this sublation must be in terms of moral and religious self-appropriation. But since psychic conversion mediates moral and religious self-appropriation, it effects once again the completion of the heuristic intent of the foundational quest.

5. *Psychic Energy and Anagogic Symbols.*

The openness of an intellectually and psychically converted consciousness permits the post-critical and post-therapeutic entrance into third-stage consciousness of the basic law of limitation and transcendence. The tension of limitation and transcendence is characteristic of all development in the concrete universe of being proportionate to human experience, human understanding, and human judgment. But in the human subject the tension itself becomes conscious. Wherever it is found, the tension is rooted in potency, i.e., in the individuality, continuity, coincidental conjunctions and successions, and non-systematic divergence from intelligible norms, that are to be known by the empirical consciousness of a mind intent on explanatory understanding.[42] Potency is the root of tension because it is the principle both of limitation and of the upwardly but indeterminately directed dynamism of proportionate being that Lonergan calls finality.[43] Moreover, the principle of limitation of the lowest genus of proportionate being is prime potency and, since each higher genus is limited by the preceding lower genus, prime potency is the universal principle of limitation for the whole range of proportionate being.[44]

Prime potency grounds energy, which, Lonergan says, "is relevant to mechanics, thermodynamics, electromagnetics, chemistry, and biology."[45] Thus, he asks, "Might one not say that the quantity of energy is the concrete prime potency that is informed mechanically or thermally or electrically as the case may be?" And he asks for an answer to this and other questions "such that prime potency would be conceived as a ground of quantitative limitation and general heuristic considerations would relate quantitative limitation to the properties that science verifies in the quantity it names energy."[46]

The relevance of the notion of energy to psychology is not without its difficulties, but it has been defended by C. G. Jung,[47] approved, it would seem, by the physicist Wolfgang Pauli,[48] and defensible in terms of Lonergan's exposition of explanatory genera and species. Nonetheless,

> . . . when one mounts to the higher integrations of the organism, the psyche, and intelligence, one finds that measuring loses both in significance and in efficacy. It loses in significance, for the higher integration is, within limits, independent of the exact quantities of the lower manifold it systematizes. Moreover, the higher the integration, the greater the independence of lower quantities. . . . Besides this loss in significance, there is also a loss in efficacy. Classical method can

> select among the functions that solve differential equations by appealing to measurements and empirically established curves. What the differential equation is to classical method, the general notion of development is to genetic method. But while the differential equation is mathematical, the general notion of development is not. It follows that while measurement is an effacacious technique for finding boundary conditions that restrict differential equations, it possesses no assignable efficacy when it comes to particularizing the general notion of development.[49]

The loss of significance and efficacy to the quantitative treatment of what remains a quantity is most apparent in humanity, where "the higher system of intelligence develops not in a material manifold but in the psychic representation of material manifolds. Hence, the higher system of intellectual development is primarily the higher integration, not of the man in whom the development occurs, but of the universe that he inspects."[50] As integrator, the human psyche develops in an underlying manifold of material events, but, as operator, the psyche is oriented to the higher integration of the universe in and through human intentional consciousness.

It is this tension between the sensitive, aesthetic psyche as integrator of physical, chemical, cytological, and neurological events and the same psyche as operator of the higher integration of the universe in human intelligence, affirmation, and decision that is the sensitive manifestation of the law of limitation and transcendence as this law becomes conscious in human development. In fact, it is through psychic energy as integrator and operator that this law *does* first become conscious. The genuineness that would accept the law into consciousness and live from it, then, is promoted by a mediated recognition of psychic energy as integrator and operator of one's own development.

Freud and Jung developed what eventually were to become dialectically opposed understandings of psychic energy and of its functioning in personal development. For Freud, psychic energy would seem to be reducible to a biological or botanical quantum (despite his inability ever to provide any quantities for it!). It is always, in all its manifestations or object relations, explained by moving backwards. Its real object is sexual, and it institutes other object-relations only by being displaced from the sexual object. Dreams, works of art, linguistic expressions and cultural objectifications dissimulate one basic and unsurpassable desire. They do not witness to a polymorphism of human desire, a capacity to be directed in several autonomous patterns of experience, and a capacity to be misdirected in the movement of life. Rather, they always disguise the unsurpassable biological instinct from which they originate. Displacement can be either neurotic or healthy. It always occurs through the agency of one or more mechanisms: repression, substitution, symbolization, or the never quite adequately explained sublimation. In each instance the primary process, governed by the pleasure principle, is superseded by a secondary process whose principle is the harsh Ananke of reality. The seat of psychic energy, then, i.e., the unconscious, is on this account never related directly to the real world. It must be adapted by the reality principle and submit in stoic resignation to things as they are. Therapy facilitates this healthy, adult stoicism, this adaptation to a cruel fate.

For Jung, in contrast, specifically psychic energy is a surplus energy from the standpoint of biological purposiveness. It is, in Lonergan's terms, a coincidental manifold at the biological level. Its original orientation is neutral, undetermined, undifferentiated. It is not aboriginally sexual, tied to a destiny in reverse,[51] but can be directed to a host of different objects in different realms of meaning. Moreover, it can be transformed. The transformation of energy is not displacement, even by sublimation, for psychic energy has no determinate object from which to be displaced. Thus Jung frequently takes issue with the Freudian notion of mechanisms of displacement, and he sharply distinguishes his own notion of transformation from even the seemingly least reductive Freudian mechanism, sublimation.[52] Sublimation is a bending of instinctual desire to a suitable form of adaptation to reality. In essence it is a self-deception, "a new and somewhat more subtle form of repression," for "only absolute necessity can effectively inhibit a natural instinct."[53] Transformation, on the other hand, is a thoroughly natural process--i.e., a process that occurs of itself when the proper attitude is adopted toward the process of energic composition and distribution (complex formation) that depth psychologists call the unconscious.[54] This proper attitude initially may be characterized as one of compassionate and attentive listening, of an effort to befriend the neglected dimensions of one's subterranean existence. Attentiveness, therapeutically tutored, puts one in touch with the upwardly but indeterminately directed dynamism or teleology that corresponds with what Lonergan calls finality. Healing thus complements creativity. Jung designates the fuller being[55] to which finality is directed as wholeness, which he characterizes as the unconscious meaning and purposefulness of the transformation of energy.[56]

Jung's explanation of symbols is related to the transformation of energy in the service of this unconscious meaning and purposefulness. I find it most instructive to compare the early and later Jung on fantasy and dream.[57] More or less in agreement with Freud, the early Jung indicated that fantasy-thinking and dreaming represent a distortion in one's relation to reality, an intrusion--welcome or unwelcome--of the nonrealistic unconscious psyche into the domain of the reality principle or ego.[58] Fantasies and dreams are thinly but subtly disguised instances of wishful thinking, symptoms of the primary process. Only the suspicious hermeneutic of reduction is required in order to reveal them for what they are.[59] But in Jung's later work, fantasies and dreams are neither distorted forms of thinking nor illegitimate relations to reality, but spontaneous products of a layer of the subject that has its own distinct meaning and purpose.[60] Fantasies and dreams, moreover, have a function: they cooperate in the interests of the transformation of energy in the direction of the wholeness of the personality.[61]

The development in Jung's thought is from symptom to symbol. If dreams and fantasies are symptoms of neurotic difficulty, they reveal the formation of substitutes for sexual energy. But if they have a meaning of their own as symbols of the course of occurrences or conjugate acts at the psychic level of finality, then they are to be interpreted as integrators and operators of a process of development, i.e., of the transformation of psychic energy in the direction of the fuller being that Jung calls wholeness. As an integrator and operator of development, the spontaneous or elemental symbol is efficacious. It does not merely point to the transformation of energy like a sign; it *gives what it symbolizes;* it is not just a symbol of transformation, but a transforming symbol. If for the moment I may neutralize a religiously charged word, we might call the symbol as integrator and operator sacramental.

Because we have made reference to and use of Lonergan's notion of finality, we should note in this context that Jung speaks explicitly of the necessity of adopting a teleological point of view in the science of the psyche. The question to be asked of the elemental symbol is not so much, What caused this distortion in the relation to reality?, as it is, What is the purpose of this symbolic expression? What is it intending? Where is it heading? The intelligibility is to be discovered in the higher system of human living that systematically assembles and organizes the psychic materials.[62] There is not, however, an either/or dichotomy between the causal point of view and the teleological approach. Jung understood that these two scientific orientations are mutually complementary. Both are necessary if the symbol, precisely as symbol, is to be understood correctly. The causal point of view displays the system of energy-composition *from which* energy has passed over into a new distribution. The teleological point of view reveals the direction of the new distribution. Where Jung differs from Freud is in considering the new distribution not as a faulty substitute for the primal system, but as a new and autonomous system in its own right, invested with energy that has become properly its own. It takes over something of the character of the old system, but in the process it radically transforms this character. To employ explanatory categories from Lonergan, we might say that, just as potency is a principle of limitation for the realm of proportionate being, while finality urges world process to new genera that are not logically derivative from former genera, so psychic energy is a principle of limitation for that domain of proportionate being that is human development, while its finality urges human development to new patterns, capacities, and differentiations that are not logically derivative from former constellations.

For Jung, then, the elemental symbol is not an inferior form of thinking, the symptom of a maladaptation to reality. It is, instead, "the best possible description or formulation of a relatively unknown fact."[63] The relatively unknown fact, in general, is the self as it is and the self as it is becoming--the story of the search for direction in the movement of life.

The process of development toward wholeness, when engaged in consciously and deliberately, Jung calls individuation. Psychic energy, as the principle of the upwardly but indeterminately directed dynamism of finality, is initially undifferentiated with respect to its specific focus or objective. But it is generically directed to a wholeness that is moved toward by individuation. Its elemental symbolic productions effect its ongoing transformation in this direction. Wholeness is a generic goal that becomes specifically differentiated through the process of individuation.[64]

The complementarity of the causal and the teleological points of view in the interpretation of elemental symbols leads to the notion of the transformation of an *object* into an *imago*. On a purely causal interpretation, the appearance or suggestion of a maternal symbol in a dream or fantasy, for example, signifies some unresolved component of infantile Oedipal sexuality, some disguised or displaced form of the primal Oedipal situation. On a teleological interpretation, the same symbol may point not just *back* to one's childhood or infancy, but also *ahead* to further development. It may not be a symptom of infantile fixation, but a symbol of the life-giving forces of nature. It may even have a meaning that is more than personal--a significance that Jung calls archetypal. One may be indeed regressing to the mother, but precisely for the sake of finding memory-traces that will enable one to move forward. In this case, "mother" is no longer an object or a cause of a symptom, but, in Jung's term, an *imago;* i.e., a cluster of memory associations through whose aid further development may take place.[65] What was once an object of one's reachings may become a symbol of the life that lies ahead. The energy once invested in an object is now concentrated in a symbol which transforms the original investment in such a way that one is propelled to an adult future. The cathexis of psychic energy is transferred--by transformation, and not just by displacement--from an object to the "relatively unknown fact" that is expressed by the symbol. Psychic energy is channeled into a symbolic analogue of its natural object, an analogue that imitates the object and thereby gains for a new purpose the energy once invested in the object.

There remains one final step in this lengthy and at times circuitous elaboration of the completion of the heuristic structure of the foundations of interdisciplinary collaboration in the third stage of meaning. We must establish the relations between this notion of the transformation of energy-become-psyche and spiritual intentionality.

To say that the transformation of psychic energy is a natural and automatic process is not to say that wholeness, the reconciliation of the opposites, will inevitably result. We have already called attention to the requisite attitude on the part of consciousness if the individuation process is to proceed from generic indetermination to specific and explanatory differentiation. Jung himself insisted on the need for a freely adopted conscious attitude toward the psychological depths and their symbolic manifestations if individuation is to occur.[66] The same point may be gathered in more explanatory fashion from Lonergan's discussion of the collaboration between imagination and intelligence in presenting to conscious discrimination the images needed for insight, judgment, and decision.[67] Earlier I characterized the proper attitude as one of therapeutically tutored attentiveness. Such contemplative listening is a function of the effective introduction into one's operative intentionality of the universal willingness that matches the unrestricted spontaneity of the desire for intelligibility, the unconditioned, and value. "There is to human inquiry an unrestricted demand for intelligibility. There is to human judgment a demand for the unconditioned. There is to human deliberation a criterion that criticizes every finite good."[68] The transformation of psychic energy may well be a natural and automatic process, but the direction which energy will assume is dependent on the orientation of the higher system of intentionality in which the psyche itself finds its integration. Thus is grounded our conviction that the science of depth psychology depends on a maieutic of intentionality.

The unrestricted demand of inquiry, judgment, and deliberation constitutes, in its very unrestrictedness, the transcendent exigence of human intentionality. Religious conversion and its development in spirituality bring one into this realm of transcendence. As fulfillment of intentionality and simultaneously as participation in the divinely originated solution to the problem of evil, religious conversion is the beginning of the therapeutic movement from above downwards, proceeding through moral and intellectual conversion to the psychic conversion that effects the therapeutically tutored attentiveness that represents the proper attitude to the symbolic deliverances of psychic finality. In this way, the divinely originated solution to the problem of evil penetrates to the sensitive level of human living. One can expect that the unfolding of the story told in one's dreams will transform one's spontaneous symbolic process so that, in the limit, it matches more and more the exigencies of the divinely originated solution. For the transformation of sensitivity and spontaneous intersubjectivity wrought by development in the realm of transcendence penetrates to the physiological level of human subjectivity.[69] The divinely originated solution to the problem of evil is a higher integration of human living that will be implemented by a converted subjectivity, an intentionality that has been transformed by the supernatural or transcendent conjugate forms of faith and hope and charity.[70] But, because the solution is a harmonious continuation of the emergent probability of world process, it must penetrate to and envelop the sensitive level where the creative movement of intentionality from below upwards begins. Spontaneous psychic images function in human consciousness in a manner analogous to the role that questions play in intelligence, reflection, and deliberation. Just as questions promote the successive sublations of lower levels of consciousness by higher levels, so psychic images, when attended to under the influence of an antecedently willing collaboration of imagination and intelligence, promote the sublation of neural demand functions by waking empirical consciousness, which in turn is sublated by intelligent, rational, and existential consciousness.

The transformation of energy under the influence of the transcendent conjugate forms introduced into intentional consciousness by the soteriological existential dimension of spiritual consciousness will enter a dimension or stage that was not adequately differentiated by Jung.[71] Jung was keenly aware of the transformation of energic compositions and distributions from personal object-relations to archetypal *imago*-relations. But beyond the archetypal stage of energic transformation, there is its anagogic stage.[72] It represents the envelopment of sensitivity itself by the divinely originated solution to the problem of evil. In this stage, there are released transformed and transforming symbols that correspond to the unrestricted intentionality of human intelligence, human judgment, and human deliberation. Anagogic symbols simultaneously reflect and bring about the conversion of human sensitivity to participation in the divinely originated solution to the problem of evil. They correspond to what Lonergan calls "the image that symbolizes man's orientation into the known unknown,"[73] and they indicate something of the finality of that orientation, its underivable, indeed supernatural origination. Lonergan aptly explains the function of these energic manifestations: "Since faith gives more truth than understanding comprehends, since hope reinforces the detached, disinterested, unrestricted desire to know, man's sensitivity needs symbols that unlock its transforming dynamism and bring it into harmony with the vast but impalpable pressures of the pure desire, of hope, and of self-sacrificing charity."[74] These symbols make of the divinely originated solution "the mystery that is at once symbol of the uncomprehended and sign of what is grasped and psychic force that sweeps living human bodies, linked in charity, to the joyful, courageous, whole-hearted, yet intelligently controlled performance of the tasks set by a world order in which the problem of evil is not suppressed but transcended."[75] Through anagogic symbols, the divine solution becomes not only living history, but living nature. Through their agency, "the emergent trend and the full realization of the solution [includes] the sensible data that are demanded by man's sensitive nature and that will command his attention, nourish his imagination, stimulate his intelligence and will, release his affectivity, control his aggressivity and, as central features of the world of sense, intimate its finality, its yearning for God."[76] In fact, since the higher system of intentionality is primarily the higher integration, not of the subject in whom development occurs, but of the universe of being that the subject knows and makes,[77] we may say that elemental anagogic symbols not only intimate but also promote the finality of the universe. Therefore, the participation of sensitivity in the divinely originated solution to the problem of evil that occurs through anagogic symbols, when sustained by the harmonious cooperation of the therapeutic movement from above downwards with the creative development from below upwards, has to be understood as the fulfilment of the process of conversion in the retrieved genuineness of the subject in the third stage of meaning.

6. *Conclusion.*

In the Preface we said that a twofold development will be required if we are to institute a world-cultural humanity: the transformation and integration of the myriad instances of common sense and the transformation and integration of the sciences, especially of the human sciences. We have shown in the course of this book how the development of Bernard Lonergan's thought leads him to speak eventually of the theological foundations of an interdisciplinary reorientation of the human sciences. We have argued that these foundations are complemented by a psychic conversion that enables the self-appropriation of the existential dimensions of consciousness and that makes possible the foundational transformation of the science of depth psychology. But we have focused only indirectly on the transformation of common sense, relating it only to the development of a practical agency in the third stage of meaning that can sublate into existential praxis the gains of the process of self-appropriation. Let us conclude, then, with a more inclusive outline of the program for establishing a world-cultural community that issues from the foundations that we have labored to establish.

To speak of the *theological* foundations of a transformation and an integration of the sciences and of the myriad instances of common sense is to imply a new, global synthesis of faith and culture. This synthesis is, in fact, the good human world that all of our efforts in this book have been devoted to envisioning as worthy of being brought into being. We are challenged by the unfolding course of intelligent emergent probability to assume the responsibility of mediating a new axial development in human consciousness, that new control of meaning grounded in interiorly differentiated consciousness that Lonergan calls the third stage of meaning. This development is the condition of the formation of a world-cultural humanity, of a global community grounded in analogously realized attainments of genuineness. This global community will supply viable alternatives to the principal agents of a post-historic humanity: to the two escalating and competing totalitarianisms of overly centralized socialism and of monolithic transnational corporations, both of which violate on the level of systemic social-structural objectifications the law of the tension of limitation and transcendence that constitutes the intrinsic intelligibility of all genuine development in the concrete universe of proportionate being.

The suprastructural component of this new community, i.e., the interdisciplinary effort at transformed human science, will go forward on several fronts. I have argued that the reorientation of depth psychology is part of the very foundations of this implementation of Lonergan's method in the human sciences. But the implementation must extend to a reorientation of the social, anthropological, and political sciences, under the guiding orientation of an intention to ground crosscultural understanding and cooperation in the transcendental constituents of human genuineness; and the science of economics must be reoriented in accord with the same vision.

As to the transformation of common sense, perhaps we can take our lead from Eric Voegelin's distinction of the three modes of symbolization through which cultures have expressed their self-understanding: the cosmological, the anthropological, and the soteriological.[78] Cultures that exist under the forms of cosmological symbolization, where the prime analogate for the cultural order lies in the rhythms and processes of nonhuman nature, have effectively displaced the tension of limitation and transcendence in the direction of limitation. Consequently, they are unable to assume responsible control of their destinies. Unless they free themselves from the dominance of the cosmological mode of symbolization, they will become the easy prey of the competing totalitarianisms. Their symbolization, however, contains an abiding truth, and it must be mediated to a crosscultural community that will counteract the displacement toward transcendence that is characteristic of modern totalitarianisms. Cosmological symbolization is archetypal, and as such it expresses the ecological exigence for a creative tension with the schemes of recurrence of nonhuman nature.

Anthropological symbolization is dependent on the axial recovery of the order of the soul as the measure of the integrity of a society, and on the recovery of the world-transcendent measure of the order of the soul itself. And soteriological symbolization forces upon us the distinction between the eros of a well-ordered interiority and the charity of a person healed by the gracious initiative of the world-transcendent measure. The differentiation and appropriation of all three modes of symbolization and their integration in a world-cultural consciousness is, I believe, the key to the common sense of a new human community. I plan to return to this issue in great detail in a future book.[79]

NOTES

PREFACE

[1]Bernard Lonergan, *Insight: A Study of Human Understanding* (London: Darton, Longman, and Todd, 1957; also in paperback with same pagination, New York: Harper and Row, 1978).

[2]Bernard Lonergan, *Method in Theology* (New York: Herder and Herder, 1972).

[3]Lewis Mumford, *The Transformations of Man* (New York: Harper Torchbooks, 1956).

[4]Lonergan, *Insight*, pp. 48, 52, 87, 117, 208-11, 533, 608. See also Robert Doran, "Aesthetics and the Opposites," *Thought* 52 (June 1977): 117-30, esp. 117-20.

[5]Lonergan, *Method in Theology*, p. 20.

[6]I have dealt with psychic conversion in *Subject and Psyche: Ricoeur, Jung, and the Search for Foundations* (Washington, D.C.: University Press of America, 1977); "Psychic Conversion," *The Thomist* 41 (April 1977): 200-36; "Subject, Psyche, and Theology's Foundations," *Journal of Religion* 57, 3 (July 1977): 267-87; "Christ and the Psyche," in Jean-Marc Laporte and Thomas A. Dunne, eds., *Trinification of the World: Festschrift in Honor of Frederick Crowe* (Toronto: Regis College Press, 1978); "The Theologian's Psyche: Notes toward a Reconstruction of Depth Psychology," *Lonergan Workshop I*, ed. Frederick Lawrence (Missoula, Montana: Scholars Press, 1978); "Dramatic Artistry in the Third Stage of Meaning," *Lonergan Workshop II*, ed. Frederick Lawrence (Chico, CA: Scholars Press, 1980).

[7]Bernard Lonergan, "Belief: Today's Issue," in *A Second Collection*, ed. Bernard Tyrrell and William Ryan (Philadelphia: Westminster, 1974), esp. pp. 91-97.

[8]Lonergan, *Insight*, p. 396.

[9]Ibid.

[10]See Karl Jaspers, *The Origin and Goal of History*, trans. Michael Bullock (New Haven: Yale University Press, 1953); Eric Voegelin, *Order and History*, 4 vols. (Baton Rouge: Louisiana State University Press, 1956-1974); Mumford, *The Transformations of Man;* John Cobb, *The Structure of Christian Existence* (Philadelphia: Fortress Press, 1967); Lonergan, "Dimensions of Meaning," in *Collection: Papers by Bernard Lonergan*, ed. Frederick Crowe (New York: Herder and Herder, 1967), pp. 252-67; *Method in Theology*, pp. 85-99.

[11]Lonergan, *Insight*, chap. 20.

CHAPTER ONE

[1]Lonergan, *Method in Theology*, p. ix.

[2]On the two phases of theology, see ibid., pp. 140-44.

[3]On the realms of meaning, see ibid., pp. 81-85. Lonergan discusses six: common sense, theory, art, scholarship, transcendence, and interiority.

[4]Ibid., chaps. 10 and 11.

[5]On the distortions that result from regression, see Lonergan's use of Newman in "Theology and Man's Future," in *A Second Collection*, ed. Bernard Tyrrell and William Ryan (Philadelphia: Westminster, 1974), esp. pp. 141-46.

[6]Eric Voegelin has studied several of these varieties of symbolic forms under the rubric of compactness and differentiation. See his *Order and History*.

[7]Hans-Georg Gadamer, *Truth and Method*, translation edited by Garrett Barden and John Cumming from the second (1965) edition of *Wahrheit und Methode* (New York: Seabury Press, 1975).

[8]On Gadamer's irony, see Frederick Lawrence, "Gadamer and Lonergan: A Dialectical Comparison," *International Philosophical Quarterly* 20, 1 (March 1980): 33, 35.

[9]See Lonergan, *Method in Theology*, chap. 5 and Part 2, *passim*.

[10]Ibid., pp. 83-84.

[11]See Gadamer, *Truth and Method*, pp. 267-74. Compare Lonergan on the critique of mistaken beliefs and of the mistaken believer, in *Method in Theology*, pp. 43-44.

[12]Bernard Lonergan, "The Transition from a Classicist World-View to Historical-Mindedness," in *A Second Collection*, pp. 1-9; see especially pp. 5-6 for the respective relations of classicist and modern empirical notions of culture to Christian revelation.

[13]In his portrayal of the classicist ideal, Lonergan has concentrated on Aristotle, and especially on the ideal of science presented in the *Posterior Analytics*. But a parallel version is found in Plato's discussion of the philosopher in Book V of the *Republic*, 474b-480. The advance beyond classicism entails a critical readjustment of Plato's notions of wisdom and science that is nonetheless quite other than a sophistical repudiation of the intention of the good.

[14]Lonergan, *Method in Theology*, p. ix. On pp. 138-40, Lonergan presents the broad sweep of the changes that have occurred within Christian theology from the original non-differentiation of religion and theology through a process of differentiation heading toward the condition heuristically outlined by Lonergan in which "the differentiated specialties function as an integrated unity." For more detail on the classicist and modern notions of culture, see Lonergan, "Dimensions of Meaning," as well as many of the papers found in *A Second Collection*.

[15]Lonergan, *Method in Theology*, p. 21.

[16]Ibid., p. 23.

[17]Ibid. Appropriation of the unrestricted quality of the transcendental field is the whole point of *Insight*. See also *Method in Theology*, pp. 83-84:

> There is to human inquiry an unrestricted demand for intelligibility. There is to human judgment a demand for the unconditioned. There is to human deliberation a criterion that criticizes every finite good. So it is . . . that man can reach basic fulfilment, peace, joy, only by moving beyond the realms of common sense, theory, and interiority and into the realm in which God is known and loved.

A theology that would deny the correlation of such biblical categories as the Kingdom of God and discipleship with these immanent and normative requirements of human intentionality is guilty of extrinsicism. The charge is applicable not only to theologies that we might spontaneously call fundamentalist but also to Barthian neo-orthodoxy and even to some tendencies in the theology of liberation. A methodical theology would ground the positive prescriptions for Christian praxis offered by liberation theology in the self-appropriation of the subject of such praxis. Such grounding, however, would also invalidate such immanentist critiques of liberation theology as that found in Alfredo Fierro's *The Militant Gospel: A Critical Introduction to Political Theologies* (Maryknoll, NY: Orbis Press, 1977). The crucial point is the place of a critical philosophy of God within systematic theology. See Bernard Lonergan, *Philosophy of God, and Theology* (Philadelphia: Westminster, 1974) and Bernard Tyrrell, *Bernard Lonergan's Philosophy of God* (South Bend: University of Notre Dame, 1974).

[18]"The basic form of alienation is man's disregard of the transcendental precepts, Be attentive, Be intelligent, Be reasonable, Be responsible. Again, the basic form of ideology is a doctrine that justifies such alienation." Lonergan, *Method in Theology*, p. 55.

[19]Plato, *The Republic*, 379a-382. See Voegelin, *The New Science of Politics* (Chicago: University of Chicago Press, 1952), pp. 69-70, for a discussion of the crucial importance for Plato of distinguishing and evaluating "types of theology."

[20]Doran, "Aesthetics and the Opposites," p. 117.

[21]Northrop Frye, *Anatomy of Criticism: Four Essays* (Princeton: Princeton University Press, 1957), pp. 115-28. See also Joseph Flanagan, "Transcendental Dialectic of Desire and Fear," in *Lonergan Workshop I*, pp. 69-91.

[22]Eric Voegelin, "The Gospel and Culture," in D. C. Miller and D. Y. Hadidian, eds., *Jesus and Man's Hope* (Pittsburgh: Pittsburgh Theological Seminary, 1971), pp. 59-101.

[23]Voegelin, *The New Science of Politics*, chap. 2.

[24]Voegelin, *Order and History, vol. I: Israel and Revelation*.

[25]Voegelin, *The New Science of Politics*, chap. 3 esp. pp. 76-80.

[26]Whether the transcendent noetic differentiation is indeed immanently generated is a disputed point. In principle, it can be; in fact, it most likely is not. See Bernard Lonergan, "Natural Knowledge of God," in *A Second Collection*, pp. 117-33. On the place of natural theology *within* Christian theology, see Lonergan, *Philosophy of God, and Theology*.

[27]Lonergan, *Method in Theology*, p. 331.

[28]On the notions of proportionate and transcendent being, see Lonergan, *Insight*, p. 391.

[29]On complementary, genetic, and dialectical relations among horizons, see Lonergan, *Method in Theology*, pp. 236-37.

[30]This is not to say that it introduces into history a principle of disharmony or radical discontinuity. See Lonergan, *Insight*, chap. 20.

[31]The discovery of the possibility of a dialectical relationship between the natural knowledge of God and the absolutely transcendent conjugate forms of faith, hope, and love will be one of the permanent achievements of Latin American liberation theology, however exaggerated this theology's denunciations of natural knowledge of God may be in their present form. See, for example, Jon Sobrino, *Christology at the Crossroads* (Maryknoll, N.Y.: Orbis Books, 1978), pp. 221-22, 349-50, 370.

[32]See Friedrich Heiler, "The History of Religions as a Preparation for the Cooperation of Religions," in *The History of Religions: Essays in Methodology*, ed. Mircea Eliade and Joseph M. Kitagawa (Chicago: University of Chicago Press, 1959), pp. 132-60. On the same issue, helpful suggestions are offered in Vernon Gregson, "A Foundation for the Meeting of Religions: A Study of Religion as Spirituality in the Intentionality Analysis of Bernard Lonergan," Ph.D. dissertation, Marquette University, 1978.

[33]Lonergan, *Method in Theology*, p. xi.

[34]Ibid., chaps. 1 and 4.

[35]Voegelin, *The New Science of Politics*, p. 107.

[36]Frederick Lawrence, "Gadamer and Lonergan: A Dialectical Comparison," p. 27. As Lawrence indicates, such an illusion relates to the Kantian presupposition that epistemology is the fundamental philosophic point of departure. Epistemology settles the *quaestio iuris* concerning how experiences of truth are valid or possible. In Lonergan's terms, epistemology asks, "Why is doing that knowing?" Clearly, on such terms, there is a prior question to be settled, the *quaestio facti*, "What am I doing when I am knowing?" This is the question of cognitional theory, and it is not answered by taking an inward look.

On Cartesian subjectivity, see Hiram Caton, *The Origin of Subjectivity: An Essay on Decartes* (New Haven and London: Yale University Press, 1973).

[37]Lonergan, *Method in Theology*, p. 8.

[38]Gadamer, *Truth and Method*, pp. 267-74.

[39]The expression, "leap in being," is Voegelin's. See *Israel and Revelation*, pp. 40-41. On emergent probability, see Lonergan, *Insight*, pp. 121-28; on intelligent emergent probability, ibid., pp. 209-11.

[40]On limitation and transcendence as a law of human development, see ibid., pp. 472-79.

[41]See ibid., p. 227.

[42]On the equivalence of dramatic artistry and existential authenticity, see my paper, "Dramatic Artistry in the Third Stage of Meaning."

[43]On neurosis and failed artistry, see Ernest Becker, *The Denial of Death* (New York: The Free Press, 1973), chap. 10.

[44]Lonergan, *Method in Theology*, pp. 14-15. For an extreme example of an attempt to explain such events on the analogy of classical mechanics, see Sigmund Freud, "Project for a Scientific Psychology," in *The Standard Edition of the Complete Psychological Works of Sigmund Freud*, translated under the general editorship of James Strachey, vol. 1: *Pre-Psycho-Analytical Publications and Unpublished Drafts* (London: The Hogarth Press, 1966), pp. 283-397. See also interpretation of this work by Paul Ricoeur, *Freud and Philosophy: An Essay on Interpretation*, trans. Denis Savage (New Haven: Yale University Press, 1970), pp. 69-86. Ricoeur shows how the latent presence of Freudian *hermeneutics* in this early (1895) text makes the "Project" stand "as the greatest effort Freud ever made to force a mass of psychical facts within the framework of a quantitative theory, and as the demonstration by way of the absurd that the content exceeds its form" (ibid., p. 73). Ricoeur's noting of the fact that Freud specifies no numerical law to govern his notion of quantity--a summation of excitation homologous to physical energy--is interesting in light of Lonergan's detailing of the manner in which, in the scientific study even of organisms, to say nothing of the psyche and intelligence, genetic method increasingly assumes priority over classical method, and the relevant heuristic notion becomes development rather than an unspecified correlation to be specified or an indeterminate function to be determined (Lonergan, *Insight*, pp. 459-63. See especially the negative observation on the significance and efficacy of measurement for genetic method, p. 463. I have generalized this observation to apply even to energy, when that energy is psychic (Doran, "Dramatic Artistry in the Third Stage of Meaning").

[45]On self-affirmation as explanatory, see Lonergan, *Insight*, pp. 334-35.

[46]Lonergan, *Method in Theology*, pp. 81-99.

[47]Ibid., pp. 47-52.

[48]Lonergan, *Insight*, chaps. 6-7, 18, and 20.

[49]Ibid., chaps. 14-17.

[50]Lonergan, *Method in Theology*, chap. 11.

[51]Ibid., p. 20.

[52] Ibid.

[53] Ibid., and chap. 4.

[54] Ibid., p. 19.

[55] Ibid.

[56] Ibid., pp. 18-20. See *Insight*, chap. 11, for the argument that the self-affirmation of the knower flows from the reflective grasp of a virtually unconditioned.

[57] Ibid., p. 596.

[58] See Bernard Lonergan, "*Insight* Revisited," in *A Second Collection*, esp. p. 277. For a detailed study of the development of Lonergan's thought on this issue, see Frederick Crowe, "An Exploration of Lonergan's New Notion of Value," *Science et Esprit*, 29, 2 (1977): 123-43.

[59] Lonergan, *Insight*, p. 391. Emphasis added.

[60] See ibid., p. 624, where Lonergan speaks of a universal willingness that "consists not in the mere recognition of an ideal norm but in the adoption of an attitude towards the universe of being, not in the adoption of an affective attitude that would desire but not perform but in the adoption of an effective attitude in which performance matches aspiration." By the time of *Method in Theology*, in contrast, feelings are what give "intentional consciousness its mass, momentum, drive, power. Without these feelings our knowing and deciding would be paper thin" (pp. 30-31). The truly effective attitude is one where affectivity is of a single piece because of the gift of God's love (p. 39).

[61] Lonergan, "*Insight* Revisited," p. 277.

[62] "The very wealth of existential reflection can turn out to be a trap. It is indeed the key that opens the doors to a philosophy, not of man in the abstract, but of concrete human living in its historical unfolding. Still, one must not think that such concreteness eliminates the ancient problems of cognitional theory, epistemology, and metaphysics, for if they occur in an abstract context, they recur with all the more force in a concrete context." Bernard Lonergan, "The Subject," in *A Second Collection*, p. 85.

[63] Lonergan, *Method in Theology*, p. 107. For the notion of a fifth level of consciousness, see Lonergan's *Philosophy of God, and Theology*, p. 38.

[64] Bernard Lonergan, "Healing and Creating in History," in *Bernard Lonergan: Three Lectures*, ed. R. Eric O'Connor (Montreal: Thomas More Institute Papers, 1975), pp. 55-68.

[65] Lonergan, *Method in Theology*, pp. 122-23.

[66] Lonergan, "Healing and Creating in History," p. 63.

[67] Ibid., p. 65.

[68] Lonergan, *Method in Theology*, pp. 83-84.

[69]Ibid., p. 240.

[70]Ibid., pp. 238-40.

[71]Ibid., pp. 241-43.

[72]Most satisfactorily to date in Doran, "Dramatic Artistry in the Third Stage of Meaning."

[73]"The impossibility of *philia* between God and man may be considered typical for the whole range of [Greek] anthropological truth. The experiences that were explicated into a theory of man by the mystic philosophers had in common the accent on the human side of the orientation of the soul toward divinity. The soul orients itself toward a God who rests in his immovable transcendence; it reaches out toward divine reality, but it does not meet an answering movement from beyond. The Christian bending of God in grace toward the soul does not come within the range of these experiences--though, to be sure, in reading Plato one has the feeling of moving continuously on the verge of a breakthrough into this new dimension. The experience of mutuality in the relation with God, of the *amicitia* in the Thomistic sense, of the grace which imposes a supernatural form on the nature of man, is the specific difference of Christian truth. The revelation of this grace in history, through the incarnation of the Logos in Christ, intelligibly fulfilled the adventitious movement of the spirit in the mystic philosophers. The critical authority over the older truth of society which the soul had gained through its opening and its orientation toward the unseen measure was now confirmed through the revelation of the measure itself. In this sense, then, it may be said that the fact of revelation is its content" (Voegelin, *The New Science of Politics*, p. 78).

[74]Lonergan, *Method in Theology*, p. 20.

[75]Voegelin, *The New Science of Politics*, p. 78.

[76]Ibid., pp. 78-79.

[77]On dramatic bias, see Lonergan, *Insight*, pp. 191-206; on individual, group, and general bias, ibid., pp. 218-42.

[78]It is perhaps Gandhi who has captured with aesthetic and mystical sensitivity, if not with explanatory exactness, what is crucial to the ecological differentiation: the creative tension between limitation and complexity in all arrangements of human affairs. See Lanza del Vasto, *Return to the Source* (New York: Simon and Schuster, 1974). For a work inchoatively representative of the ecological differentiation, see E. F. Schumacher, *Small is Beautiful: Economics As If People Mattered* (New York: Harper and Row, 1973).

[79]Lonergan, *Method in Theology*, p. 254.

[80]Ibid., pp. 79-80.

[81]Mumford, *The Transformations of Man*, pp. 120-68.

[82]On genuineness or authenticity as conditional and analogous, see Lonergan, *Insight*, pp. 475-79.

[83]Alfred North Whitehead, *Religion in the Making* (Cleveland and New York: World Publishing Company, 1969), p. 16.

84 Ibid., pp. 14-15.

85 Ibid., p. 23.

86 Ibid., p. 28.

87 Ibid., p. 16.

88 Soren Kierkegaard, *The Sickness Unto Death*, in *Fear and Trembling and The Sickness Unto Death*, trans. Walter Lowrie (New York: Doubleday Anchor Books, 1954), p. 147.

89 Becker, *The Denial of Death*, esp. chap. 5.

90 Part of the difficulty would seem to be that for Becker the original experience consists in the terror of death on the part of a dualistically conceived self-conscious animal. For the methodical theologian, the original experience is rather the search for integral direction in the movement of life on the part of the triple compound-in-tension of spirit, psyche, and organism. For an argument that the anticipation of death is derivative from a more fundamental experience, see Voegelin, *Israel and Revelation*, pp. 4-5.

91 See above, n. 38. On the dramatic pattern of experience, see Lonergan, *Insight*, pp. 187-206.

92 See ibid., pp. 472-79.

93 Lonergan, *Method in Theology*, p. 52. Details of Lonergan's notion of the human good will be presented below in Chapter Three.

94 Lonergan, *Insight*, p. 391; see also pp. 398-401.

95 See David Tracy, *Blessed Rage for Order: The New Pluralism in Theology* (New York: Seabury, 1975), pp. 8, 19.

96 Lonergan, *Method in Theology*, p. 333.

97 Voegelin speaks in *Israel and Revelation*, pp. 491-512, of a moment in the history of Yahwistic faith when what was demanded was an exodus of Israel, not from Egypt, but from Israel.

98 On positions and counter-positions, see Lonergan, *Insight*, pp. 387-90.

99 Bernard Lonergan, "Lectures in the Philosophy of Education," unpublished lectures given at Xavier University, Cincinnati, August, 1959. Lecture 2, pp. 19-20. Emphasis added. These lectures have recently been edited and are available at the Lonergan Center, Regis College, Toronto.

CHAPTER TWO

1 Lonergan, *Insight*, p. xxiii.

2 Ibid., p. xiii.

3 Ibid., p. 748.

[4]Bernard Lonergan, *Verbum: Word and Idea in Aquinas*, ed. David B. Burrell (Notre Dame: University of Notre Dame Press, 1967), pp. ix-x.

[5]See, for instance, Voegelin, *The New Science of Politics*, chaps. 4-6.

[6]Lonergan, *Method in Theology*, p. 85.

[7]Voegelin, *The New Science of Politics*, p. 123.

[8]See Lonergan, *Insight*, pp. 387-90.

[9]Ibid., p. 386.

[10]On the realms of meaning, see Lonergan, *Method in Theology*, pp. 81-85 and p. 272; on the realm of interiority, p. 83.

[11]The definition of metaphysics is stated and elaborated in Lonergan, *Insight*, pp. 390-96.

[12]On the homogeneous expansion and the higher viewpoint, see *ibid.*, pp. 13-19. Admittedly, I am here interpreting the significance of the later development. I am led by the course of my own developing thought over the past decade to believe that the differentiation that I wish to suggest would not be possible had there not first occurred a basic shift to a higher viewpoint in the structure of Lonergan's thought on the human subject.

[13]On the metaphor of upper and lower blades, see Lonergan, *Insight*, pp. 312-13, 523, 577-78.

[14]Ibid., pp. 392-93.

[15]Lonergan, *Method in Theology*, p. 254.

[16]Lonergan, "Dimensions of Meaning," p. 255. This 1965 paper can convincingly be interpreted as marking a definitive transition in Lonergan's thought, for it is here that the constitutive function of meaning is acknowledged as such. The distinction of four functions of meaning--cognitive, constitutive, effective, and communicative--emerges in *Method in Theology*, pp. 76-81. In the 1968 lecture, "The Subject" (esp. pp. 79-84), existential subjectivity is declared to be a further level of consciousness beyond the empirical, intelligent, and rational levels; it is acknowledged as sublating the other three levels into its own distinct intention and as enjoying a primacy vis-a-vis the other levels because of its responsibility for determining the character of the self.

[17]A mutually exclusive statement of the dialectic between the existential and the political is thus discredited. For such a statement, see Fierro, *The Militant Gospel*, pp. 3-47.

[18]Lonergan, *Method in Theology*, pp. 30-37.

[19]Lonergan, "*Insight* Revisited," p. 277.

[20]Thus in the Jungian typology, thinking and feeling are opposed functions. If either is developed and differentiated, the other remains undeveloped and compact and enters into the constitution of "the shadow." See C. G. Jung, *Collected Works*, vol.6: *Psychological Types*, trans. R. F. C. Hull (Princeton: Princeton University Press, 1970). See also Doran, "Aesthetics and the

Opposites." Jung does not adequately thematize, though he does acknowledge, the moments of decision in the individuation process, through which opposed functions are integrated.

[21]See Lonergan, *Insight*, pp. 472-79.

[22]Lonergan, *Method in Theology*, p. 52. On the crucial distinctions, particular good, good of order, and value, see ibid., pp. 47-52. As already indicated, Lonergan's notion of the structure of the human good will be studied in the next chapter.

[23]See ibid., p. 15.

[24]On metaphysics as a basic semantics, see Lonergan, "The Subject," p. 86.

[25]Lonergan, *Insight*, pp. 181-206.

[26]See Doran, "Dramatic Artistry in the Third Stage of Meaning."

[27]In *Insight*, the expression "the existential subject" refers to a subject short of the intellectual pattern and its self-recognition in the self-affirmation of the knower. See, for example, p. 385.

[28]Ibid., chap. 12.

[29]Lonergan, "Healing and Creating in History."

[30]Lonergan, *Method in Theology*, pp. 30-34.

[31]Ibid., p. 55.

[32]Bernard Lonergan, "Foreword" to *The Achievement of Bernard Lonergan* by David Tracy (New York: Herder and Herder, 1970), p. ix.

[33]See Lonergan, *Insight*, pp. 387-88. In *Insight*, Lonergan does not use the term, foundations, in this context, but refers to cognitional theory as the *basis* for metaphysics, ethics, and theology.

[34]Ibid., pp. 3-6.

[35]See ibid., pp. 332-35, for Lonergan's account of the move from description to explanation in his exposition of human knowing.

[36]Ibid., pp. 334-35.

[37]It is well to recall here that I am not attempting to bring the reader to this foundational position. It can be arrived at only by reading the first eleven chapters of *Insight* as Lonergan intended them to be read.

[38]On the reducibility of the position on objectivity to those on being and on the subject, and the reducibility of the position on being to that on the subject, see Lonergan, *Method in Theology*, p. 20. Among the foundational positions, then, that on the subject is the most radical.

[39]Lonergan, *Insight*, p. 348.

[40]Ibid., p. 361.

[41]Ibid., p. 350.

[42]Ibid.

[43]Ibid.

[44]Ibid., pp. 348-49.

[45]Ibid., p. 352.

[46]"The idea of being is the content of an unrestricted act of understanding" (ibid., p. 644).

[47]Ibid., p. 352.

[48]Ibid., p. 364.

[49]Ibid., p. 361.

[50]Ibid., p. 355.

[51]Ibid., p. 377.

[52]Ibid.

[53]Ibid., p. 380.

[54]Ibid.

[55]Ibid.

[56]Ibid., pp. 381-83.

[57]Ibid., p. 385.

[58]Ibid.

[59]Ibid.

[60]Ibid., pp. 400-401.

[61]Lonergan, *Method in Theology*, p. 77.

[62]Lonergan, *Insight*, p. 386.

[63]Ibid., p. xx.

[64]Ibid., p. xxi. For the theological pertinence of this realization in the interpretation of Christological doctrine, see Bernard Lonergan, *The Way to Nicea: The Dialectical Development of Trinitarian Theology* (Philadelphia: Westminster, 1976).

[65]Lonergan, *Insight*, pp. xxi-xxii. See also *Method in Theology*, pp. 3-4.

[66]Lonergan, "Dimensions of Meaning," p. 268.

[67]Lonergan, *Method in Theology*, p. xi.

[68]Lonergan, "Dimensions of Meaning," pp. 258-59.

[69]Ibid., pp. 259-60.

[70]Ibid., p. 261.

[71]Ibid., p. 262.

[72]Ibid., p. 259.

[73]Lonergan, *Insight*, pp. 387-88.

[74]Lonergan, "Dimensions of Meaning," p. 264.

[75]Ibid.

[76]Ibid., pp. 265-66.

[77]Ibid., p. 266.

[78]Lonergan, *Method in Theology*, pp. 239-40.

[79]See, for example, ibid., p. 21: "To take the simplest instance, Hume thought the human mind to be a matter of impressions linked together by custom. But Hume's own mind was quite original. Therefore, Hume's own mind was not what Hume considered the human mind to be."

[80]Lonergan, *Insight*, p. 389.

[81]Ibid., p. 388. In fact, there is an ambiguity in the basic position on the subject as it is expressed on this page. First it is said that "the subject becomes known when it affirms itself intelligently and reasonably." Later the basic position on the subject is referred to as the basic position on knowing. But presumably the subject can affirm more about himself or herself than one's own intelligence and reasonableness. Thus, without denying that only intelligent and reasonable affirmation gives rise to self-knowledge, already we are inclined to ask whether the basic position on the subject will not contain more than the intelligent and reasonable affirmation of intelligence and reasonableness.

[82]On the complete intelligibility of the real, see ibid., pp. 499-502.

[83]Lonergan, *Method in Theology*, p. 365.

[84]Ibid., p. 9.

[85]Ibid., p. 15. Emphasis added.

[86]On Lonergan's use of the term, notion, as specifying the heuristic anticipation expressed in questions, and on the distinction of notion and concept, see ibid., pp. 11-12.

[87]Bernard Lonergan, "The Response of the Jesuit as Priest and Apostle in the Modern World," in *A Second Collection*, pp. 165-87; quotation from p. 168. The entire first section of this paper is quite helpful on the notion of self-transcendence.

[88]Ibid.

[89]Lonergan, *Insight*, pp. 218-22.

[90]See Becker, *The Denial of Death*.

[91]Lonergan, *Insight*, pp. 222-25.

[92]Lonergan, *Method in Theology*, p. 107. On the scale of values, ibid., pp. 31-32.

[93]The pattern is similar to that which Lonergan discovers in the relations between healing and creating in history. See above, chap. 1, n. 64.

[94]Lonergan, *Method in Theology*, pp. 17-18; *Insight*, pp. 326-28.

[95]Lonergan, *Method in Theology*, p. 13.

[96]Lonergan, *Insight*, pp. 623-24.

[97]Ibid., p. 606.

[98]Lonergan, *Method in Theology*, p. 37: "Judgments of value differ in content but not in structure from judgments of fact. They differ in content, for one can approve of what does not exist, and one can disapprove of what does."

[99]Lonergan, *Insight*, p. 606.

[100]Ibid., pp. 623-24.

[101]Voegelin, *The New Science of Politics*, p. 186.

[102]Ibid., pp. 185-86. As variants, Voegelin lists La Rochefoucauld's psychology of the worldly man, "the French psychology of the *moralistes* and novelists, the English psychology of pleasure-pain, associationism and self-interest, and the German enrichments through the psychology of the unconscious of the Romantics and the psychology of Nietzsche" (ibid., p. 185). The extension to Freudian psychology, and even to the ambiguities of Jungian archetypal psychology, unless its deficient assumptions regarding intentionality are transcended, is evident. Witness, for example, the derailments of Jungian thought in the work of James Hillman, *Re-Visioning Psychology* (New York: Harper and Row, 1975).

[103]Lonergan, *Method in Theology*, p. 65.

[104]Ibid., p. 31.

[105]Ibid.

[106]Ibid.

[107]"There are three conditions which often look alike
Yet differ completely, flourish in the same hedgerow:
Attachment to self and to things and to persons, detachment
From self and from things and from persons; and, growing
between them, indifference
Which resembles the others as death resembles life,
Being between two lives--unflowering, between
The live and the dead nettle." T. S. Eliot, "Little Gidding," *Four Quartets* (New York: Harcourt, Brace and World, 1971), p. 55.

[108]Lonergan, *Method in Theology*, p. 31.

[109]Ibid., pp. 83-84.

[110]Ibid., p. 28.

[111] Ibid., p. 32.

[112] Ibid., p. 36.

[113] Ibid., p. 35.

[114] Ibid., p. 237.

[115] Ibid., p. 40.

[116] Ibid., pp. 236-37.

[117] Ibid., p. 236.

[118] On simple and comparative judgments of value, see ibid., p. 36.

[119] Ibid., p. 237.

[120] Ibid., p. 80.

[121] Ibid.

[122] Ibid.

[123] Ricoeur, *Freud and Philosophy*.

[124] Lonergan, *Method in Theology*, p. 39.

[125] Ibid.

[126] Ibid., p. 40.

[127] Ibid., p. 33:

> According to Max Scheler, ressentiment is a re-feeling of a specific clash with someone else's value-system. The someone is one's superior physically or intellectually or morally or spiritually. The re-feeling is not active or aggressive but extends over time, even a life-time. It is a feeling of hostility, anger, indignation that is neither repudiated nor directly expressed. What it attacks is the value-quality that the superior person possessed and the inferior not only lacked but also feels unequal to acquiring. The attack amounts to a continuous belittling of the value in question, and it can extend to hatred and even violence against those that possess that value-quality. But perhaps its worst feature is that its rejection of one value involves a distortion of the whole scale of values and that this distortion can spread through a whole social class, a whole people, a whole epoch.

[128] Ibid., p. 37.

[129] Lonergan, *Insight*, pp. 604-7.

[130] Ibid., p. 385.

[131] Lonergan, *Method in Theology*, pp. 241-44.

[132] Lonergan, *Insight*, pp. 431-37.

CHAPTER THREE

[1]Mumford, *The Transformations of Man*, p. 132.

[2]Allan Bloom, "The Failure of the University," *Daedalus* 103 (1974): 59, quoted in Frederick Lawrence, "Political Theology and 'The Longer Cycle of Decline,'" *Lonergan Workshop I*, p. 223.

[3]See Robert Doran, "Faith, Education, and Freedom: Jesuit Spirituality in Higher Education" (to be published in a forthcoming collection of essays). On the series of ever less comprehensive viewpoints, see Lonergan, *Insight*, pp. 231-32, and "The Role of a Catholic University in the Modern World," in *Collection*, pp. 114-20, esp. pp. 116-17. On Lonergan's account, liberal democracy and communist totalitarianism constitute respectively the penultimate and ultimate stages in a longer cycle of sociocultural decline. See Lawrence, "Political Theology and 'The Longer Cycle of Decline,'" p. 237. We can now view the ultimate stage as consisting in the competing and escalating totalitarianisms of the multinational corporations and the Soviet alliance.

[4]On conceptualism, see Lonergan, "The Subject," esp. pp. 73-75.

[5]Lonergan, *Method in Theology*, p. 55. Note the careful choice of words: the *progress* of modernity in science has been turned into *decline* in the social order.

[6]Lonergan, *Insight*, p. 624.

[7]Ibid., pp. 627-30.

[8]Ibid., chap. 20.

[9]Ibid., p. 666.

[10]The dynamics of this aspect of decline are outlined in ibid., pp. 222-25.

[11]On the constitutive conditions of revolution as opposed to reform, see ibid., p. 225.

[12]Thus Lord Keynes' defense of the *methodically* narrow scope of the judgments of economic science: "They give vastly more weight to the short than to the long term, because in the long term, as Keynes put it with cheerful brutality, we are all dead" (cited by Schumacher, *Small is Beautiful*, p. 41. Compare Lonergan:

> "Man can discover emergent probability; he can work out the manner in which prior insights and decisions determine the possibilities and probabilities of later insights and decisions; he can guide his present decisions in the light of their influence on future insights and decisions; finally, this control of the emergent probability of the future can be exercised not only by the individual in choosing his career and in forming his character, not only by adults in educating the younger generation, but also by mankind in its consciousness of its responsibility to the future of mankind. Just as technical, economic, and political development gives

> man a dominion over nature, so also the advance of knowledge creates and demands a human contribution to the control of human history" (*Insight*, p. 227).

[13]I have in this section interpreted the pages on group bias and general bias in *Insight* in the light of Lonergan's more recent existential differentiation. There is much in his treatment of practical common sense that I have not treated. I am particularly impressed with his critique of Marx: namely, that in Marxism the roots of the shorter and longer cycles are lumped together, and the corrective principle of the shorter cycle is assumed to be able to reverse the longer cycle of decline as well. On the other hand, I find that Lonergan's later existential differentiation, and especially the construction of the scale of values, permits a better integration of the long-range point of view with Marx's concern to reverse the shorter cycle. Much more work must be done at the level of the social praxis of the oppressed so as to correct *their* general bias and to introduce into liberating praxis an integral concern for religious, personal, and cultural values. "No one is really working for peace unless he is working primarily for the restoration of wisdom" (Schumacher, *Small is Beautiful*, p. 30). On this score, I suspect that we have not begun to learn from Gandhi what he has to teach us. At the same time, much work also needs to be done to preserve the minds and hearts of those concerned with religious, personal, and cultural values from a group bias that would encourage them to pursue these higher levels of value without regard for the social and vital values of all members of the series of social orders in our world. That is to say, while those concerned with economic and political liberation need to acknowledge the manner in which religious, personal, and cultural values condition the possibility of that liberation, those concerned with these higher levels of value need to integrate their pursuit of them with the concerns of economic and political liberation. It is entirely in keeping with the scale of values that emerges from the normative order of inquiry that existential authenticity demands an effective *Parteilichkeit* for the economically and materially oppressed. Without this partiality, one is not responding authentically to the normative scale of values.

[14]Becker, *The Denial of Death*. Toward the end of Chapter 1, above, I indicated that Becker himself does not entirely transcend the confusion.

[15]Voegelin, *The New Science of Politics*, pp. 182-84. I quote from these pages. Voegelin inserts excerpts from Hobbes. Hobbes' constriction of feelings to passions results in

> a few distinctions concerning the meaning of the term "person." "A person, is he, whose words or actions are considered, either as his own, or as representing the words and actions of another man, or of any other thing." When he represents himself, he is a natural person; when he represents another, he is called an artificial person. The meaning of person is referred back to the Latin *persona*, and the Greek *prosopon*, as the face, the outward appearance, or the mask of the actor on the stage. "So that a person, is the same that an actor is, both on the stage and in common conversation; and to personate, is to act, or represent himself, or another."
>
> This concept of a person allows Hobbes to separate the visible realm of representative words and deeds from the unseen realm of processes in the soul, with the consequence that the visible words and actions, which always

must be those of a definite, physical human being, may represent a unit of psychic processes which arises from the interaction of individual human souls. In the natural condition every man has his own person in the sense that his words and actions represent the power drive of his passions. In the civil condition the human units of passion are broken and fused into a new unit, called the commonwealth. The actions of the single human individuals whose souls have coalesced cannot represent the new person; its bearer is the sovereign. The creation of this person of the commonwealth, Hobbes insists, is "more than consent, or concord," as the language of contract would suggest. The single human persons cease to exist and merge into the one person represented by the sovereign. "This is the generation of that great Leviathan, or rather, to speak more reverently, of that *mortal god*, to which we owe under the *immortal God*, our peace and defence." The covenanting men agree "to submit their wills, everyone to his will, and their judgments to his judgment." The fusion of wills is "a real unity of them all"; for the mortal god "hath the use of so much power and strength conferred upon him, that by terror thereof, he is enabled to form the wills of them all, to peace at home, and mutual aid against their enemies abroad."

The style of the construction is magnificent. If human nature is assumed to be nothing but passionate existence, devoid of ordering resources of the soul, the horror of annihilation will, indeed, be the overriding passion that compels submission to order. If pride cannot bow to Dike, or be redeemed through grace, it must be broken by the Leviathan who "is king of all the children of pride." If the souls cannot participate in the Logos, then the sovereign who strikes terror into their souls will be "the essence of the commonwealth." The "King of the Proud" must break the *amor sui* that cannot be relieved by the *amor Dei*.

[16]Lonergan, *Method in Theology*, pp. 23-24. The same insight appears with unmistakable clarity in, for example, Plato's *Gorgias*.

[17]Ibid., p. 50.

[18]Lonergan, *Insight*, p. 599.

[19]Lonergan, *Method in Theology*, p. 50.

[20]The essential difference from Marxist analysis should not be overlooked. Lonergan and Frederick Lawrence both call attention to the "artificial intersubjective basis" of Marxist theory. See Lonergan's "The Role of a Catholic University in the Modern World," p. 118, and Lawrence's "Political Theology and 'The Longer Cycle of Decline,'" p. 237. For the modes of interaction among the three levels of culture, see *Insight*, chap. 7, and Lonergan's "Belief: Today's Issue," esp. pp. 91-97, and "The Absence of God in Modern Culture," esp. pp. 111-116. See also Lonergan's comments on economic determinism, above, chap. 1, n. 99.

[21]Lonergan, *Insight*, pp. 222-23.

[22]Lonergan, *Method in Theology*, pp. 50-51.

[23]Ibid., p. 51.

[24]Ibid., pp. 51-52.

[25]Ibid., p. 53.

[26]Ibid.

[27]Ibid., p. 55.

[28]Ibid.

[29]Lonergan, *Insight*, p. 601.

[30]Lonergan, *Method in Theology*, p. 50.

[31]Ibid., p. 51.

[32]Ibid., p. 52.

[33]Ibid.

[34]Mumford, *The Transformations of Man*, pp. 136-37.

[35]Ibid., p. 142.

[36]Ibid., p. 143.

[37]Ibid., p. 138.

[38]Ibid., p. 144. As we shall see in Part Two, Mumford's position is thus already distinguished from the unfortunate final conclusions of Jung, on whom Mumford relies. Jungian psychology makes a false distinction between the impulse to perfection and transcendence, on the one hand, and the psyche's urge toward wholeness, on the other.

[39]Materials are abundant in Jung's writings. One might begin by reflecting on Jung's sympathy with a Native American's conviction of the insanity of the white man. See C. G. Jung, *Memories, Dreams, Reflections*, trans. Richard and Clara Winston (New York: Vintage Press, 1963), pp. 246-53.

[40]See John Dunne, *The Reasons of the Heart* (New York: Macmillan, 1978), p. 103.

[41]On defensive circles in emergent probability, see Lonergan, *Insight*, pp. 118-21. The defensive circles in the development of the human compound-in-tension of spirit and matter are found in the psyche that mediates between these opposites, elevating neural demand functions to a consciously energic level, from which standpoint they can be attended to, interpreted, affirmed, and decided upon.

[42]See C. G. Jung, "Synchronicity: An Acausal Connecting Principle," in *The Collected Works of C. G. Jung, vol. 8: The Structure and Dynamics of the Psyche*, 2d ed., trans. R. F. C. Hull (Princeton, NJ: Princeton University Press, 1969), pp. 419-519; "On Synchronicity," ibid., pp. 520-31.

[43]In effect, the matter is more complicated than this. For there is a dialectic of the social order that is more dominant than the dialectic of the subject and that "gives rise to the situations that stimulate neural demands and . . . moulds the orientation of

intelligence that preconsciously exercises the censorship" (Lonergan, *Insight*, p. 218). Consequently, the individual's aesthetic disintegration may be largely the result of the social surd, as R. D. Laing has so dramatically argued. The psychotic may be saner than the normal run of men and women. Such is the extent of the reaches of the longer cycle of decline in our own day. The sins of the fathers are visited upon their children to the third and fourth generations--and far beyond that! It is precisely a *longer* cycle of decline that we must today reverse if we are not to suffer the loss of all that has been achieved in the course of the substance of history.

[44]Mumford is thus in agreement with Lonergan's heuristic prescriptions for the study of the organism, the psyche, and the human person. See Lonergan, *Insight*, pp. 451-83, on "The Notion of Development" and "Genetic Method."

[45]Mumford, *The Transformations of Man*, p. 132.

[46]Lonergan, *Method in Theology*, p. 31.

[47]Ibid., p. 33.

[48]Ibid., p. 64.

[49]Ibid., p. 66.

[50]Ibid., pp. 66-67.

[51]Lonergan, *Insight*, p. 624.

[52]Ibid., p. 627.

[53]Ibid., p. 629.

[54]Ibid., p. 630.

[55]Ibid., p. 666.

[56]Ibid., pp. 698-703.

[57]Lonergan, *Philosophy of God, and Theology*, p. 38.

[58]Lonergan, *Method in Theology*, p. 106.

[59]Ibid., p. 105.

[60]Ibid.

[61]In *Insight*, pp. 622-24, Lonergan distinguishes four sources of such determinism: external circumstance, psychoneurosis, the limitations of intellectual development, and unwillingness.

[62]Ibid., pp. 379-80, 513-14.

[63]See Paul Ricoeur, *Fallible Man*, trans. Charles Kelbley (Chicago: Regnery).

[64]"Intellectual conversion" is used in two senses in Lonergan's writings, and they are not always clearly distinguished. *In actu exercito* the Church achieved intellectual conversion at the Council of Nicea. *In actu signato* intellectual conversion is coincident with the explanatory self-affirmation of the knower

and the consequent positions on being and objectivity. The latter is probably more precisely termed a philosophic conversion. See Walter E. Conn, "The Ontogenetic Ground of Value," *Theological Studies*, 39, 2 (June 1978): pp. 313-35.

[65]The expression, affective conversion, first occurs in Lonergan's writings, to my knowledge, in "Natural Right and Historical-Mindedness," paper presented to the American Catholic Philosophical Association, April 1977.

[66]In the transcript of the dialogue sessions of the 1977 Lonergan Workshop held at Boston College, available at Lonergan Center, Regis College, Toronto.

[67]Lonergan, *Method in Theology*, p. 115.

[68]On the relations among the supernatural conjugate forms of faith, hope, and love, see Lonergan, *Insight*, pp. 698-721.

[69]Lonergan, "Healing and Creating in History," p. 63.

[70]Lonergan, *Insight*, pp. 728-29.

[71]On the canon of selection in modern natural science, see ibid., pp. 71-74.

[72]On pure and experiential conjugates, see ibid., pp. 79-82.

[73]Eugene Gendlin, *Experiencing and the Creation of Meaning* (Toronto: Free Press of Glencoe, 1962), p. 4.

[74]On this problem, see Voegelin, *The New Science of Politics*, chap. 1.

[75]See Pedro Arrupe, *A Planet to Heal: Reflections and Forecasts* (Rome: Ignatian Center of Spirituality, 1975).

[76]Lonergan, *Insight*, pp. 249-50.

PART TWO, INTRODUCTION

[1]Bernard Lonergan, *Method in Theology*, p. 77.

CHAPTER FOUR

[1]Schumacher, *Small is Beautiful*, p. 146. The context is a discussion of the neglect of limitation *and so* of the long-range view in the development of technology.

[2]Lonergan, *Insight*, p. 181.

[3]Ibid., p. 182.

[4]Ibid., p. 456.

[5]Ibid., p. 183. To this list, I add associations and spontaneous intersubjective responses.

[6]Ibid.

[7]See ibid., pp. 514-20.

[8]Becker, *The Denial of Death*, p. 26.

[9]"With Freud I know where I am and where I am going; with Jung everything risks being confused: the psychism, the soul, the archetypes, the sacred." Ricoeur, *Freud and Philosophy*, p. 176.

[10]We shall hint later that Jung extends the negotiation of the opposites into one particular dimension that demands an entirely different set of procedures, the opposition of good and evil.

[11]C. G. Jung, "On the Nature of the Psyche," in *The Structure and Dynamics of the Psyche*, pp. 159-234.

[12]Lonergan, *Insight*, pp. 475-79.

[13]Dunne, *The Reasons of the Heart*, chaps. 6-7; James Hillman, *The Myth of Analysis* (Evanston, Ill.: Northwestern University Press, 1972) and idem, *Re-Visioning Psychology*.

[14]Hillman, *Re-Visioning Psychology*, p. x.

[15]Dunne, *The Reasons of the Heart*, p. 98. I do not wish to imply that Dunne and Hillman are about the same thing, for I believe there is a vast gap between their respective projects whose only resolution is dialectical. There is to Dunne's journey an integrity of purpose that, if persevered in, would have as its by-product the integration of the totality of body and mind, of matter and spirit. Hillman's recent abandonment of the integration of the totality as a futile enterprise is at its roots a renunciation of integrity. Moreover, Hillman reifies the soul as a mythical in-between mediating what is "in here" with what is "out there," thus betraying in the epistemological order the same defective notion of objectivity that distorts his psychological quest into a variant of the romantic agony.

[16]Jung, *Memories, Dreams, Reflections*, p. 256.

[17]Lonergan, *Insight*, p. 443.

[18]"A theory of emergent probability exhibits generically the intelligibility immanent in world process. Emergent probability is the successive realization of the possibilities of concrete situations in accord with their probabilities. The concrete intelligibility of Space is that it grounds the possibility of those simultaneous multiplicities named situations. The concrete intelligibility of Time is that it grounds the possibility of successive realizations in accord with probabilities. In other words, concrete extensions and concrete durations are the field or matter or potency in which emergent probability is the immanent form or intelligibility." Lonergan, *Insight*, pp. 171-72.

[19]Ibid., pp. 513-14.

[20]Doran, "Aesthetics and the Opposites," p. 121.

CHAPTER FIVE

[1]Martin Heidegger, *Being and Time*, trans. John Macquarrie and Edward Robinson (New York: Harper and Row, 1962), pp. 171-72.

[2]On being dragged through life and walking through life upright, see John Dunne, *The Way of All the Earth* (New York: Macmillan, 1972), p. 152.

[3]On the notion of the world mediated by meaning, see Lonergan, "Dimensions of Meaning." Paul Ricoeur tends to ascribe to *writing* the fact that human consciousness alone has a world and not just a situation. See his *Interpretation Theory: Discourse and the Surplus of Meaning* (Fort Worth, Texas: Texas Christian University Press, 1976), pp. 34-37. While there is no denying the great extension of the scope of reference that is opened by writing, it must also be said that spoken language too opens a world. It is not true that "all references of oral language rely on monstrations" (p. 35), as if spoken language were limited to what Lonergan calls the world of immediacy. For Ricoeur, "the world is the ensemble of references opened up by every kind of text, descriptive or poetic, that I have read, understood, and loved" (p. 37). Ricoeur makes too sharp a distinction between the dialogical situation and the hermeneutical appropriation of meaning. The dichotomy may be rooted in an exaggerated notion of the distantiation or semantic autonomy of the text. A hermeneutic theory constructed on the basis of the structure of conscious performance would make its primary distinction that of the world of immediacy and the world mediated by meaning. The latter world is opened up by all language, spoken or written, though surely vastly extended through literacy.

[4]Lonergan, *Method in Theology*, p. 28:

> Operations are said to be immediate when their objects are present. So seeing is immediate to what is being seen, hearing to what is being heard, touch to what is being touched. But by imagination, language, symbols, we operate in a compound manner; immediately with respect to the image, word, symbol; mediately with respect to what is represented or signified. In this fashion we come to operate not only with respect to the present and actual but also with respect to the absent, the past, the future, the merely possible or ideal or normative or fantastic. As the child learns to speak, he moves out of the world of his immediate surroundings towards the far larger world revealed through the memories of other men, through the common sense of community, through the pages of literature, through the labors of scholars, through the investigations of scientists, through the experience of saints, through the meditations of philosophers and theologians.

[5]See Lonergan, *Insight*, pp. 189-191.

[6]It must be kept in mind that the factors that distort the dramatic pattern are manifold and complex. The relative dominance of the dialectic of history over the dialectic of the subject (Lonergan, *Insight*, p. 218) means that many never are given much opportunity for dramatic art. Their inauthenticity is a function more of personal, familial, social, political, and cultural

victimization than it is of unwillingness. The number of such human tragedies is going to increase as a civilizational course nears or reaches the last stages of the longer cycle of decline.

[7]Johann Baptist Metz, "A Short Apology of Narrative," in *Concilium 85: The Crisis of Religious Language*, ed. Johann Baptist Metz and Jean-Pierre Jossua (New York: Herder and Herder, 1973), pp. 84-96.

[8]Ibid., pp. 85-86. Metz's reliance on Theodor Adorno in this context makes clear that "technique" is here opposed to "praxis."

[9]Ibid., p. 87.

[10]Ibid., pp. 88-89.

[11]Ibid., p. 90.

[12]Ibid., p. 92.

[13]Ibid., p. 93.

[14]Ibid.

[15]Ricoeur, *Freud and Philosophy*. For my own radicalizing of Ricoeur's conclusions in the light of transcendental method, see Doran, *Subject and Psyche*, chap. 3.

[16]But see Ernest Jones, *The Life and Work of Sigmund Freud* (New York: Basic Books, 1953), 1: 269-71, for an argument supporting Freud's approach in this regard. Jones does not acknowledge even the possibility of proceeding from a preliminary account of well-being to a science of neurosis. Freud himself admitted that philosophers have done little to prepare the way for a "Neurosis-Psychology" (ibid., p. 269). But see Plato, *The Republic*, Book IX, and Aristotle, "On Dreams," and "On Prophesying by Dreams," in *The Basic Works of Aristotle*, ed. Richard McKeon (New York: Random House, 1941), pp. 618-30, where dreams are treated quite intelligently, albeit most incompletely, from the overall perspective of an understanding of human well-being.

[17]Lonergan, *Insight*, p. 190. On correspondence and emergence, see ibid., pp. 451-52.

[18]Ibid., p. 190.

[19]Ibid., p. 191.

[20]Ibid., p. 188.

[21]Ibid.

[22]Ibid., p. 218.

[23]Ibid., pp. 188-89.

[24]Ibid., p. 189.

[25]Ibid.

[26]Ibid., pp. 194-96.

[27]Ibid., p. 210.

[28]Even extraordinary remedies, of course, can be subverted by religious and moral corruption and by intellectual inauthenticity.

[29]Lonergan, *Method in Theology*, p. 177:

> There is succession in the flow of conscious and intentional acts; there is identity in the conscious subject of the acts; there may be either identity or succession in the object intended by the acts. Analysis may reveal that what actually is visible is a succession of different profiles; but experience reveals that what is perceived is the synthesis (*Gestalt*) of the profiles into a single object. Analysis may reveal that the sounds produced are a succession of notes and chords; but experience reveals that what is heard is their synthesis into a melody. There results what is called the psychological present, which is not an instant, a mathematical point, but a time-span, so that our experience of time is, not of a raceway of instants, but a now leisurely, a now rapid, succession of overlapping time-spans. The time of experience is slow and dull, when the objects of experience change slowly and in expected ways. But time becomes a whirligig, when the objects of experience change rapidly and in novel and unexpected ways.
>
> Whether slow and broad or rapid and short, the psychological present reaches into its past by memories and into its future by anticipations. Anticipations are not merely of the prospective objects of our fears and our desires but also the shrewd estimate of the man of experience or the rigorously calculated forecast of applied science. Again, besides the memories of each individual, there are the pooled memories of the group, their celebration in song and story, their preservation in written narratives, in coins and monuments and every other trace of the group's words and deeds left to posterity.

[30]The existentially negligible exception lies in the "dreams of the night," which are purely expressive of biological exigence. Again, the purely biological pattern of experience is independent of direct existential determination.

[31]Lonergan, *Insight*, p. 190.

[32]Ibid., p. 476.

[33]Ibid., p. 477.

[34]Ibid., p. 478.

[35]Lonergan, "Dimensions of Meaning," p. 259.

[36]Bernard Lonergan, "Self-Transcendence: Intellectual, Moral, Religious," lecture, quoted in Philip McShane, "The Psychological Present of the Academic Community," *Lonergan Workshop I*, p. 57.

[37]Lonergan, *Method in Theology*, p. 83.

[38]On the therapeutic exigence, see Doran, "Psychic Conversion."

[39]Lonergan, *Insight*, p. 473.

[40]Ibid., pp. 473-74.

[41]Ibid., pp. 723-24.

[42]On potency, see ibid., pp. 432-33; on central potency (individuality), conjugate potency (other aspects of the empirical residue), ibid., p. 437; on a coincidental manifold of conjugate acts (occurrences) as potency for a higher integration by an emergent conjugate form, ibid., p. 438. The remainder of the present chapter is a slight modification of the conclusion of my paper "Dramatic Artistry in the Third Stage of Meaning."

[43]Ibid., pp. 442-51.

[44]Ibid., pp. 442-43.

[45]Ibid., p. 443.

[46]Ibid., p. 444.

[47]C. G. Jung, "On Psychic Energy," in *The Structure and Dynamics of the Psyche*, pp. 3-66.

[48]C. G. Jung, "Synchronicity: An Acausal Connecting Principle," ibid., pp. 419-519; see p. 514.

[49]Lonergan, *Insight*, p. 463.

[50]Ibid., p. 469. In the light of the later expansion of the analysis of consciousness to the fourth level, "intellectual development" as used throughout Lonergan's treatment of human development in Chapter 15 of *Insight* must include the existential development of the subject as originating value.

[51]See Ricoeur, *Freud and Philosophy*, p. 452.

[52]For a representative critique of the notion of sublimation, see C. G. Jung, "Analytical Psychology and the 'Weltanschauung,'" in *The Structure and Dynamics of the Psyche*, p. 365.

[53]Ibid.

[54]Jung, of course, initially agreed with Freud that psychic energy is displaced from sexual object-relations to other distributions, but he soon abandoned this notion in favor of the natural process of transformation. His early agreement with Freud on the notion of sublimation can be seen in some original 1909 footnotes to a paper Jung revised and expanded in 1949, "The Significance of the Father in the Destiny of the Individual," in *Collected Works, Vol. 4: Freud and Psychoanalysis*, pp. 320-321, nn. 21-22.

[55]Lonergan, *Insight*, p. 445.

[56]Cf. ibid., p. 477: "*Unconsciously operative* is the finality that consists in the upwardly but indeterminately directed dynamism of all proportionate being." Emphasis added. The context is the tension of limitation and transcendence in human development.

[57]Approximately, the early Jung is the Jung prior to the "confrontation with the unconscious" detailed in Chapter 6 of the autobiographical *Memories, Dreams, Reflections*.

[58]"Ego" is here used differently from the way Lonergan uses it (*Insight*, p. 191), where the ego *is* a day-dreamer or fantasizer, and not in a particularly helpful way.

[59]On the hermeneutic of suspicion, see Ricoeur, *Freud and Philosophy*, pp. 32-36. Jung's early interpretation of fantasies and dreams is still present in the 1912 book that generally is acknowledged as his definitive break with Freud, *Wandlungen and Symbole der Libido*. An English translation of the work by Beatrice M. Hinkle, *Psychology of the Unconscious*, appeared in 1916 (New York: Moffatt Yard). Jung extensively revised this work in 1952. The revision appears as vol. 5 of his *Collected Works* under the title *Symbols of Transformation*. The revision puts forth the later interpretation of fantasies and dreams.

[60]The dream "is a typical product of the unconscious, and is merely deformed and distorted [i.e., not constituted] by repression. Hence any explanation that interprets it as a mere symptom of repression will go very wide of the mark." Jung, "Analytical Psychology and the 'Weltanschauung,'" p. 365.

[61]Jungian analyst John Weir Perry has argued persuasively that this it the case even--or especially--with the fantasies of psychotics. See his *The Far Side of Madness* (Englewood Cliffs, N.J.: Prentice-Hall Spectrum Books, 1974). If Perry is correct, he has contributed another facet to the critique of the usual treatment of schizophrenia that has been offered by Thomas Szasz and R. D. Laing.

[62]See Lonergan, *Insight*, pp. 264-67.

[63]C. G. Jung, *Psychological Types*, p. 474.

[64]Cf. Lonergan, *Insight*, pp. 452-53:

> The course of development is marked by an increasing explanatory differentiation. The initial integration in the initial manifold pertains to a determinate genus and species; still, exclusive attention to the data on the initial stage would yield little knowledge and less understanding of the relevant genus and species. What is to be known by understanding, is what is yet to come, what may be present virtually or potentially but, as yet, is not present formally or actually. Accordingly, if one attends simply to the data on each successive stage of a development, one finds that the initial integration can be understood only in a generic fashion, that subsequent integrations are increasingly specific intelligibilities, that the specific intelligible differentiation of the ultimate stage attained is generated in the process from the initial stage.

[65]Paul Ricoeur's notion of the archeological-teleological unity-in-tension of the concrete symbol helps me understand the complex constitution and function of the dream (see *Freud and Philosophy*, pp. 494-551). The tense unity of regressive and progressive aspects is rooted in what Ricoeur calls the overdetermination of the symbol, a factor which in turn I would root in the coincidental character of psychic energy from a prepsychological standpoint.

[66]C. G. Jung, "The Relations between the Ego and the Unconscious," *Collected Works, vol. 7: Two Essays on Analytical Psychology*, pp. 123-241.

[67] Lonergan, *Insight*, pp. 187-96.

[68] Lonergan, *Method in Theology*, pp. 83-84.

[69] Lonergan, *Insight*, pp. 741-42.

[70] Ibid., pp. 696-703.

[71] I have offered a preliminary critique of Jung on this issue and the related problem of his treatment of evil in "Christ and the Psyche" and "The Theologian's Psyche: Notes toward a Reconstruction of Depth Psychology."

[72] My initial exposure to the contrast of archetypal and anagogic symbols was through Northrop Frye's *Anatomy of Criticism*, pp. 95-128. I was introduced to Frye by Joseph Flanagan's "Transcendental Dialectic of Desire and Fear," in *Lonergan Workshop I*, pp. 69-92. For my own purposes, I will articulate the distinction in its most simple form as follows: archetypal symbols are taken from nature and imitate nature (e.g., the example of the mother-*imago)*; anagogic symbols are taken from nature but point to its transformation in the light of its transcendent finality. I do not intend, however, to ascribe that precise interpretation to Frye. In my next book, I will attempt to show that Jung's failure to make some such distinction leads to a displacement of the tension of limitation and transcendence that is every bit as erroneous as Freud's reductionism. On displacement of the tension as failure in genuineness, see Lonergan, *Insight*, p. 478.

[73] Ibid., p. 723.

[74] Ibid.

[75] Ibid., pp. 723-24.

[76] Ibid., p. 724.

[77] Ibid., p. 469.

[78] Voegelin, *Israel and Revelation*, pp. 5-6.

[79] See Robert Doran, "Theological Grounds for a World-Cultural Humanity," in *Creativity and Method*, ed. Matthew Lamb (Milwaukee: Marquette University Press, 1981).